JOHN D. W. O'MEARA

Metrical phonology: a coursebook

D1550902

Metrical phonology:
a coursebook

Richard Hogg and C. B. McCully

Department of English Language and Literature
University of Manchester

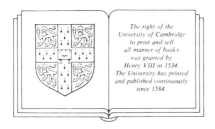

Cambridge University Press

Cambridge

London   New York   New Rochelle

Melbourne   Sydney

Published by the Press Syndicate of the University of Cambridge
The Pitt Building, Trumpington Street, Cambridge CB2 1RP
32 East 57th Street, New York, NY 10022, USA
10 Stamford Road, Oakleigh, Melbourne 3166, Australia

© Cambridge University Press 1987

First published 1987

Printed in Great Britain by
Bath Press, Bath, Avon.

British Library cataloguing in publication data

Hogg, R. M.
Metrical phonology: a coursebook.
1. Grammar, Comparative and general – Phonology
I. Title   II. McCully, C. B.
414   P217

Library of Congress cataloguing in publication data

Hogg, Richard M.
Metrical phonology.
Bibliography
Includes index.
1. Grammar, Comparative and general – Phonology.
2. Accents and accentuation.
3. Language and languages – Rhythm.
4. Generative grammar.
I. McCully, C. B.   II. Title.
P217.6.H6   1986   414   86–14701

ISBN 0 521 30363 X hardcovers

ISBN 0 521 31651 0 paperback

Contents

1   *Segmental approaches to stress*

1.1   *Introduction*

Consider the pair *blackboard* and *black board*. If a phonologist were to analyse these items simply as strings of consonants and vowel segments, then he or she might well wish to transcribe the first as something like /blækbɔd/, the second as something like /blæk bɔd/. Ignoring the gap in the second transcription, the two transcriptions are identical. Yet nobody would wish to claim that the two were pronounced identically, or that speakers of English could only distinguish them in their written forms. On the contrary, all speakers of English can easily distinguish between them on phonological grounds. Our failure to represent the manner in which the distinction is made because we have concentrated solely on the sequence of phonological *segments* and therefore failed to note the crucial feature, namely the distinct patterns of *stress* which serve to differentiate the two strings. In *blackboard* the stress is strongest at the beginning of the string – or, more accurately, there is a falling stress contour, whilst in *black board* there is a rising stress contour (with the stress strongest towards the end of the string). There are many different ways in which we can transcribe stress patterns. For example, some linguists would show the contrasting patterns as ˈ*black* ˌ*board* vs. ˌ*black* ˈ*board*, whilst others would show the contrast as *bláckbòard* vs. *blàck bóard*. In fact we shall use neither of these here, but instead a system of numbering, where the lowest integer (i.e. 1) indicates strongest stress, and higher degrees indicate correspondingly weaker stress. In this system the opposition we have been discussing will be transcribed as *bláckbȯard* vs. *blȧck bóard*.

However, before we go any further we should say what we mean by stress. Unfortunately that is rather difficult. Whilst it is true that for the speaker stress has one distinct physical correlate, namely that a stressed syllable occurs when the speaker pushes more air out from his lungs (in comparison with the amount of air pushed out for the pronunciation of adjacent syllables), for the hearer this can have any one of three results, or any combination of the three. Any one or all of the following might be heard: (i) an increase in vowel length, (ii) an increase in pitch, (iii) an increase in loudness. In other words, stress is associated with an increase in respiratory activity on the part of the speaker which causes an increase in

1

any one or other of the following: vowel length, pitch, loudness. And since each of these can be influenced by other factors (often, admittedly, of a nonlinguistic nature), the position is complex.

Q.   Despite all these problems, there is no real difficulty in claiming that stress is an isolable phonological phenomenon. Not only are there definable physical and acoustic correlates, but hearers find it relatively simple to pick out patterns of stress. Consider, for example, the following sentence:

> (1.1) The goal of the descriptive study of a language is the construction of a grammar

Where do the primary or main stresses occur in that sentence?

A.   If we simply mark such stresses by ', then the most plausible answer seems to be that given in (1.2). Indeed, we would be surprised if anyone had an analysis *markedly* different from ours:

> (1.2) The 'goal of the des'criptive 'study of a 'language is the con'struction of a 'grammar

If we simply set out (1.2) as a sequence of stressed (/) and unstressed (x) syllables, then another characteristic of stress patterning is made clear:

> (1.3) x / x x x / x / x x x / x x x x / x x x / x

Note how regular this pattern is – only the short gap between the stressed syllable of *descriptive* and the stressed syllable of *study* disrupts the general pattern in which stressed syllables tend to occur every fourth or fifth syllable. This is by no means unusual. Try marking the following sentences in the same way and note their patterns. You should find that, despite inevitable variations, yet again a stressed syllable tends to occur at approximately every fourth syllable:

> (1.4) The grammar of the language is the system of rules that specifies this sound–meaning correspondence.

> (1.5) The performance of the speaker or the hearer is a complex matter that involves many factors.

From what we have said already it should be clear that we regard stress as a *suprasegmental* phenomenon. That is to say, unlike an ordinary phonological feature such as [±voice], which is a property of individual segments (at least that is the traditional belief), so that in, say, *cats* /kæts/ we can claim that /æ/ is the only segment which is [+voice], stress is a property of a string of segments. Nevertheless, in the earlier generative treatments of stress (e.g. Chomsky & Halle 1968; Halle & Keyser 1971; Halle 1973) stress is indeed described as a property of individual segments, more specifically vowels. Probably the most radical claim which has been made by metrical phonologists is that any such purely segmental approach, i.e. any approach which treats spoken sequences as only a linear sequence of individual segments, is inadequate, and that reference has to be made to some kind of phonological hierarchy, including, for example, a syllable constituent. In this chapter, however, we shall be introducing the strictly segmental approach, and in chapters 2 and 3 especially we shall consider the limitations and inadequacies of such an approach.

Q.   There is another issue which we must discuss now. Consider the following two sentences:

(1.6) Presidents Gorbachev and Reagan are to meet next month

(1.7) John says that he is a communist and that he admires Mrs Thatcher

What words are stressed in each of those sentences? More importantly, there is one word which the two sentences have in common. Is it unstressed on both occasions, or stressed on one and not on the other?

A.   The word, of course, is *and*. What we would want to say is that it is unstressed both in (1.6) and in (1.7). But, it has to be admitted, it is perfectly reasonable to claim that in (1.7) *and* could be stressed. In order to resolve this we need to distinguish between *normal* stress and *emphatic* stress. In this book we shall always, henceforth, be talking about normal stress, but a few words about emphatic stress are needed now, if only to justify its future exclusion from the discussion.

There are two crucial differences between normal stress and emphatic stress. Firstly, emphatic stress seems usually to be connected with pragmatic factors. Thus if in (1.7) *and* receives emphatic stress, then this is presumably because the speaker perceives some contradiction between John being a communist and John admiring Mrs Thatcher. This can only be because of the speaker's feelings about, in this case, politics, and what he thinks may be compatible and incompatible political beliefs. But other speakers might well feel that John's beliefs were by no means incompatible, in which case *and* would not receive emphatic stress. The primary task of emphatic stress is to draw attention to events, objects, beliefs, etc. which the speaker feels are especially worthy of note. As such, anything can receive emphatic stress, and this brings us to the second difference between emphatic and normal stress. As we shall see very shortly, usually only certain word-classes can receive normal stress. Sentence (1.6) shows as well as any other sentence that conjunctions do not form one of those word-classes. But a conjunction like *and* can receive emphatic stress, because emphatic stress, being pragmatically based, does not pay attention to syntactic categories in any strictly definable way. Even individual syllables of words can receive emphatic stress if the occasion demands, for example: 'I said *reflate*, not *inflate*.' Finally, we should note that wherever emphatic stress occurs in a sentence, it over-rules normal stress. Undoubtedly, much more can be said about emphatic stress, but for the present only one point needs to be made, that it is clear that normal stress and emphatic stress are systematically different. This should not be taken to imply that both types of stress cannot be encompassed within one over-arching theory, specifically the theory we shall be discussing in later chapters, but the issues which are raised and the possible solutions are too complex to be seriously considered within the covers of this book. Readers who are interested in emphatic stress, however, might like to take the following rather ordinary and uninteresting sentence and give each word in turn emphatic stress. What effect is this differing placement of emphatic stress likely to have on the hearer's interpretation of the sentence?

(1.8) John and Mary didn't walk to London yesterday

1.2   *The generative approach: basic principles*

Consider again the pair *bláckbòard* and *blàck bóard*. To these we might add many other examples: *rédhèad* and *rèd héad*, *bíg-hèad* and *bìg héad*, *yéllowhàmmer* and *yèllow hámmer*, etc. In each case there is the same contrast between a 1 2 stress pattern and a 2 1 pattern. This contrast correlates exactly with a syntactic contrast, for in each case the first member of the pair is a compound noun and the second member of the pair is a noun phrase (containing an adjective plus noun). Thus we can immediately observe one of the most striking characteristics of stress: the placement of stress in English sentences and phrases is related to the syntactic structure of the sentence or phrase concerned. If we take the first pair yet again, then *blackboard* will have the structure of (1.9a) and *black board* will have the structure of (1.9b):

(1.9) a.   N   b.   NP

              A   N   A   N
            black   board   black   board

These trees are notationally equivalent to labelled bracketing as in (1.10a, b):

(1.10) a.   [$_N$[$_A$black]$_A$ [$_N$board]$_N$]$_N$

(1.10) b.   [$_{NP}$[$_A$black]$_A$ [$_N$board]$_N$]$_{NP}$

This, however, is not enough. Even the very few examples which we have discussed so far suggest that the crucial distinction which has to be made is that between the operation of stress within words and the operation of stress over units larger than words. Therefore we need to show the beginnings and ends of words in the bracketing. There is in fact a quite simple way of doing these, which is as follows. If we symbolise a word-boundary as #, then we can state the following *Word-Boundary Insertion Rule* (Chomsky & Halle 1968:366):

(1.11) The boundary # is automatically inserted at the beginning of every string dominated by a major category, i.e. by one of the lexical categories 'noun', 'verb', 'adjective', or by a category such as 'sentence', 'noun phrase', 'verb phrase', which dominates a lexical category.

If we insert word-boundaries into (1.10a) and (1.10b) according to the above rule, we then have the following bracketing:

(1.12) a. $[_N\#[_A\#black\#]_A [_N\#board\#]_N\#]_N$

(1.12) b. $[_{NP}\#[_A\#black\#]_A [_N\#board\#]_N\#]_{NP}$

We can then define the minimal structure of a word as a string bounded on either side by two word-boundaries, that is: ## —— ##, where that string does not itself contain ##. Note, by the way, that this definition of word takes no account, at least for the present, of bracketing configurations. Thus *black* is followed by two word-boundaries just as much as *board* is, despite the different configuration of brackets, i.e. #][# vs. #]#].

Let us now suppose that in any word with the minimal structure as above, one and only one vowel receives the strongest stress of the word. We shall call this stress *primary stress*. If we take this as a rule of English grammar and apply it to (1.12a), then we shall obtain the following result:

(1.13) $[_N\#[_A\#bl\overset{1}{a}ck\#]_A [_N\#b\overset{1}{o}ard\#]_N]_N$

But *blackboard* is itself a word, for it is a compound word, i.e. it forms a single unit which behaves both syntactically and semantically as an independent word (note, for example, that a blackboard need not be *black*). Therefore, since it is a single word, albeit a compound, it should contain only one primary stress. How can this be achieved? Chomsky & Halle (1968) suggest one interesting method, namely the introduction of what they call the *transformational cycle*, and they suggest that stress assignment rules operate within such a cycle, i.e. they are *cyclic*.

What exactly does this mean? We have already noted that stress assignment is in some way related to the surface syntactic structure of the string concerned. That syntactic structure can be represented by the kind of labelled bracketing which we have just been using. If a rule, such as a rule of stress assignment, applies cyclically, then all that this means (but see here chapter 3) is that it can apply over and over again in the following manner. First of all the rule applies to the longest or maximal strings containing no brackets. When all the relevant rules have applied, those brackets are then erased and the rules now apply once more to maximal strings containing no brackets. Then the brackets are deleted, and the process continues until all brackets are deleted. We can therefore delete the innermost sets of brackets in (1.13), giving us:

(1.14) $[_N \#\#\text{bl}\overset{1}{\text{a}}\text{ck}\# \ \#\text{b}\overset{1}{\text{o}}\text{ard}\#\#]_N$

Exactly the same procedure for *black board* would give us:

(1.15) $[_{NP}\#\#\text{bl}\overset{1}{\text{a}}\text{ck}\# \ \#\text{b}\overset{1}{\text{o}}\text{ard}\#\#]_{NP}$

Given the stress patterns which we wish to obtain, it would appear that the following happens. If we are dealing with the syntactic category NP, then the rightmost primary stress of the category is most strongly stressed; if we are dealing with the syntactic category N, then the primary-stressed vowel which precedes another primary-stressed vowel in the same phrase is the most strongly stressed.

What we find in the case of a compound like *blackboard*, therefore, is that the penultimate primary-stressed vowel in the compound receives the strongest stress of the compound. What, then, about the other primary-stressed vowels? In traditional terms, the vowels in any constituent which are stressed but do not receive the strongest stress of the constituent are said to bear *secondary stress*. Thus if we adopt the notation *bláckbòard* referred to at the beginning of this chapter, the acute accent signifies primary stress, the grave accent secondary stress. The question thus arises of how we assign primary stress to one vowel but secondary stress to all other vowels in the constituent. Should we, for example, have a rule which directly assigns secondary stress in some given context? The answer appears to be no, and for at least one very good reason. Consider a compound such as *chambermaid*, which is parallel to *blackboard* in every respect except one, namely that there is, in addition to a primary-stressed vowel and a secondary-stressed vowel, a completely unstressed vowel (the medial /ə/). What that kind of example points out for us is that only vowels which are initially assigned primary stress can, in some larger context, bear secondary stress. Thus in the example of *chambermaid* the medial /ə/ cannot bear secondary stress since it has not been assigned primary stress (or secondary stress) in the simple lexeme *chamber*.

The way generative phonologists have solved this problem is by suggesting that stress assignment rules always and only assign primary stress. Remembering that we notate stress by a system of integers, where the strongest stress is marked 1, we can propose that all rules assigning stress are of the general form:

(1.16) V $\longrightarrow$ [1stress] in some specified context

This, of course, supposes that there is some means of ensuring that all the other stresses, i.e. the stress contour of the whole phrase or word, can be determined from the (cyclic) application of rules of the form of (1.16). This is in fact quite simple to do, by means of the following *Stress Subordination Convention* (Chomsky & Halle 1968:16–17):

> (1.17) When primary stress is placed in a certain position, then all other stresses in the string under consideration at that point are automatically weakened by one.

We can now suggest the following rule to give us the correct representation of the noun phrase *black board*, which provides a more precise description than the informal one that we gave above:

(1.18) $V \longrightarrow$ [1stress] $/ \overset{1}{V} X \overline{} Y]_{NP}$

where X and Y contain any (string of) segments not containing V. It is then possible to provide the following derivation of *black board*:

(1.19) $[_{NP}\#[_A\#black\#]_A [_N\#board\#]_N\#]_{NP}$

$[_{NP}\#\#bl\overset{1}{a}ck\# \#b\overset{1}{o}ard\#\#]_{NP}$ Word-Stress Rule (not yet given)

$\#\#bl\overset{2}{a}ck\# \#b\overset{1}{o}ard\#\#$ Rule (1.18)

A point of interest which we shall not pursue in any detail at present is that in one sense rule (1.18) does not so much assign [1stress] to *board* as, by virtue of the Stress Subordination Convention (1.17), assign [2stress] to *black*. It should also be noted that at some stage the word-boundaries will have to be deleted (in order to provide the phonetic output), but for the present, at least, it need only be assumed that this takes place after the operation of all stress rules. In fact, we shall ourselves often omit word-boundaries where these are of no direct relevance.

At this stage it is important to note one of the crucial features of this generative approach to stress – that in assigning the stress pattern of some particular constituent or constituents we proceed from an initial or *underlying* string of segments, unmarked for stress but together with appropriate word-boundaries (and any other syntactic information which may be relevant). Then in a step-by-step operation, stress assignment rules are applied to those underlying strings or representations so that eventually we reach, or are able to *derive*, the appropriate phonetic output. Thus the surface form *black board* is said to be derived from underlying $[_{NP}\#[_A\#black\#]_A [_N\#board\#]_N\#]_{NP}$, and that is shown by the *derivation* in (1.19).

Q. Once more let us consider *blackboard*. From our informal description of stress assignment in noun compounds, it would appear that the exact counterpart of (1.18) should be:

(1.20) $V \longrightarrow$ [1stress] $/ \overline{} X \overset{1}{V} Y]_N$

Attempt now to give a derivation of the stress pattern of this compound.

A. Omitting word-boundaries, the correct derivation should be:

(1.21) $[_N[_A\text{black}]_A\ [_N\text{board}]_N]_N$

$[_N\text{bl}\overset{1}{\text{a}}\text{ck b}\overset{1}{\text{o}}\text{ard}]_N$ \qquad Word-Stress Rule

$\text{bl}\overset{1}{\text{a}}\text{ckb}\overset{2}{\text{o}}\text{ard}$ \qquad Rule (1.20)

Rules (1.18) and (1.20), even in a more refined form, have much more generality than we have so far suggested. If we examine such compound adjectives as *heartbroken, bed-ridden, sea-sick, God-fearing*, or such compound verbs as *horsewhip, typewrite, sight-see, baby-sit*, these too have the stress pattern 1 2. And if we examine verb phrases, such as *kicked the cat*, or adjective phrases such as *very fat*, or even sentences such as *Jesus wept*, these all have the stress pattern 2 1.

If you recall the word-boundary rule given above as (1.11), it can be seen that the contrasting stress patterns correlate exactly with a contrast between on the one hand the lexical categories 'noun', 'adjective', 'verb' (N,V,A,) and on the other hand phrasal categories such as 'noun phrase' (NP) or 'verb phrase' (VP), even 'sentence' (S), which dominate a lexical category. When we are dealing with a lexical category the stress pattern is 1 2, when we are dealing with a phrasal category the stress pattern is 2 1. Let us therefore generalise (1.18) and (1.20) as follows, where L stands for one of the defined lexical categories and P stands for one of the defined phrasal categories. The revision of (1.18) is given as (1.22), which is usually referred to as the *Nuclear Stress Rule*; the revision of (1.20) is given as (1.23), which is usually referred to as the *Compound Stress Rule*.

(1.22) *Nuclear Stress Rule (NSR)*

$\text{V} \longrightarrow [\text{1stress}] / \overset{1}{\text{V}}\ \text{X} \underline{\qquad} \text{Y}]_P$

(1.23) *Compound Stress Rule (CSR)*

$\overset{1}{\text{V}} \longrightarrow [\text{1stress}] / \underline{\qquad} \text{X}\ \overset{1}{\text{V}}\ \text{Y}]_L$

You should work out for yourself examples such as *sea-sick* and *very fat*, in order to be certain that the rules work.

As we have already mentioned, these rules apply cyclically, i.e. over and over again, each time the innermost brackets are removed. In order to see how the cyclical application of rules operates, let us now consider the compound *blackboard duster*. In this and all such examples the crucial first step seems to be some way removed from phonology, for it is that we have to make sure that we have the correct syntactic bracketing. Recall, however, that we have already noted that stress placement is critically dependent upon the syntactic structure of the string concerned.

Q.   In the present case the correct bracketing is:

(1.24) $[_{NP}[_N[_A black]_A [_N board]_N]_N] [_N duster]_N]_{NP}$

Given that structure, attempt now to give a detailed derivation of the stress pattern of the string.

A.   The first step is to assign primary stress within each word, and then remove the innermost set of brackets:

(1.25) $[_{NP}[_N bl\overset{1}{a}ck\ boa\overset{1}{r}d]_N\ d\overset{1}{u}ster]_{NP}$

The innermost set of brackets now demarcates *blackboard* and labels it as an N, i.e. a member of a lexical category. Therefore the Compound Stress Rule (henceforth CSR) applies, assigning [1stress] to *black*, and the Stress Subordination Convention (henceforth SSC) reduces all other stresses in the string by one. It is especially important to note here that the string under consideration is that string which is bound by the innermost set of brackets – therefore the primary stress on *duster* remains unaffected. The result of the application of the CSR is therefore:

(1.26) $[_{NP} bl\overset{1}{a}ckb\overset{2}{o}ard\ d\overset{1}{u}ster]_{NP}$

The final set of brackets contains an NP, and therefore the Nuclear Stress Rule (NSR for short) applies, assigning [1stress] to *duster*:

(1.27) $bl\overset{2}{a}ckb\overset{3}{o}ard\ d\overset{1}{u}ster$

In order to see how crucial syntactic bracketing is (at least within this approach to stress assignment), you should now try to assign the correct stress pattern to *black board-duster* (i.e. a board-duster which is black).

The rules which we have given above can apply to an extraordinarily wide range of syntactic structures above the word level. In order to see this you should attempt to derive the stress patterns of the following quite varied sentences and phrases:

(1.28) a. John loves Mary
       b. white elephant
       c. Mary likes red roses
       d. Anne-Marie is a redhead

At this point it may be convenient to give a brief summary of the generative account of stress assignment as we have discussed it so far.

(i)   Stress is assigned by rule to vocalic segments.
(ii) Primary stress is indicated by [1stress], absence of stress (more properly, weak stress) by [0stress]; all other stress levels are derived by convention – see (vi) below.
(iii) The assignment of stress is dependent upon syntactic structure.

(iv) Stress is assigned cyclically, working from the innermost set of brackets outwards.

(v) In strings of greater than word length, there are two main rules of stress assignment: (a) CSR, which applies to strings dominated by a lexical category; (b) NSR, which applies to strings dominated by a phrasal category.

(vi) Whenever [1stress] is assigned by rule, all other stresses in the relevant string are reduced by one, according to the SSC.

We would not be so foolish as to deny that the assignment of stress above the word level is less simple than we have suggested or that there are many problems that we have not yet discussed. Nor could it possibly be maintained that we have outlined fully the principles of such stress assignment as given in works such as Chomsky & Halle (1968) and Halle & Keyser (1971). All that we have done, in fact, is demonstrate the general principles of such analyses. Towards the end of this chapter we shall have a further and more detailed look at the workings of these rules, when we shall discover that some of the above points need to be amended, but for the present we shall leave this discussion at the level of general principles.

1.3   *Primary word-stress*

Q. Let us now move on to the topic of stress assignment within (minimal) words. Consider firstly the following pair of sentences:

(1.29) a. John promised success
       b. John achieved success

What is the stress pattern of each, as given by the stress rules discussed so far?

A. In both cases the stress pattern is 2 3 1, by virtue of repeated application of the NSR. This, of course, is correct, but not entirely so, for we have failed to note one important point, and we have equally failed to demonstrate how that point might be handled within the theory. This is that in (1.29a) [3stress] must be assigned to the *first* vowel of the verb (*promised*), whereas in (1.29b) [3stress] must be assigned to the *second* vowel of the verb (*achieved*). This contrast cannot conceivably be a function of either the NSR or the CSR. The NSR's job, which it has done quite properly, is to assign less stress to the main stress of the verb than to the main stresses of the other items in the string. Neither string here contains by any stretch of the imagination a compound, and therefore the CSR can have played no role in the derivation. Clearly, therefore, what we must be concerned with here is the placement of *word-stress*.

Q. Let us start by considering the location of the primary stress in the following nouns:

(1.30) (a)   (b)   (c)   (d)

design   ellípsis   muséum   polýgamy

ballóon   inspéctor   aróma   élephant

cocáine   repúblic   flúid   précipice

domáin   propagánda   stúpid   levíathan

Can you determine any general principles about the location of primary stress in these words? In other words, can you say why the words in column (a) have stress on the final vowel, why the words in columns (b) and (c) have stress on the penultimate vowel, and why the words in column (d) have stress on the antepenultimate vowel?

A. It is easiest to start with the words in column (d). In what ways do they contrast with the words in the other columns? One point of contrast is that it is noticeable that all the vowels which occur to the right of the primary-stressed vowel are short. Thus, compare *muséum*, where we may infer that primary stress is prevented from occurring on the first vowel when there is a long vowel to its right. This suggests that primary stress occurs on the leftmost [+long] vowel (where this definition includes diphthongs). If that were the case, then *precipice* could be regarded as an example of a default mechanism: primary stress is assigned to the leftmost vowel even if it is [−long], since the stress has to be assigned somewhere! But that won't do. If it were so, then an example such as *polygamy* would be inexplicable. This latter example seems to prove that stress must be assigned to one of the last three vowels (for otherwise the stress pattern would be **pólygamy*). You might like to try to pronounce this example with stress on the first syllable – you are almost certain to give some stress to the third syllable as well, which, very weakly, tends to support the claim that stress must be assigned to one of the three rightmost vowels. There is another contrast. Consider the words in column (b): as with the words of column (d), the two rightmost vowels are [−long]. This might lead us to suppose that they too should have stress on the third vowel from the right. But they do not. Is there any explanation for this? The answer is to be found by looking to see what consonants follow the second vowel from the right. In the case of the words in column (d) the second vowel is always followed by a single consonant; but in the case of the words in column (b) the second vowel is always followed by two (or more) consonants. This suggests that if the penultimate vowel is [−long], then it can still receive stress provided that it is followed by two or more consonants. The same, however, is not true of the final vowel; compare here *elephant*. All this suggests that the following rule can be proposed for assigning stress to words of the type exemplified in column (d):

(1.31) $V \longrightarrow$ [1stress] $/ \underline{\hspace{1cm}} C_0 \, \check{V} \, C \, \check{V} \, C_0]_N$

where $\check{V}$ indicates [V, $-$long] and C_0 indicates zero or more consonants.

If we then turn to the words in columns (b) and (c), it looks at first sight as if the parallel rule to (1.31) should be, given the facts as stated above :

(1.32) $V \longrightarrow / \underline{\hspace{1cm}} \langle C_2 \rangle_b \, \check{V} \, C_0]_N$
$\langle +\text{long} \rangle_a$

where the angled brackets ($\langle \ \rangle$) and the subscripts indicate disjunction: that is to say, either all the material in $\langle \ \rangle_a$ or all the material in $\langle \ \rangle_b$ must be taken, but not both. Rule (1.32) looks rather complicated, and indeed it is. Fortunately there is a simpler solution. Let us suppose that rule (1.31) applies first, and that it assigns [1stress] correctly to all examples of the type in column (d). The consequence of this is that we need only deal with the types represented in the other three columns, and those in columns (b) and (c) are characterised by having to their right a vowel which is [$-$long]. Thus we can assign stress to those words by the following rule, much simpler than that in (1.32), provided that we assume that this rule applies if and only if rule (1.31) has failed to assign [1stress] (by virtue of the word concerned failing to meet the structural description of (1.31)):

(1.33) $V \longrightarrow$ [1stress] $/ \underline{\hspace{1cm}} C_0 \, \check{V} \, C_0]_N$

If we assume that rules (1.31) and (1.33) apply first, then the examples in column (a) fall out nicely, for stress will correctly be assigned by the following rule, which comes into play only if [1stress] is not assigned by (1.31) or (1.33):

(1.34) $V \longrightarrow$ [1stress] $/ \underline{\hspace{1cm}} C_0]_N$

Q.   In our account immediately above it will be noticeable that we have left unresolved one rather obvious difficulty: we have not given any formal means of ensuring that rule (1.33) only comes into play if rule (1.31) fails to apply and that rule (1.34) only comes into play if both rule (1.31) and rule (1.33) fail to apply. We shall show how we can resolve this difficulty quite simply, but first of all it is worth giving a wider range of examples to show that the rules as we have stated them apply. For the following forms, consider where the primary stress is located and which rule will in each case correctly assign that primary stress: *ballyhoo, England, America, phonology, volume, asparagus, horizon, divine, alien, potato.*

A.   The best way to approach the correct answer to this question is to test each word to see whether or not the longest environment can apply.

This environment is, of course, found in rule (1.31). You should have worked out that the following words are assigned [1stress] on their antepenultimate vowel by that rule: *América, phonólogy, aspáragus*. The next longest rule is (1.33), which assigns [1stress] to the penultimate vowel of *England, vólume, horízon*. Finally, rule (1.34) assigns [1stress] to the final vowel of *ballyhóo, divíne*. What about *potato* and *alien*? There can be no doubt about the location of primary stress in either: in *potáto* it is the penultimate vowel which is stressed, and in *álien* it is the first vowel which is stressed. But surely in the case of *potato* the final vowel (diphthong) should be stressed, since it is [+long], i.e. [pəteɪtəʊ]? And this is not the only example; note also *tomáto* (in either English or American pronunciation), *albíno, cíty, macaróni*, etc. One point that we might note here is that there is considerable variation amongst speakers: some speakers, for example, will say [sɪtiː] whilst others will say [sɪtɪ]. This variation is more common for the high vowel than the mid vowel, where in general the diphthong is the usual (RP) pronunciation (with forms such as [oː] in other dialects). This variation suggests that there is a rule in English (subject to sociolinguistic variables) which converts a final [−long] vowel into a [+long] vowel, with consequent diphthongisation, etc., so that the underlying form of *potato* would have underlyingly a final short vowel. The rule will be of the form:

(1.35)   V $\longrightarrow$ [+long] / ——— #
          [−low]

Some further evidence from this comes from the minimal pair *Mary* and *Marie*. *Marie* always has final [iː] and for those speakers who implement rule (1.35) for [+high] vowels *Mary* too will have final /iː/. But in the case of *Mary* the underlying vowel will be /ɪ/ as against /iː/ in *Marie*. It is this difference in underlying form which creates the different stress pattern, and the different stress pattern is fully accounted for by our rules provided that stress assignment is carried out at the level of underlying representation. The case of *alien* seems somewhat simpler, for surely its usual pronunciation in British English is either [eɪlɪən] or [eɪljən], suggesting that the penultimate vowel is underlyingly (and on the surface in one case) short. However, many American phonologists suggest a pronunciation where the second vowel is long, i.e. /iː/. For dialects where that is the case it would appear that we have another instance of a non-low vowel becoming [+long], this time immediately before another vowel, i.e.:

(1.36) V $\longrightarrow$ [+long] / ——— V

Rules (1.35) and (1.36) can be collapsed together, but for British English at least we see no reason for doing so. Words such as *potato* and *alien* interest us because they demonstrate the necessity for stress assignment rules to operate at the level of underlying representation.

As we have already said, we still need to find some way of ensuring that our stress rules interact correctly with one another. Take an example such as *elephant*. The way we have stated our rules so far would mean that by rule (1.31) [1stress] would be assigned to the antepenultimate vowel, then by rule (1.33) [1stress] would be assigned to the penultimate vowel, and then by rule (1.34) [1stress] would be assigned to the final vowel. Assuming that the SSC operates, this would give the hopelessly incorrect pattern 3 2 1! Compare now the environments for the three rules (1.31), (1.33), (1.34):

(1.37) a. $/ \text{———} C_0 \: \breve{V} \: C \: \breve{V} \: C_0]_N$

b. $/ \text{———} \qquad C_0 \: \breve{V} \: C_0]_N$

c. $/ \text{———} \qquad\qquad C_0]_N$

Even a cursory glance at (1.37a–c) is probably sufficient to make everyone aware that the environments concerned are very similar. Indeed, the environment for (1.37c) is a subpart of the environment for (1.37b), which in turn is a subpart of the environment for (1.37a) – and, of course, the actual change is in every case identical. This means that with the appropriate use of brackets we can collapse three rules into one, namely:

$(1.38) \quad V \longrightarrow [1stress] \: / \text{———} C_0 \: (\breve{V} \: (C)) \: (\breve{V} \: C_0)]_N$

Within the conventions of generative phonology this rule is to be interpreted as follows: material within brackets is optional (i.e. need not be present for the rule to apply) and the rule applies disjunctively, that is to say, in any given case the rule applies only once and it applies with the longest environment which the structure of the string under consideration matches. Thus, in the case of a word such as *hippopotamus*, the longest environment, i.e. (1.37a) can, and therefore must, apply, and so [1stress] is assigned to the antepenultimate vowel. And in the case of a word such as *England* the longest environment which can apply, and therefore must apply, is (1.37b), whereby [1stress] is assigned to the penultimate vowel. Similarly, in the case of *ballyhoo* the longest environment which can apply is (1.37c), which assigns [1stress] to the final vowel. You should check for yourself that rule (1.38), which we shall call (after Halle 1973, although our formulation is different from his and much nearer to that of the English Stress Rule in Liberman & Prince 1977) the *Primary Stress Rule* or PSR, correctly places [1stress] on the other words which we have just been discussing.

Q.   Unfortunately the PSR by no means covers all the words in the language. Consider firstly the following pairs: *tòrment/tormènt*, *àbstract/*

ábstráct, súrvey/survèy, pérmit/permìt, cóntent/contènt. Can you determine any syntactically based reasons for the contrasting stress patterns (it should be clear that there are no phonological reasons)?

A. Three of the pairs all show the same syntactic contrast, for in the case of *torment, permit* and *survey,* the first member of each pair is a noun, the second member a verb. On the other hand, in the case of *content,* although the first member of the pair must be a noun, the second member may be either an adjective or a verb, and in the case of *abstract* the first member is an adjective and the second member is a verb. In fact these pairs demonstrate what appears to be a fairly general property of English, that although nouns do follow the PSR as in (1.38), with only a few fairly marginal exceptions, verbs to a very great extent tend to show primary stress nearer the end of the word. Adjectives tend to vacillate between the nominal type and the verbal type.

Q. If what we have just said is correct, then it would seem that rule (1.38) will not satisfactorily apply to most verbs (and many adjectives). The obvious solution, therefore, is to suggest a different version of the PSR for verbs. Adjectives will then have to be specially marked in the lexicon for which version of the PSR they undergo (e.g. *content* will be marked as undergoing the verbal version of the rule whereas *abstract* will be marked as undergoing the nominal version of the rule), as will the inevitable cases where nouns and verbs are exceptions to their rules. We might note in passing that exceptions are inevitable in almost any phonological process – this is not in itself troublesome, provided that the number of exceptions is limited. Given this situation, therefore, consider the following verbs and suggest a version of the PSR which will properly predict their stress assignment: *torment, practise, abstract, edit, elicit, astonish, molest, swallow, allege, maintain.*

A. These verbs fall into two groups: (a) those with penultimate stress, namely *práctise, édit, elícit, astónish, swállow;* (b) those with final stress, namely *tormènt, abstràct, molèst, allège, maintàin.* Recalling that *swallow* will be like *potato* and have an underlying short final vowel which is lengthened by rule (1.35), all the words in group (a) will have in common the fact that underlyingly they end in a short vowel plus no more than one consonant. All the words in group (b) violate this by having in final position either a long vowel (or diphthong), as in *maintain,* or a consonant cluster, as in *torment.* Note, by the way, that this assumes that in *allege* the final consonant /ʤ/ is analysed as a cluster (and therefore /dʒ/) rather than a single consonant. We can therefore suggest the following PSR for verbs:

(1.39) $V \longrightarrow [1stress] / \underline{\hspace{1cm}} C_0 \, (\check{V} \, (C))]_V$

If, however, one compares (1.38) and (1.39), it is noticeable that the only difference between the two is that (1.39) omits the final elements V C_0. This means that the two rules can be collapsed together as:

(1.40) *Primary Stress Rule (PSR)*

$$V \longrightarrow [1stress] / \text{―――} C_0 \ (\check{V} \ (C)) \ (_a\check{V} \ C_0)_a\#$$

We can then simply state a condition that all those items which preferentially undergo (1.39) rather than (1.38) are marked as [~a] in the lexicon, i.e. that the part of the environment labelled $(_a \ldots)_a$ is not applied to them. Generally speaking, the vast majority of verbs and a very considerable number of adjectives will be so marked – only a small number of nouns will be so marked.

Q.   The pair *tórment/tormènt* and others like it pose other problems beside that of determining the location of the primary stress. Compare with that pair the following pair: *Aúgust/augúst*. What differences can you perceive in the stress patterns? Why might that be so?

A.   The second members of each of the above pairs are similar, in that they have primary stress on the final vowel, presumably because both are [~a]. But the first members are different, although not in the location of primary stress, which in each case is on the first vowel. In *August* the first vowel is primary-stressed because, being a noun, *August* is not marked [~a] and therefore [1stress] can be assigned to the penultimate vowel in the environment: ――― C_0 V $C_0]_L$. In the case of *torment*, however, this is not enough, for the final vowel, although not primary-stressed, does have secondary stress (unlike the final vowel of *August*). Now, as we have already suggested above, in the system within which we are working the only way for a vowel to acquire secondary stress is for it first to acquire primary stress and then, by appropriate application of the SSC (1.17), have that primary stress reduced. In the present context that must produce two questions. Firstly, why is it that the noun *torment* acquires two primary stresses (one of which is reduced), whilst the noun *August* acquires only one primary stress? Secondly, how is it that *torment* acquires its second primary stress?

The crucial difference between the two pairs seems to be that in the case of *torment* the noun and verb are synchronically related to one another and that indeed the noun is derived from the verb, whereas in the case of *august* the noun and adjective are synchronically unrelated (whatever their ultimate historical origins might be). Thus in the case of *august*, which is marked [~a], stress will be assigned to the final vowel by the PSR, whereas in the case of *August* stress will be assigned to the penultimate vowel, since that word is not marked [~a]. That is entirely possible, since the two words will have independent lexical entries. In the case of *torment/torment*, however, we start off with only one lexical entry, namely the verb *torment*, which is marked [~a]. Therefore application of the PSR will give *tormént*. We need, however, to assign [1stress] to the first vowel too, both in the obvious case of the noun and in the less obvious case of the verb, for it turns out that the first vowel of the verb has secondary stress. In order to solve this problem we shall have to turn away from this particular example and consider a much wider set of examples. We will, however, return to the case of *torment/torment* later in this chapter.

1.4   *Multiply-stressed words*

Q. So far we have assumed that lexical items and primary stresses stand in a one-to-one relationship to each other. Whilst this is obviously true in a great number of instances (and most obviously, indeed almost tautologically, in the case of lexical monosyllables), there are also a great many examples where there is more than one primary stress. The SSC will, of course, reduce all but one of these primary stresses. Nevertheless primary stress will need to be assigned more than once within such words. Consider, therefore, the following examples. In each case we have indicated where primary stress will be assigned by virtue of the PSR (in some cases by an exceptional application of the PSR). Attempt now to determine whether there are any other primary stresses in each word and, if so, their location. Furthermore, attempt to formulate a rule which might account for the location of these primary stresses. Note, by the way, that for the moment we are not interested in the relative strength of each of these primary stresses; therefore, do not apply the SSC.

(1.41) (a)	(b)	(c)	(d)
catamarán	Ecclesiástes	ukuléle	champágne
hullaballóo	Seringapátam	balaláika	tycóon
abracadábra	Monongahéla	hogmanáy	tormént
mulligatáwny	laryngoscópe	debonáir	baróque
Popocatepétl	decompósable	caraván	políce

A. In all except two cases, namely, the last two examples in column (d), there is indeed an additional primary stress, and indeed in the instance of the last example of column (a) there are two additional primary stresses.

These additional stresses are located as follows:

(1.42)

(a)	(b)	(c)	(d)
catamaran	Ecclesiastes	ukulele	champagne
hullaballoo	Seringapatam	balalaika	tycoon
abracadabra	Monongahela	hogmanay	torment
mulligatawny	laryngoscope	debonair	baroque
Popocatepetl	decomposable	caravan	police

Let us consider firstly the examples in column (a), for the moment excluding the last example *Popocatepetl*. In each case there are two unstressed syllables (vowels) between the primary stresses. Furthermore, these cases are all differentiated from the cases in the other columns by virtue of the fact that they map on to the structure: # C V̆ C V̆ C V̆ C immediately followed by a primary-stressed vowel. Notice here especially the words in column (b). These contrast with the words in column (a) in, apart from anything else, the fact that the vowel two syllables away from the rightmost primary-stressed vowel is either [+long] or followed by more than one consonant. Furthermore, the example of *Popocatepetl* would seem to suggest that the maximum number of unstressed vowels intervening between two stressed vowels is two; if this were not the case, then we might expect *$\overset{1}{P}$opocatep$\overset{1}{e}$tl. All this suggests that we could account for the stress pattern of the words in (1.42) by means of the following rule:

(1.43) V $\longrightarrow$ [1stress] / ——— C_0 V̆ C V C $\overset{1}{V}$

Let us now look again at the examples in column (b). Not only is it the case that in all these examples the stressed vowel is either [+long] or followed by more than one consonant, as we have already remarked; it is also the case that the structure of the following sequence is irrelevant. Thus, in the case of *Seringapatam* the newly stressed vowel is followed (after the consonant cluster) by V̆ C; in the case of *laryngoscope* the sequence is V̄ C C; and in the case of *decomposable* the sequence is V̆ C C. This suggests the following rule:

(1.44) V $\longrightarrow$ [1stress] / ——— C_0 V $C_0\overset{1}{V}$

If one now turns to the words in column (c), it turns out that they too will have their stress correctly assigned by rule (1.44). This leaves us with the words in column (d). Let us ignore for the moment the last two words, namely *baroque* and *police*. In the other cases there is a very attractive solution which rests upon the following generalisation. If in any polysyllabic word primary stress is assigned by the PSR to some vowel in that word, then at least one vowel to the left of that primary-stressed vowel must also receive primary stress. This clearly applies to the words in columns (a–c) (that is not completely true – there is one interesting exception to which we shall return later). If this generalisation is indeed significantly true, then it follows that there should be, as it were, a 'default' version of (1.43) and (1.44), i.e. a version of these rules which would apply just in case both these rules failed to assign [1stress] anywhere in the word (cf. the discussion of *precipice* on p. 11). This rule would have the form:

$$(1.45) \quad V \longrightarrow [\text{1stress}] \ / \ \underline{\qquad} C_0 \overset{1}{V}$$

Recall now our earlier discussion of the PSR (1.40), where we started off with three separate rules and then collapsed these separate rules into a single rule. Clearly, the same process is possible here. Liberman & Prince (1977:278; henceforth LP) suggest that the processes we have been discussing above can be collapsed together as a single rule; they in fact call this rule the Long Retraction Rule (LRR), and it is formulated by them as follows:

$$(1.46) \quad V \longrightarrow [\text{1stress}] \ / \ \underline{\qquad} C_0 \ (\check{V} \ (C)) \ (V \ C_0) \overset{1}{V}$$

Q. We have already hinted that words such as *baroque* and *police* are apparent exceptions to (1.46). This is indeed the case, since in both words the LRR (1.46) will, apparently counterfactually, assign [1stress] to the first vowel, which should in fact be unstressed. Let us also assume that (1.46) operates iteratively. What we mean by this is that (1.46) not only assigns [1stress] to some vowel to the left of a vowel assigned [1stress] by the PSR; it will also assign [1stress] to some vowel to the left of the vowel assigned [1stress] by the first application of (1.46) itself. This process will then be repeated (or re-iterated) until the left boundary of the word is reached. Under this assumption, there are four further words in (1.42) where a vowel appears to be incorrectly assigned [1stress] by (1.46). What words are these?

A. These words, in addition to *baroque* and *police*, are *Ecclesiastes*, *Seringapatam*, *Monongahela* and *laryngoscope*, for in each case the subrule which assigns [1stress] in the environment: $\underline{\qquad} C_0 \overset{1}{V}$ will apply. Thus we will find the following:

$$(1.47) \quad \overset{1}{\text{ba}}\overset{1}{\text{ro}}\text{que} \qquad\qquad \text{po}\overset{1}{\text{li}}\overset{1}{\text{ce}} \qquad\qquad \overset{1}{\text{E}}\text{cc}\overset{1}{\text{le}}\text{si}\overset{1}{\text{a}}\text{stes}$$

$$\overset{1}{\text{Se}}\text{rin}\overset{1}{\text{ga}}\text{pa}\overset{1}{\text{tam}} \qquad \overset{1}{\text{Mo}}\text{non}\overset{1}{\text{ga}}\text{he}\overset{1}{\text{la}} \qquad \overset{1}{\text{la}}\text{ryn}\overset{1}{\text{go}}\text{sco}\overset{1}{\text{pe}}$$

The problem is clearly that rule (1.46) overgenerates, that is to say, it creates instances of [1stress] which should not exist. On the other hand, it is usually argued, the LRR expresses quite elegantly a generalisation about the placement of primary stress which we should be loth to lose. Therefore, what we should have is some kind of 'housekeeping' rule which will tidy up the mess created by the overgenerating rule (1.46). The function of such a rule is quite clear: it should reduce certain initial [1stress] vowels to [0stress].

Q. This rule, which we shall call the Initial Destressing Rule (IDR), must have the form: [V, 1stress] ⟶ [0stress]. Taking into account the words above and also the following words, can you suggest the environment in which the rule operates: *fandango, articulate, Belfast, Caithness, maidan?*

A. As the very name of the rule suggests, it only applies to the first vowel of a word, and furthermore it applies regardless of the number of consonants that precede that vowel. It is also the case that the rule only applies if the next following vowel is [1stress]; note, here all the examples under (1.42c). Therefore there appear to be only two variables involved. One of these concerns the length of the first vowel. Not only do all the examples above of Initial Destressing involve a [−long] vowel, there is also the example of *maidan*, which does not show Destressing even although the next following vowel has (exceptionally) been assigned [1stress]. Therefore we shall have to indicate that only [−long] vowels undergo Destressing. If we then consider the other examples where Destressing does not apply, then it is noticeable that in each case two or more consonants intervene. This suggests that the formulation of the Initial Destressing Rule should be as follows:

$$(1.48) \quad \begin{matrix} V \\ [-\text{long}] \end{matrix} \longrightarrow [\text{0stress}] \: / \: \# \: C_0 \text{——— (C)} \: \overset{1}{V}$$

Unfortunately, as you may have noticed, (1.48) does not always work as it stands. Rather than trying to rectify this at present, all that we wish to do is point out the problem and the general method of solution. The one example above which is not amenable to (1.48) is *Ecclesiastes*, for according to our formulation, since more than one consonant intervenes, (1.48) should not apply. Now there are in fact many similar examples, such as *asparagus, mosquito*, and *astronomy*. It seems to us undeniable that, as LP (287) point out, the rule as it is presently stated cannot cope with the problem and that it ought to be formulated in terms of syllable structure. This is not the first time that we have noted such difficulties, and we shall return to the question of syllable structure at a later stage, since it should be becoming increasingly clear that a resolution of the nature of syllable structure is imperative. However, for the moment we shall let matters stand, and simply ask you to reflect on the issues involved and, perhaps, think about what syllable-based solution might be possible.

Q.   Not all words appear to follow exactly the above pattern. This is especially, but by no means exclusively, the case with verbs having the (stressed) suffix *-ate*. Consider therefore the following forms and determine the location of stressed vowels. Furthermore, see if it is possible to modify (1.46), the LRR, to account for the location of these stresses:

(1.49) manipulȧte   articulȧte   syllabicȧte   officiȧte

      Afghanistȧn   Scheherazȧde   supposititious

A.   The location of stresses in the above examples is as follows:

(1.50) manipulȧte   articulȧte   syllȧbicȧte   officiȧte

      Afghȧnistȧn   Scheherȧzȧde   suppȯsititious

What we find in each of the above cases is that stressed syllables occur alternately, regardless of the nature of the relevant syllables. If we assume, as above, that this variation of the LRR operates iteratively, and also that the same requirement still holds that at least one vowel to the left of any primary-stressed vowel must also carry primary stress (although this is not without its problems – consider the case of *Afghanistan*), then we can propose a rule of the form:

(1.51) V ⟶ [1stress] / ─── C_0 (V C_0) $\overset{1}{V}$

If you compare (1.51) with rule (1.46), then it is clear that the same environment is present in both cases; the only difference is that (1.46) permits a longer expansion (containing V̌ (C)). We can therefore collapse the two rules together, and mark the longer expansion by some index, say *a*. This gives us:

(1.52) V ⟶ [1stress] / ─── $C_{0\ a}$(V̌ (C))$_a$ (V C_0) $\overset{1}{V}$

It is then a quite straightforward matter to mark all words containing the suffix *-ate*, together with other words of the same type, [~a]. This will ensure that they only undergo the variant of the LRR given under (1.51). This type of retraction we shall call *Strong* or *Alternating Retraction*. This variation of SRR is essentially that given by LP (275–6). You may well have noticed that it is often difficult to tell whether a word undergoes Long Retraction or Strong Retraction. The examples in (1.42b–d) and also *Popocatepetl* in (1.42a) could well have been analysed as Strong Retractors. Which pattern is the more fundamental is an important question, which we shall leave until chapter 3. Whatever the answer, it is certain that the two types of retraction are closely related.

Q.   There is another group of words which show another pattern of Stress Retraction. These are best typified by examples with the suffix *-oid*, although again there are other exceptional items to be added to the list (and regularly in American English, occasionally in British English, the list should be extended by items with the suffix *-ite* – see the last line of examples below). Again, for the following examples determine the location of stressed vowels, and then see if it is possible to modify (1.52) so as to account within one rule for the location of these stresses:

(1.53) ellipsóid   pyramidóid   cylindróid   epicyclóid

        Adiróndacks   peróxide   Orestés   electrón

        tripartíte   archimandríte   stalagmíte   gelignîte

A.   The location of the stresses in the above examples is as follows:

(1.54) ellípsóid   pyrámidóid   cylíndróid   épicyclóid

        Adiróndacks   peróxide   Oréstés   eléctrón

        tripártíte   archimándríte   stálagmíte   gélignîte

As with Strong Retraction, primary stresses are placed not more than one syllable away from a primary stress to the right. Thus we have an example such as *pyramidoid*. On the other hand, primary stress is located immediately to the left of another primary stress if the relevant vowel is [+long] or is followed by more than one consonant. The rule to account for this is as follows:

(1.55) $V \longrightarrow [\text{1stress}] / \underline{\quad\quad} C_0\ (\breve{V}\ (C))\ \overset{1}{V}$

If we now compare this rule with (1.46) you will be able to see that the only difference between this rule and (1.46) is that (1.46) permits a longer expansion including the sequence: $V\ C_0$. Since (1.55) and (1.51) are in complementary distribution with regard to the portion of rule (1.46) which is omitted, we can now provide a single rule which covers all three types of retraction. This rule will have the form:

(1.56) *Stress Retraction Rule*
        $V \longrightarrow [\text{1stress}] / \underline{\quad\quad} C_{0\ a}(\breve{V}\ (C))_{a\ b}(V\ C_0)_b\ \overset{1}{V}$

Then items of the type listed in (1.54), which undergo, as LP term it, Weak Retraction, will be marked [~b] just as Strong Retractors were marked [~a]. Note that in British English *stalagmite* and *gelignite* undergo Strong Retraction and not Weak Retraction, although *tripartite* and *archimandrite* do indeed undergo Weak Retraction. This will have to be specified for each item individually in the lexicon. If LP are correct in assuming that in American English words with the suffix -*ite* regularly undergo Weak Retraction and only exceptionally undergo some other form of retraction, then the lexical marking will be more economically specified. You should determine for yourselves the stress patterns of *stalagmite* and *gelignite* in those American English dialects where Weak Retraction is the norm.

Q.   Compare now the SRR (1.56) and the PSR (1.40). Is it possible to combine these two separate rules into one single rule?

A.   It should be clear that there are very few differences between the two rules, and therefore that in principle they should be combinable into a single rule. These differences are as follows: (i) whereas the PSR has as its rightmost element the word-boundary #, the SRR has as its rightmost element a primary-stressed vowel; (ii) whereas in the PSR the vowel before the word-boundary must be [−long], in the SRR the vowel before the primary-stressed vowel may be either [+long] or [−long]. There is also a complication which concerns the indexation of exceptions. Let us assume that, as in the SRR, Strong Retractors are marked [~a] and Weak Retractors marked [~b]. It is still necessary to indicate that many verbs and some adjectives undergo (1.39), the 'short' version of the PSR. One almost absurdly simple point is that we shall have to relabel these, since [~a] now has a different signification. Let us relabel them [~n] (where *n* stands for nominal). This leads to the following single rule, which applies iteratively (like the PSR) and which covers all the work of the two single rules. We may therefore call it the *English Stress Rule* (ESR):

(1.57) *English Stress Rule*

$$ V \longrightarrow [\text{1stress}] / \underline{\hspace{2em}} C_0 \, (_a \check{V} \, (C))_a \, (_b, \, \langle n \rangle \begin{bmatrix} V \\ \langle -\text{long} \rangle \end{bmatrix} C_0)_b, \, \langle n \rangle \left\{ \begin{matrix} \overset{1}{V} \\ \langle \# \rangle \end{matrix} \right\} $$

To this rule must be attached the following conditions:

(i) [~a], [~b] are lexically or morphologically marked
(ii) [~n] is lexically marked

Note also that there is a standard convention by which either all the material in angled brackets (⟨. . .⟩) is included or none of it is. Thus values for [*n*] will be relevant only in the case that the rightmost element in the environment is #.

1.5   *Secondary stress*

At this point, except for one problem, we wish to end our discussion of stress within words in this chapter. But, as we shall see in chapter 3, the above account of English word-stress is essentially the same as that in at least the early versions of metrical phonology. You should therefore check for yourselves that (1.57) does indeed encapsulate all the observations that we have made about English word-stress. You might also wish to consider whether it is indeed appropriate to combine the PSR and the SRR into one rule. True enough, the formalism of generative phonology makes that a relatively simple task. But is the subsequent claim, that in each word the assignment of primary stress by the PSR and the assignment of further primary stresses by the SRR are merely subparts of a single process, a valid one?

Q. You will have noticed that throughout our discussion of word-stress we have carefully avoided implementing (1.17), the Stress Subordination Convention (SSC). For many of our examples this avoidance must seem simply perverse. Take, for example, the following words: *catamaran, debonair, tycoon, gelignite*. If we apply the English Stress Rule (ESR) to these words, then we obtain the following representations on the first iteration: *catamarán, debonáir, tycoón, gelígnite*. On the second iteration of the ESR [1stress] will be assigned to some other vowel, and, if we apply the SSC, then the following (correct) representations will result: *cátamarán, débonáir, tycóon, gélignite*. In order to see why our refusal to apply the SSC is not simply perverse, consider the following examples and show why the application of the SSC according to (1.17) is inappropriate: *Popocatepetl, tripartite, epicycloid, Adirondacks, laryngoscope, Seringapatam, baroque, police*.

A. Let us start off by considering the first four examples. The assignment of stress in each will have the same effect if we apply the ESR and simultaneously apply the SSC, so we show only one example:

(1.58) Underlying   epicycloid

      ESR, 1st iteration   epicycl**ó**id

      ESR, 2nd iteration   epic**ý**cl**ò**id

      ESR, 3rd iteration   **é**pic**ỳ**cl**ò**id (=output)

This is, of course, quite wrong: clearly, it is the third syllable which is most strongly stressed, and therefore a stress pattern more like, say, 2 1 2 is desirable. However, the application of the SSC makes that, or anything like it, impossible. An even worse situation arises with a word such as *laryngoscope*. Initially the assignment of stress follows the same pattern as in *epicycloid*:

(1.59) Underlying   laryngoscope

      ESR, 1st iteration   laryngosc**ó**pe

      ESR, 2nd iteration   lar**ý**ngosc**ò**pe

      ESR, 3rd iteration   l**á**r**ỳ**ngosc**ò**pe

But then, you will recall, in such a case rule (1.48), the Initial Destressing Rule, ought to apply. But (1.48), since it requires a following V which has [1stress], will not be able to apply. And if we were to modify the rule nevertheless, then *laryngoscope* would turn up without any primary stress at all, namely as *lar$\overset{2}{\text{y}}$ngosc$\overset{3}{\text{o}}$pe*, when the desired pattern must surely be something like *lar$\overset{1}{\text{y}}$ngosc$\overset{2}{\text{o}}$pe*. It should be a relatively simple matter to see that the same unfortunate results occur with words such as *baroque*.

Before we attempt to remedy the position, it is worth considering another set of words which, in a more complicated fashion, pose the same problem. Earlier we briefly discussed a set of words typically exemplified by the pair *t$\overset{1}{\text{o}}$rm$\overset{2}{\text{e}}$nt/t$\overset{2}{\text{o}}$rm$\overset{1}{\text{e}}$nt*. Pairs such as this contrasted with pairs such as *$\overset{1}{\text{A}}$ugust/a$\overset{2}{\text{u}}$g$\overset{1}{\text{u}}$st*, and we suggested that the only explanation for this is that the members of the pairs of the first type were synchronically related, while the members of the pairs of the second type were not synchronically related.

Of the four words [t$\overset{1}{\text{o}}$rm$\overset{2}{\text{e}}$nt]$_N$, [t$\overset{2}{\text{o}}$rm$\overset{1}{\text{e}}$nt]$_V$, [$\overset{1}{\text{A}}$ugust]$_N$, [a$\overset{2}{\text{u}}$g$\overset{1}{\text{u}}$st]$_A$, only *August* is unproblematic, since the ESR will straightforwardly give *$\overset{1}{\text{A}}$ugust*. In the case of *august*, there will be an entirely different derivation, since the pair are not synchronically related. Since the word will be, in terms of the ESR, marked as [~n], the first application of the rule will give *aug$\overset{1}{\text{u}}$st*. But the second application of the rule will apparently give *a$\overset{1}{\text{u}}$g$\overset{2}{\text{u}}$st*, because of the way that the SSC operates. One question, therefore, is how to undo that result? In the case of the two forms of *torment*, since they are synchronically related, both will have the same applications of the ESR, which will produce – so long as we assume (apparently correctly) that the verb form, which is [~n], is basic and the noun form is derived – first of all *t$\overset{1}{\text{o}}$rment*, and then, as in the case of *a$\overset{1}{\text{u}}$g$\overset{2}{\text{u}}$st*, *t$\overset{1}{\text{o}}$rm$\overset{2}{\text{e}}$nt*. Let us suppose that we can somehow adjust the SSC to give the correct results, i.e. *a$\overset{2}{\text{u}}$g$\overset{1}{\text{u}}$st* and *t$\overset{2}{\text{o}}$rm$\overset{1}{\text{e}}$nt*. Even if that were possible, we would still have a problem, for how then would we derive the nominal form *t$\overset{1}{\text{o}}$rm$\overset{2}{\text{e}}$nt* from the verbal form *t$\overset{2}{\text{o}}$rm$\overset{1}{\text{e}}$nt*?

Quite honestly, the problems relating to the SSC as it stands seem too great to offer any hope of a reasonable solution. Sanford A. Schane, in an unpublished paper (1972) reported on in Halle (1973), has suggested instead that we revise the SSC as follows:

(1.60) *Stress Subordination Convention (revised version)*
    When [1stress] is assigned to a vowel which already bears [1stress], then and only then all other stresses in the string under consideration at that point are automatically weakened by one.

If you look back over examples such as *baroque*, you will be able to see that they are no longer problematic. However, all the other cases remain so.

The basic difficulty which remains is now to ensure that only the appropriate syllable in each word is assigned [1stress]. For the position that we have now reached is one where the ESR assigns [1stress] to one or more (as appropriate) vowels in a word without any process of stress subordination taking place. Further, there is the Initial Destressing Rule (1.48) which may delete an initial [1stress]. This too, fairly obviously, will not cause stress subordination. The only two rules which we have invoked and which assign [1stress] to an already [1stress] vowel are the NSR and the CSR, given in a very basic form as (1.22) and (1.23). Under the revised version of the SSC, these are the only rules which will cause the SSC to come into play. This, of course, would make it impossible to apply the SSC within words, since the domains of both the NSR and the CSR extend beyond the word. What we need, therefore, is a rule which will re-assign [1stress] to only one (appropriate) vowel in a word. Then the revised SSC will weaken all other stresses in the word. This rule, whose formulation we shall consider in a moment, has been rather quaintly called the Detail Rule by Schane (1972), followed by Halle (1973).

Q. Consider the following words, which by the ESR will have primary stresses assigned as indicated: *télephòne, nìghtingàle, trìpartìte, èpicýclòid, àbracadàbra, bàlalàika.* Try to determine which vowel has the primary stress and which must therefore be re-assigned [1stress] by the Detail Rule. Then attempt to provide a formulation of the Detail Rule which will indeed re-assign [1stress] to the desired vowels.

A. The primary-stressed vowels appear to be as follows: *télephone, nìghtingale, tripàrtite, epicýcloid, abracadàbra, balalàika.* All that the first two words seem to tell us is that the primary stress must not be on the final vowel. Only when we consider the next pair can we see that the position is more precise than that, for they tell us, apparently, that the primary stress must be on the penultimate stressed vowel. We could, therefore, handle all four words by suggesting a form of the rule which re-assigns [1stress] to the penultimate [1stress] vowel. Unfortunately, as *abracadabra* and *balalaika* demonstrate, this is not correct, for in these cases the primary-stressed vowel is the last [1stress] vowel. Why might that be? What is the difference between these examples and the others? The answer to this is that in these two cases the final [1stress] vowel is not the final vowel of the word. This suggests that what happens is that primary stress is assigned to the last [1stress] vowel in the word which does not occur in the final syllable. We can formulate the Detail Rule as follows:

(1.61) *Detail Rule*

$$\overset{1}{V} \longrightarrow [\text{1stress}] / \underline{\hspace{2em}} Q \ V \ C_0]_L$$

Conditions: Q is a string of zero or more segments not containing [1stress].

L is any lexical category.

In fact this formulation of the rule is not entirely satisfactory as it stands, but we shall not go into the reasons for this at present. Rather, what we want to do is draw attention to another aspect of the Detail Rule. Recall, therefore, our initial presentation of the CSR in (1.23), which is repeated here for convenience:

(1.23) *Compound Stress Rule (CSR)*

$$\overset{1}{V} \longrightarrow [1stress] / \text{——} X \overset{1}{V} Y]_L$$

A rather fuller version of this rule, which would make clear that [1stress] is, by virtue of the CSR, re-assigned to the last primary-stressed vowel in the first element of the compound (more precisely, the penultimate element of the compound), would be:

(1.62) $\overset{1}{V} \longrightarrow [1stress] / \text{——} Q \ (\#\#P)]_L$

Conditions: Q is a string of zero or more elements not containing [1stress].

P is a string of zero or more segments not containing ##.

L is any lexical category.

It should be clear that (1.62) and (1.23) can be combined as a single rule, which, following Halle (1973:457), we shall continue to name the Compound Stress Rule, although in fact it assigns stress not only in compounds but also in simple words. The rule is as follows:

(1.63) *Compound Stress Rule (revised version)*

$$\overset{1}{V} \longrightarrow [1stress] / \text{——} Q \ (\#\#PP) \ V \ C_0]_L$$

Conditions: as under (1.62)

Although it would be possible to refine further both the CSR and the version of the NSR given as (1.22), we shall not do so here. For, in fact, despite this possibility, we have now given a fairly full account of the assignment of stress in words and phrases within the theoretical framework first proposed in Chomsky & Halle (1968) and then modified by papers such as Halle (1973). Furthermore, as we shall see in chapter 3, it is this account of stress which Liberman & Prince (1977), in the first full presentation of a metrical or nonlinear account of English stress, take as their starting-point. We need not, therefore, worry unduly, at least for the present, about problems which affect both approaches equally.

1.6   *Conclusion*

Let us conclude this chapter by a brief resumé of the principal features of this approach to stress which we have just been discussing. In essence this approach contains the following features.

(i)   Stress is a segmental property of vowels which is assigned by a set of rules.

(ii)   Primary stress is indicated by the feature [1stress]; absence of stress (more properly, weak stress) is indicated by the feature [0stress]; all other stress values are derived by convention.

(iii)   The assignment of stress is dependent upon morphological and syntactic structure, and all and only all lexical category words must contain at least one [1stress] vowel.

(iv)   Stress is assigned cyclically, working from the innermost set of syntactic bracketing outwards.

(v)   From (iv) it follows that stress is first assigned to simple words, then to words plus (certain types of) affixes, then to compounds, and then to larger and larger syntactic strings.

(vi)   All stress assignment rules assign [1stress] to some vowel (see (ii)), but they are of two types: (a) rules which assign [1stress] to a vowel not already bearing [1stress]; (b) rules which assign [1stress] to a vowel already bearing [1stress].

(vii)   The rule which assigns [1stress] to a vowel not already bearing [1stress] is the ESR (1.57), which operates iteratively assigning [1stress] to all vowels within a word.

(viii) The (principal) rules which assign [1stress] to a vowel already bearing [1stress] are the CSR (1.63) and the NSR (1.22). The CSR applies not only to compounds, but also applies to words so that one and only one vowel in any word has [1stress] (before the application of the CSR and the NSR to strings of greater than word length).

(ix)   When rules of type (vib) apply, the stress values of all other vowels in the string under consideration are weakened by 1 (i.e. [1stress] > [2stress] etc.) by application of the SSC (1.60).

(x)   The environment over which stress rules apply is an indefinitely long string of phonological elements; see the application of the NSR and the corresponding application of the SSC.

Notes and further reading

1.1 Although it does not deal in any great detail with the question of stress, Ladefoged (1982) is a good introduction to phonology and phonetics. Lass (1984) gives an excellent and wide-ranging introduction to phonological theory, whilst Kenstowicz & Kisseberth (1979) provide a valuable introduction to generative phonological theory. For comprehensive accounts of English stress, but not within the generative tradition, Kingdon (1958) is very useful, whilst a first-class recent account, primarily aimed at foreign learners of English but of great interest to all, is Fudge (1984).

1.2 The generative account of stress which has been presented here is most fully articulated in Chomsky & Halle (1968), of which chapters 1 and 2 are most relevant. To a fair extent chapters 3–5, which elaborate considerably the outline of the earlier chapters, can probably now be skipped. On the other hand, the modifications introduced in Halle (1973) are essential reading.

Chomsky & Halle (1968) and others working within the same tradition would assign *blackboard* the stress pattern 1 3. Such assignment seems to derive from the work of earlier American structuralists, notably Trager & Smith (1951: 38–9), who suggest four phonemic levels of stress: primary (= [1stress]), secondary (=[2stress]), tertiary (=[3stress]), and weak. For reasons that will become apparent at the beginning of chapter 3, such absolute assignment of stress values seems to us irrelevant, and indeed incorrect. We shall, therefore, ignore this particular feature of the Chomsky–Halle system here.

1.3 The rules used here for assigning stress are most closely based on Liberman & Prince (1977: §2.3), for which see chapter 3. More immediately you should consult Halle (1973), whose rules bear a close family resemblance to those used here.

For the question of how we might derive appropriate underlying representations, see Kenstowicz & Kisseberth (1979), but in addition Zwicky (1975) gives a brilliant demonstration of the complexity of the issues even for an apparently straightforward case such as the English plural inflection.

Lass (1984: 91–2, and further references therein) provides a starting-point for the analysis of long vowels and diphthongs, for which see also chapter 2.

1.4 Compare here Liberman & Prince (1977: §3.3).

Essay and discussion topics

1. Does it matter that stress has no single phonetic correlate?

2. The stress pattern in isolation of the phrase *sad plight* is, by the NSR, 2 1. By repeated applications of the NSR in the sentence *My friend can't help being shocked at anyone who would fail to consider his sad plight*, the same phrase has the pattern 8 1 (Chomsky & Halle 1968: 23). Try, if you can, to confirm this, and then consider the claim by the same authors that the actual internal relations of stress are in both cases presumably the same.

3. Throughout this chapter we have given the stress patterns of compounds such as *blackboard* as 1 2. However, it is usual to claim that the stress pattern in such cases is 1 3. Consider how such a pattern might be assigned by the rules that we have presented (modified if necessary) and then evaluate the validity of this claim.

4. There are a considerable number of apparent compounds, such as *apple pie*, *still life*, *hard-boiled*, which appear to have the stress pattern 2 1. How best might such 'exceptions' be treated in the grammar? Fudge (1984: 140–9) is a good source of examples, and see also Quirk *et al.* (1972: 1039ff).

5. What makes the rules discussed above characteristically different from all other types of generative phonological rules?

2 Segments and syllables

2.1 Introduction

The word *syllable* has been in the English language since at least the time of Chaucer, and it is frequent in linguistic descriptions, yet in chapter 1, although we made considerable informal use of the term, we did not use it in formal phonological descriptions. On the other hand, we made it clear on many occasions that a syllable-based description would be preferable to a segment-based description, on grounds both of simplicity and of adequacy, and this is a position which is now generally accepted by linguists.

Q. In order to obtain a first, albeit rough, impression of the preferability of a syllable-based description, at least for English stress, consider again the stress placement of nouns such as *design, ellipsis, museum, polygamy* (see (1.32)). We saw earlier that the assignment of primary stress in these nouns could be described by a rule of the (1.38), reproduced here as (2.1):

(2.1) $V \longrightarrow$ [1stress] $/ \underline{\hspace{1cm}} C_0 \, (\breve{V} \, (C)) \, (\breve{V} \, C_0)]_N$

Can you now suggest an informal statement in terms of syllables which might equally well account for the assignment of stress?

A. If we consider the first three examples, we can see that primary stress falls on the last syllable which contains either a long vowel or a short vowel followed by two consonants. Let us suppose that any syllable which meets these conditions (or exceeds them) is a *heavy* syllable and that any syllable which fails to meet these conditions is a *light* syllable. We could then say that primary stress is assigned to the first heavy syllable counting from the right, with a condition that no more than two syllables may be skipped.

What we wish to do now is take a look at the issues raised by assuming the existence of syllables as phonological constituents and then provide a basis for a syllable-based description sufficiently adequate for the discussion in later chapters. There are two areas, however, which we shall not consider in depth. Firstly, we shall not attempt to consider in any detail the reason why earlier work in generative phonology virtually ignored the syllable (for example, the word *syllable* does not appear as a separate entry in the subject index to Chomsky & Halle 1968), since this seems to us a matter of linguistic historiography. Secondly, though what we shall be presenting here is a description of the syllable associated with the theory of metrical phonology and, to some extent, the competing but not incompatible theory of autosegmental phonology, we shall not make a detailed comparison of metrical and autosegmental theories, nor shall we compare either with a third theory called dependency phonology. See, however, the notes and further reading at the end of this chapter.

2.2   *Syllables and sonority*

There is no shortage of definitions for the syllable. For example, Pike (1943: 116) defines a syllable as 'a single unit of movement of the lung initiator . . . which includes but one crest of speed'; but he notes elsewhere (1943: 54) that 'other criteria . . . have been advanced for the syllable, such as relative loudness of the phonemes, sonority, prominence (made up of inherent sonority, length, stress, special intonation, or a combination of some of these), and change in stress or pitch'. We wish to suggest that the principal criterion for defining pitch is the feature of *sonority*. A useful definition of sonority can be found in Ladefoged (1982: 221): 'The sonority of a sound is its loudness relative to that of other sounds with the same length, stress and pitch.'

It has, indeed, long been known (see, for example, Saussure 1966: 44–62) that it is possible to classify the sounds of language in terms of their sonority relative to each other. For example, it is quite uncontroversial that the most sonorous sounds are low (open) vowels (e.g. /a, ɑ/) whilst the least sonorous sounds are the voiceless stops (e.g. /p, t, k/). Experimentally it is rather difficult to determine a very detailed and precise ranking of the relative sonority of sounds, but there has been more than enough progress in this area for us to be fairly confident about the results. Since sonority is in part to be correlated with degrees of obstruction of the airstream, it follows that high vowels are less sonorous than low vowels, that nasals are more sonorous than their corresponding oral stops, etc. Also, voicing naturally increases sonority, and so voiced fricatives, for example, are more sonorous than their voiceless counterparts. Further evidence can be found from certain phonological developments. For instance, Vennemann (1972) demonstrates that it is possible to account for a series of sound changes in Old Icelandic by postulating a 'strength hierarchy' amongst consonants, where the 'weakest' consonant is /r/ and the strongest are the voiceless stops. Now, as Hooper (1976: 203) points out, such a strength hierarchy corresponds inversely to a sonority hierarchy: the 'strongest' consonants, in Vennemann's terms, are the least sonorous.

With evidence such as these three sources we can then propose a sonority scale (2.2), where the most sonorous elements are given the highest value and the least sonorous the lowest value (you might like to compare this scale with that in Selkirk 1984a: 112, which we shall return to later).

(2.2) *Sonority scale*

Sounds	Sonority values	Examples
low vowels	10	/a,ɑ/
mid vowels	9	/e,o/
high vowels	8	/i,u/
flaps	7	/r/
laterals	6	/l/
nasals	5	/n,m,ŋ/
voiced fricatives	4	/v,ð,z/
voiceless fricatives	3	/f,θ,s/
voiced stops	2	/b,d,g/
voiceless stops	1	/p,t,k/

Q.   The usefulness of this concept of a sonority scale in the definition of a syllable lies in the fact that where sonority is greatest we have the centre of a syllable, whereas where sonority is lowest we are near the edge of a syllable. This, of course, can easily be deduced from the fact that whereas vowels are to be closely associated with syllable centres, voiceless stops are never so associated. However, it is possible to say rather more than this. Consider, therefore, the following examples:

(2.3)

modest	complain	petty	elastic	elasticity	petrol	button	bottle
/modest/	/kompleːn/	/peti/	/əlæstik/	/iːlæstisiti/	/petrəl/	/bʌtn/	/botl/

In each example assign every segment a value for sonority according to the scale in (2.2). How many syllables are there in each word? Also, does the number of syllables in each word in any way relate to the sequencing of sonority values in each word?

A.   You should have obtained the following results: for *modest* 5–9–2–9–3–1; for *complain* 1–9–5–1–6–9–5; for *petty* 1–9–1–8; for *elastic* 8–6–10–3–1–8–1; for *elasticity* 9–6–10–3–1–8–3–8–1–8; for *petrol* 1–9–1–7–9–6; for *button* 2–9–1–5; for *bottle* 2–9–1–6. The number of syllables in each word is as follows: *modest* – two; *complain* – two; *petty* – two; *elastic* – three; *elasticity* – five; *petrol* – two; *button* – two; *bottle* – two. Let us define what we shall call a *sonority peak*. If some segment X has a sonority value which is higher than the sonority values of both of its immediately adjacent segments (or its only adjacent segment) just in case it is at the edge of a word (as, for example the final vowel in *petty*), then that segment X constitutes a sonority peak. If we now reconsider the words above, what we find is that the number of sonority peaks and the number of syllables coincide exactly. Thus there are two sonority peaks in the bisyllabic words *modest, complain, petty, petrol, button, bottle*. Therefore, we can indeed equate a sonority peak with the centre of a syllable, and we shall call the latter a *syllabic nucleus*.

Q.   But we can say rather more about syllable structure than this. Consider the following English monosyllables: *id, bad, bread, band, brand, I, isle, bye, bide, bind, bride, grind*. Can you deduce from these examples any generalisations about the structure of Modern English monosyllables in terms of the sequence of sonority values?

A.   As would be expected, there is in each example one sonority peak. But that is not all there is to say, for it is also the case that where we find a sequence of segments preceding or following that sonority peak, then sonority values increase as one nears that peak, and decrease as one moves away from that peak. Thus in the example *brand* we find the sequence 2–7–10–5–2. This highly consistent phenomenon has led many linguists (see here Bell & Hooper 1978: 8–13) to establish what Selkirk (1984a: 116) called a *Sonority Sequencing Generalisation* or SSG. Selkirk states this SSG as follows:

> (2.4) In any syllable, there is a segment constituting a sonority peak that is preceded and/or followed by a sequence of segments with progressively decreasing sonority values.

As we shall see later, there is one regular exception to this SSG (you might like to work out for yourself what that exception is). Nevertheless, if we accept it we can take a further important step forward, for we can now explain examples such as *button* and *bottle*. At first sight, since they contain only one vowel, we might suppose that they contain only one syllable. But look again at the sequence of sonority values in these two words, namely 2–9–1–5 and 2–9–1–6. Not only is it the case that they both contain two sonority peaks, which confirms our treatment of them as bisyllabic, it is also the case that if they were in fact monosyllabic, the SSG in (2.4) would be violated. Thus the acceptance of sonority values as playing a crucial role in the internal structure of syllables doubly ensures that we can correctly determine the number of syllables in a word.

2.3   The internal structure of the syllable

The examples above allow us to say more about syllable structure. Amongst segments we can make a major class division between, on the one hand, vowels and glides and, on the other hand, all other segments: in terms of distinctive features the first two types of segment are [−consonantal] whereas all other segment types are [+consonantal]. Let us use V as a shorthand description for [−cons] segments and C as a shorthand description for [+cons] segments. If we then take the first five words above, *id*, *bad*, *bread*, *band*, *brand*, we can suggest that they have the following sequence of segments respectively: VC, CVC, CCVC, CVCC, CCVCC. If we turn to the next set of examples, all of which involve diphthongal pronunciations: *I*, *isle*, *bye*, *bide*, *bind*, *bride*, *grind*, then we can state that these have the following sequence of segments respectively (where, following on from above, diphthongs are represented as VV, since they consist of two vowels, the second less prominent than the first and therefore often called a glide): VV, VVC,. CVV, CVVC, CVVCC, CCVVC, CCVVCC.

Thus we can say that the minimal structure for a stressed monosyllable is either VC (*id*) or VV (*I*). Furthermore, we could state that provided that minimal structure is observed, the only obligatory element is one V segment, that the regular structure is (C)V(C) and that there may be up to two segments of the same type adjacent to one another, i.e., that the maximal structure is CCVVCC. If we accept the above, then we can suggest, for instance, that the syllabic structure of *grind* is as follows (where $ represents a syllable-boundary): $CCVVCC$ = /graind/. An alternative way of representing *grind* might be to use a tree diagram, thus (where we use σ to represent syllable):

(2.5)

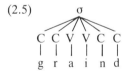

The tree representation in (2.5) says no more than the segmental sequence represented immediately above, except in one important respect. This is that it introduces the possibility of a *hierarchical* structure for segments: it claims that phonological sequences are not merely concatenated strings of segments, but also that there is a higher level element, namely the syllable, present, which has its own internal structure, e.g. CCVVCC, which determines the possible sequence of segments. Thus the following string is ruled out because it does not conform to any possible syllable structure: */pfraind/. If we posit the maximal syllable structure as suggested above, there is one segment left unattached to the syllable:

(2.6)

This, together with the SSG, which will rule out additional examples such as */rgaind/ (since /r/ is more sonorous than /g/), enables us to make a number of interesting statements about the phonotactics of English.

For instance, if we simply take the sequence CCVVCC, it is possible to note that there is a strong case for claiming that such a sequence is in fact divisible into three parts, namely CC–VV–CC. The reason for this is that there appear to be much stricter constraints operating between, say, the initial consonant segments than between any initial consonant segment and the following vowel. Thus if the initial consonants are /br/ then any vowel (sequence) can follow (*brim, bread, bran, brock, brunt*, etc.); but if the initial consonant is /b/ then there are very strict constraints on what consonant might follow. And by no means all of these are a matter for the sonority hierarchy, e.g. */bnik/. This type of collocational restriction can be repeated for all the elements, and it leads us to suggest that the syllable has an internal hierarchy of its own which determines possible CV sequences. We can claim that the syllable is composed of three parts, namely an initial consonant sequence or *onset*, a sequence of nonconso-nantal segments, the *nucleus*, and a final sequence of consonantal segments which is called the *coda*.

Q. Given the above suggestion we might suppose that the syllabic structure of, say, *grind*, might be represented by means of a tree diagram of the form in (2.7):

(2.7)

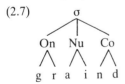

However, just as there are good distributional reasons for supposing that there are at least three separate constituents which go to make up a syllable, there are also good distributional reasons for supposing that these three constituents do not merely stand in a linear relationship to one another but rather are related by some kind of hierarchy. Can you think of any such reasons? The following distribution of stressed monosyllables in English should help: *ba, ban, bay, bane, Anne, aye*.

A.   The obvious point to note is that only one of the above examples is unacceptable in English, namely *ba. What makes it different from all the others? The answer is surely that the nucleus consists of a short vowel and the coda is empty. In all other cases either the nucleus contains a long vowel or diphthong (e.g. *bay*, *aye*) or the nucleus contains a short vowel but the coda contains at least one element (e.g. *ban*, *Anne*). In one case, of course, the nucleus contains a long vowel (diphthong) and the coda is non-empty (i.e. *bane*). Note that it is entirely irrelevant whether or not there is any segment in the onset. It might have been the case that if the nucleus contained a short vowel only, then the syllable would be acceptable if either the coda contained a segment, as in the case of *Anne* or the onset contained a segment, as in the case of *ba. This is obviously not so. Finally, it is worth noting that given monosyllabic *ba, there is a strong tendency to make the sequence acceptable by lengthening the vowel (as in *Baa*, *baa*, *black sheep*). The consequences of this we shall return to in a moment.

The clear conclusion to reach from the above is that the nucleus and the coda are more closely related to one another than either of them is to the onset. Let us suppose, therefore, that the nucleus and the coda form together a single constituent which we can call the *rhyme*. The name itself, of course, reminds us of a further reason for supposing that the nucleus and the coda form a single constituent, for that constituent plays an important role in verse (. . . *have you any wool?* / *Yes sir, yes sir, three bags full*). All this suggests that we should restructure (2.7) so that it has the shape:

(2.8)

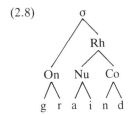

A structure such as (2.8) has one further and very important advantage. It has long been known that we ought to make a distinction between *heavy* and *light* syllables. This distinction is important for all sorts of phonological processes, most obviously, and as we have already noticed at the beginning of this chapter, for stress assignment, but also for all sorts of sound changes, such as, for example, loss of final vowels. Thus, for example, in Old English disyllabic words ending in either /u/ or /i/ lose their final vowel after a heavy syllable but retain their final vowel after a light syllable, e.g. *scipu* > *scipu* 'ships', but *wordu* > *word* 'words'. We can now make a more systematic distinction between heavy and light syllables than the one we made earlier, by stating that a heavy syllable is one in which the rhyme (or, in case the rhyme does not itself directly branch, the constituent dominated by the rhyme, namely the nucleus) branches, that is, contains more than one segment, and that a light syllable is one in which neither the rhyme nor the nucleus branches, that is, contains one and only one segment. The traditional observation about stressed monosyllables in English, namely that they must contain a heavy syllable, converts straightforwardly to the statement that the rhyme (nucleus) of such words must branch.

So far all the examples that we have discussed have contained in their nucleus either a short vowel or a diphthong. What, then, about cases involving a long vowel? Now where we have transcribed diphthongs as a sequence of two vowels, e.g. *grind* = /graind/, some phonologists would describe these diphthongs as a sequence of vowel plus glide, hence /grajnd/, or in American and most generative transcriptions, as /graynd/. Many of these same phonologists would then argue that in English even the so-called 'pure' long vowels consist in fact of a short vowel plus glide, so that *bead* might be transcribed as /bijd/. If that were done, then, of course, the so-called long vowels would be treated on a par with the other, more obvious, diphthongs. Here, however, we wish to claim that there are indeed 'pure' long vowels, at least at the underlying phonemic level, e.g. /iː, uː, oː, eː, aː/. It might be argued that this is purely a matter of taste, and therefore not worth discussing. But in fact it raises some interesting issues which are undoubtedly worth confronting.

Q.   Consider the following words, all of which might be considered to contain phonemically long vowels: *you, eat, fierce, fiend*. How might you represent their syllabic structure? Note that you should assume that *fierce* does indeed have underlyingly a long vowel /iː/. The diphthongal surface phonetic form should be assumed to be derived by later phonological rules which, however interesting they might be, are not relevant to our purposes here.

A.   If we take a simple example such as *eat*, then we might be tempted to suppose that its structure is as follows:

(2.9)

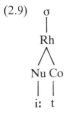

But then consider the case of *you*, which we might phonemicise as /juː/. Note here that the /j/ is consonantal and cannot be part of the nucleus.

There are several reasons for supposing this, but we shall only mention one. It is well known that in present-day English the indefinite article has two forms, namely *a* and *an*, the first of which occurs before a consonant, the second elsewhere. Note then the following examples: *a year, a youth* vs. *an apple, an orange*. The same is true of /w/; compare *a wind, a willow*. For further notes on this point see Gimson (1980: 211). Under the circumstances it looks as if we should have the following structure for *you*:

(2.10)

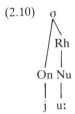

But if we do that, what we find is a structure which does not meet our earlier requirement that the rhymes of stressed monosyllables must branch. On the other hand, traditional statements would indeed class /juː/ as a heavy syllable since the vowel is long.

The answer to this problem lies in our discussion immediately above, where we mentioned that many phonologists would transcribe the 'pure' long vowels as simple vowel plus glide, e.g. *you* would be transcribed as /juw/. What we propose is not radically different from that, namely to transcribe *you* as containing two identical vowels, i.e. as /juu/. We can then suggest the following syllable structure, which overcomes our objections immediately above:

(2.11)

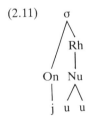

Similarly, the other three examples can be transcribed as follows:

(2.12)

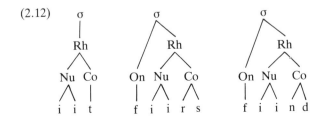

Given this possibility, it would indeed then be possible to suggest that the so-called 'true' diphthongs have the same phonological status, so that, for example, *bide* would have the representation /baid/. Then the parallelism between long vowels and diphthongs would be clear: long vowels would have a sequence of two identical short vowels, whereas diphthongs would have a sequence of two non-identical short vowels. How, then, can we account for the existence of so-called glides? Or, to put it another way, when analysing diphthongs, how can we determine which of the two elements of the diphthong has more prominence, that is to say, how can we distinguish between falling diphthongs (the norm in English) and rising diphthongs? As Selkirk (1984a) points out, this problem is easily resolvable if we make use of the sonority scale and the associated SSG. Consider the diphthong in a word such as *bide* = /baid/. In terms of sonority values the sequence we find there is 2–10–8–2. Hence the sonority peak is filled by the vowel /a/. The vowel /i/, although it is also contained within the nucleus, is less sonorous, and therefore less prominent, thus resulting in a falling diphthong. The fact that falling diphthongs are the norm in English is easily accounted for by stating that in English the leftmost member of the nucleus must be the most sonorous. We can also account for the fact that in English second elements of diphthongs are filled by high vowels, but not by mid or low vowels, thus /ai, au/ but not */ea, oɑ/, by stipulating that the second member of the nucleus, unless it is identical to the first member (as in long vowels), must not be filled by a segment whose sonority value is greater than 8.

If we represent long vowels as /VV/, i.e. two short vowels, then we are saying that phonologically two short vowels are equivalent in length to one long vowel. In other words, we have adopted a position where vowel segments (at least) have a constant phonological unit of length. This position is by no means new, and indeed has been long applied to consonants, so that it is generally recognised that geminate consonants may be represented either as a single long consonant or as two short consonants. Thus in Old English the verb *fremman* 'to perform' might be represented either as /frem:an/ or as /fremman/. The factors which dictate each linguist's choice here are not really relevant at present. Much more important is that it is quite commonplace to suppose that each segment occupies the same unit of phonological length. Thus *fremman* in Old English occupies seven units of length and *you* in present-day English occupies three. Of course these units of length are not phonetic: the time which it takes to say a particular word will change drastically according to context, and there are also phonological environments which may cause a long vowel to shorten or a short vowel to lengthen. For example, in present-day English the word *bite* occupies, other things being equal, less time than the word *bide*, although their phonological transcriptions (/bait/ and /baid/) suggest that this is not the case. The choice between a following voiceless and voiced consonant determines the phonetic output.

These units of phonological length, at least within the rhyme, are usually called *morae* (singular *mora*). The analysis of segments into morae is not usually extended to onsets, for the simple reason that length, although crucial to the constitution of the rhyme components, appears to play no part in the construction of the onset. Furthermore, the number of segments in the onset has no bearing on the 'weight' of a syllable, i.e., whether it is heavy or light. If we accept this mora-based analysis, we can say something further about the kind of syllable structure trees which we have drawn: namely that each terminal node dominates a single mora. As we have hinted, this is of interest for our distinction between heavy and light syllables, for now we can also say that a heavy syllable contains two morae in its rhyme, whereas a light syllable contains only one mora.

2.4 Templates

Let us now return to our example of *grind*. As we have already seen, we can give such a word the following syllable structure:

(2.13)

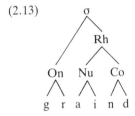

This, we have suggested, is the normal maximal structure for an English stressed syllable. We have also seen various other trees of varying shapes and sizes for other monosyllables. What we now have to ask ourselves is whether we can do no more than this, that is to say, no more than draw a variety of differing tree structures which, perhaps, we might be able to classify into various differing types. Surely it would be preferable if we could do more than this, if we could somehow make a general statement about the possible structure of English monosyllables. What we are looking for is what several linguists have called a *template*. A template would in this case be an abstract tree structure onto which all syllables would have to fit in order to be recognised as acceptable syllables in English.

Following the proposals of a number of linguists, most recently Selkirk (1984a), what we should like to suggest is that such a syllable template for

English can be organised in terms of the sonority scale in (2.2). We have already noted that the English syllable appears to be organised into (maximally) a sequence of six segments, which we earlier stated as CCVVCC. Given this, we were then able to suggest that the syllable was organised hierarchically into Onset + Nucleus + Coda, where the latter two formed a Rhyme constituent. Such an analysis makes it possible to suggest a template of the following kind where slots are numbered outwards from the N_1 position:

(2.14)

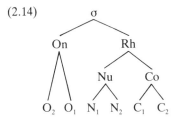

At this point we can introduce the sonority scale by stipulating a maximum (or minimum) sonority value for each segment. For example, if we were to state the following condition:

(2.15) SV $(N_1) \geqslant 8$

this would represent a claim that the sonority value of N_1, the leftmost element of the nucleus, could not be less than 8, i.e., that that segment must be a vowel of some kind, but could not be /r/ or any other segment less sonorous than a high vowel.

Q. Consider the following range of words: *true, glue, flue, threw, *vrue, *nrue, twin, swim, *zwin, *nwin, *gvin.* Taking the onsets only, work out the sonority values of the onset segments. Can you then give a provisional statement of the range of sonority values for O_2 and O_1?

A. The sonority values are as follows: *true* 1–7; *glue* 2–6; *flue* 3–6; *threw* 3–7; **vrue* 4–7; *twin* 1–8; *swim* 3–8; **zwin* 4–8; **nwin* 5–8; **gvin* 2–3. From these and other similar results we can claim that the O_2 position must be filled by a segment which is no more sonorous than a voiceless fricative, i.e., a segment whose maximum sonority value is 3. Further, we can claim that the O_1 position can only be filled by a lateral, flap or /j, w/, that is to say, the consonantal versions of the high vowels /i, u/. The minimum sonority value for O_1 must be 6, the maximum value must be 8. Of course, it is always possible to find only one consonant in the onset, in which case that consonant may be anything from a voiceless stop (*tin*, etc.) to an approximant (*win*, etc.). This can be accounted for by stating that if O_2 is empty, then the minimum sonority value for O_1 does not apply. Further, it is always possible for there to be an empty onset (*inn*, etc.), where neither

O_1 nor O_2 is filled. This enables us to make the following formal statement about onsets in English:

(2.16) Onset template conditions
    (i) O_1 is optionally filled.
    (ii) O_2 is filled iff (if and only if) O_1 is filled.
    (iii) Sonority Value (SV) of $O_1 \leqslant 8$.
    (iv) (SV) of $O_1 \geqslant 6$ iff O_2 is filled.
    (v) SV of $O_2 \leqslant 3$.

You should have realised by now, although we have not given any relevant examples, that these onset conditions are sometimes violated. There are two classes of violations which are especially interesting. One, which occurs only when /s/ fills O_2, we shall discuss later, for the status of /s/ is complex and raises issues above and beyond its position in onsets. The other, however, we shall discuss immediately, because the problem is one which is restricted to onsets. This class of violation always involves /j/. We might expect that /j/ would behave exactly like /w/, for that is what the sonority scale (they have the same value, 8) would imply. And in many cases that is indeed true – consider, for example, British English *cue* /kjuː/, *dew* /djuː/ and *few* /fjuː/. However, other examples, such as *new* /njuː/ and *lewd* /ljuːd/, clearly violate (2.16), since in them O_2 is filled by a segment with a sonority value greater than 3.

In order to understand such examples we have to consider very briefly the history of English. In the Middle English period there was a large number of words which had a falling diphthong of the form /iu/. In the seventeenth century this diphthong, contrary to the usual pattern, became a rising diphthong, very similar to the sequence found in words such as *youth* /juːθ/, which has always had initial consonantal /j/. In consequence, the first element of the rising diphthong became treated as a consonant, that is to say, as part of the onset. This initially gave rise not only to examples such as the above, but also, for a while, to forms such as /θrjuː/ for *threw*.

One synchronic analysis might be to treat /j/ in *new*, etc. as merely an historical anomaly which violates the template conditions of the present-day language. But there is a more interesting approach which will both help to explain the anomaly and keep the template inviolate. Let us assume that *new* has an underlying representation with a rising diphthong /iu/:

(2.17)

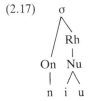

We can now propose a synchronic rule of English which applies at a later stage than the process of basic syllabification, whereby /i/ is shifted from the nucleus to the onset. This rule might have the form:

(2.18)

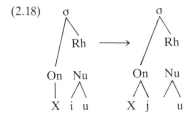

Note that although we have moved the /i/ into the onset, we have retained the node in the nucleus which previously dominated /i/. But we can now apply what Ingria (1980:471) terms the Empty Node Convention. In the form we wish to use that convention, it is in fact a mirror image of the convention proposed by Ingria, but that does not seem problematic. Let us state the convention as follows:

(2.19) *Empty Node Convention.* If some segment is moved leftwards out of the nucleus into the onset, then the empty node which remains in the nucleus is filled by a copy of the segment which fills the sister node in the nucleus.

Applying this convention, we get the following result:

(2.20)

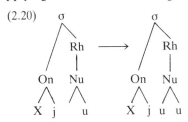

where X is any segment or zero. By this we can obtain the surface form /njuː/.

This analysis is not merely a device to avoid violation of the onset conditions stated above. There are several interesting consequences and predictions which flow from it. Firstly, it explains why sequences of consonant+/j/ are always followed by a long vowel, since the Empty Node Convention automatically supplies such a long vowel. Secondly, since, as Selkirk (1984a) points out, /i/ and /u/ are the only vowels in English which can fill the N_2 position, and since /uu/ would represent a long vowel, this gives us the prediction that sequences of consonant+/j/ can only be followed by long /uː/. Thirdly, the absence in almost all dialects of a consonant cluster plus /j/ can be explained by noting that the template allows onsets to contain only two segments. Hence, in the case of, say, *threw*, the conditions in (2.15) will immediately delete /j/. Finally, there is, as is well known, considerable variation between dialects as to the presence or absence of this /j/, and the above synchronic analysis enables us to give a more systematic and explanatory account of that variability than would a simple statement of historical anomaly.

Before we move on to consider the nucleus and coda, we should note that there is a further group of cases where, although the SSG and the specifically English conditions on the structure of onsets are not broken, certain sequences of consonants are nevertheless impossible. For example, it is impossible to start off an English word with the sequences /bw–, dl–/, although sequences such as /dw–, bl–/ are perfectly possible initially. In cases such as */bw–/ it would appear to be the case that the impossibility arises because of place of articulation problems. Note that */bw–/ has bilabial followed by labio-velar and that */dl–/ has alveolar followed by alveolar. The restriction would appear to be one on onset clusters where both members share the same place of articulation. The sonority scale, since it deals primarily with manner of articulation rather than place of articulation, cannot be expected to cope with such cases; rather, they have to be accounted for by means of what Fudge (1969) calls 'collocational restrictions'. Although such collocational restrictions obviously play an important role in English phonology, we shall not deal with them here.

So far we have claimed that the rhyme can be divided into two parts: the nucleus and the coda. Current research, however, suggests that this is a false division. Note, for example, that earlier in this chapter we claimed that a syllable is heavy if either the rhyme branches, or failing that, the nucleus branches. If, however, there is no subdivision of the rhyme we can simplify that statement into the claim that a syllable is heavy if and only if the rhyme branches. Thus a more adequate description of English syllables might be as follows:

(2.21)

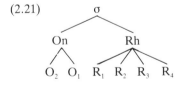

Q. Consider the following examples: *clamp*, **claimb* (cf. *climb*), *grunt*, *ground*, *punk*, **pounk*. Firstly, how might such examples be analysed if we assume (a) separate nucleus and coda constituents; (b); a unitary rhyme constituent? Secondly, what evidence do the above examples give us concerning the possible number of morae in English rhymes?

A. Examples such as *grunt* would, assuming a division between nucleus and coda, appear to be best analysed as in (2.22) (in discussing rhyme structures we shall usually, for convenience' sake, ignore onsets):

(2.22)

On the other hand, an example such as *ground* would best be analysed as:

(2.23)

This looks fine; but now consider the unacceptable examples **claimb* and **pounk*. These should, if they follow the above, have exactly the same structure as (2.23). And the acceptable parallel examples with a short vowel, *clamp* and *punk*, would have the same structure as in (2.22). But, as has been noted by, especially, Fudge (1969) and Selkirk (1982), there appears to be a constraint on English rhymes to the effect that if there are four morae in the rhyme, then the fourth mora must be filled by a consonant which is [+coronal], in effect, dental or alveolar. If we take structures (2.22–3) as our analysis, then the unacceptability of **claimb* and **pounk* and other similar examples can only be clumsily stated.

There are two options open. Firstly, we could state the following as a condition: the coda may branch only if either (a) the nucleus does not branch; or (b) the C_2 position is filled by a [+coronal] obstruent. Secondly, we could claim (as does Selkirk 1982:350–2) that in examples such as *clamp* the /m/ is not part of the coda, but in fact fills the N_2 position. This would give the structure:

(2.24)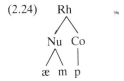

In order to account for *ground*, where the nasal could not be part of the nucleus (since that contains a diphthong), we would still have to have the condition that the C_2 position could only be filled by a [+coronal] obstruent. Clearly, either solution is unsatisfactory: the first because it makes the internal structure of one constituent, i.e. the coda, dependent upon the internal structure of another constituent, i.e. the nucleus; the second because it allows nasals (and also laterals and flaps, e.g. *wilt*, *old*, and in dialects with post-vocalic /r/, *bird*, *beard*) to be systematically ambiguous as to their position in syllable structure.

On the other hand, let us suppose a structure such as (2.21). In that case *grunt* would have the structure of (2.25a), *ground* that of (2.25b), *clamp* that of (2.25c), and **claimb* that of (2.25d):

(2.25)

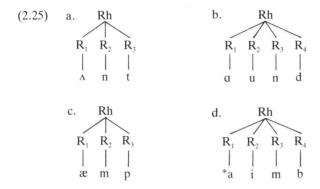

We then need only to apply the single condition that R_4 can only be filled by a [+coronal] obstruent. This solution thus gives us an excellent argument for assuming that the rhyme is a single constituent which is not to be divided up further into nucleus and coda. Informally we shall nevertheless sometimes retain the latter division and terms, because they are often helpful for purposes of exposition where the precise nature of the constituency of the rhyme is not at issue.

One interesting question arising out of the above discussion is why only [+coronal] obstruents are permitted to appear in the R_4 position. In earlier stages of English the final obstruents in words such as *climb* were indeed pronounced and their loss is to be dated round about the time of Chaucer. Examples such as Scottish *chiel* 'lad' perhaps suggest that dentals could be lost as well as labials and velars. Consider in this respect, therefore, inflected forms in Modern English such as *weaned*. One of the oddities of English since around the time of Chaucer is that inflectional endings, if they do not form a separate syllable, as in the case of *-ing*, always contain (underlyingly) a single [+coronal] obstruent. It may be, therefore, that the type of syllable structure found in a word such as *wind* (/waind/) has been protected through analogy with inflected forms such as *weaned*. This does not mean, however, that we wish to treat inflectional endings as part of basic syllable structure. As both Fudge and Selkirk show, albeit in different ways, inflectional endings such as *-s* and *-d* do not form part of basic syllable structure, but should be regarded as separate entities. Exactly how they should be attached to the basic syllable structure is not relevant to our present concerns, and therefore we shall not discuss that issue here, but see further Fudge (1969) and Selkirk (1982).

At this point, although it would be perfectly possible to consider how we might further develop our syllable template along the lines discussed earlier in respect of the onset, only now concentrating on the rhyme, we shall not do so, for two reasons. Firstly, the basic principles we discussed with relation to the onset apply equally to the rhyme. Secondly, Selkirk (1984a: 119ff) gives a clear and concise account of sonority relations within the rhyme. Therefore, we would simply refer you to her discussion and also to the essay and discussion topics at the end of this chapter.

Q.   Let us instead return to a problem which we have so far only mentioned, and that briefly. It occurs most obviously in onsets, where it concerns onsets containing /s/. Consider firstly, therefore, words such as *spin*, *stile*, *scowl*. How do these violate the template in (2.16)? Then consider the following words: *sprint*, *splay*, *strip*, *squid*. In what ways do these violate the template? How could the template violations occasioned by all these words be removed at, as it were, the stroke of a pen?

A.   In the examples *spin*, *stile*, *scowl* the template is violated because /s/ has the sonority value 3 (it is a voiceless fricative) and the following voiceless stop has the sonority value 1. This means not only that the SSG is broken, but also that the O_1 position is filled by a segment whose value is less than the required value of 6. In examples such as *sprint* we find yet again that the SSG is broken, for the reasons immediately above. But in addition there are now, apparently, three segments in the onset, which is not permissible. Notice, however, that all these violations are created solely by the presence of /s/. If we simply remove /s/, then not only will we end up with ordinary English words, but also with words which in no way violate the template: *pin*, *tile*, *cowl*, *print*, *play*, *trip*, *quid*.

Our first reaction to this might be to suggest that in some way /s/ did not 'count' in terms of basic syllable structure. Although such a proposal is attractive and, as we shall see in chapter 3, metrical phonology does have a method of allowing for such a possibility, there seem to be good reasons for supposing that this is not the correct answer. Most crucially, it is notable that /s/ appears to have extremely close links with the following stop consonant. Thus that stop consonant must always be voiceless – sequences such as /sb–/ are not permissible in English. If we look at the history of English, we discover the interesting fact that in Old English alliterative poetry initial consonants alliterated freely: that is to say, /b/, for example, alliterated with /b/ regardless of the nature of any following consonant, so that /br/ alliterated with /bl/, except if that consonant was /s/ followed by a voiceless stop. In those circumstances the onset cluster only alliterated with itself, so that /sp, st, sk/ could only alliterate with /sp, st, sk/ respectively, and none of them could alliterate with /s/ alone in the onset or with other clusters such as /sw/.

Facts such as these have led many linguists of widely differing theoretical stances (e.g. O'Connor & Trim 1953; Selkirk 1982) to suggest that /sp, st, sk/ should be treated as single constituents in syllable onsets. If we do that, then no matter what sonority value we attach to the single constituent, it will be clear that the template will not be violated. For instance, *sprint* will have the structure of:

(2.26)

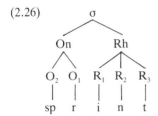

This analysis could equally well be extended to the rhyme, so that examples such as *next* and *sixth* could be analysed as:

(2.27) a.   b.

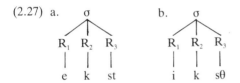

This, it has to be admitted, is not quite as convincing, largely because there would in these examples be no difficulty in assuming that the final consonant, since it is, always, [+coronal], could occupy the R_4 position. Furthermore, if we gave a bimoric analysis to such clusters, then the fact that such sequences as the above cannot have a long vowel would be explained, for they would be assigned the impermissible structure of, for instance:

(2.28) *

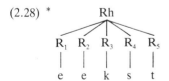

It might be better, therefore, if the single constituent analysis in the onset were regarded as being the mirror image of the structure in the rhyme, which might very reasonably be supposed to occur in words such as *chintz*:

(2.29)

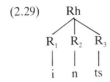

Here it is important to note that the assignment of /ts/ in rhymes to a single position can be independently argued for. Even if we leave aside examples from other languages, such as German, where /ts/ might be considered to be a single-position affricate, in English we have words such as *prince* where it is frequently the case that an epenthetic /t/ appears between the nasal and /s/. If we were to treat that /t/ as an additional segment in the rhyme this would increase the weight (length) of the syllable by the addition of an extra mora, but this does not happen. This strongly suggests that in such positions /ts/ should be treated as monomoric (occupying one mora only). Nor is the idea that the rhyme should present a mirror image of the onset merely arbitrary. If you have examined sonority sequences in the rhyme you will have already discovered that the rhyme does indeed in many ways pattern parallel to the onset, but in reverse order.

We have now presented an account of English monosyllables in sufficient detail for you to be able to see the basic principles of a syllable-based approach. The most important points to note are as follows. Firstly, this approach claims that syllables are a well-defined unit in English phonology (and, of course, in the phonology of any language). Secondly, it claims that syllables are internally organised on a hierarchical basis. The third claim is that there is a language-particular template which defines the basic structural possibilities of English syllables. Fourthly, it claims that there may be several collocational restrictions or permissions which contract or expand upon the basic template. Finally, as our discussion of /s/ immediately above should have made you realise, there are still several unresolved problems. Thus, exactly how we might best analyse a word such as *next* remains, we believe, a live and difficult issue. Nevertheless, we wish to leave this area of description behind us now, in order to move on to another area where a syllable-based description must provide an adequate analysis.

2.5   *Ambisyllabicity*

Consider the following examples:

(2.30) honest   gymnast   jetty   elastic   elasticity   petrol
       petroleum   apron   bottle

We have already seen that a syllable-based description does not face any major problems in determining how many syllables each of these words has. But there certainly do seem to be problems in determining where the boundary between each syllable (in a polysyllabic word) might lie. Interestingly, this is not always the case. For example, we doubt that anyone would disagree with our claim that *gymnast* is divided up into syllables as [gym][nast]. But how about *honest*, or *petrol*?

In order to start a plausible analysis of this problem, it is necessary to assume that in polysyllabic as well as monosyllabic words the syllable structure which we create must conform to the basic principles of syllable structure such as we have outlined above. Thus, for example, *gymnast* must have the following structure, since that is the only structure permitted by the principles discussed above:

(2.31)

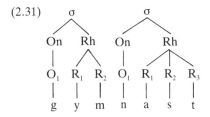

But consider the cases of *honest* and *petrol*. It would be possible, in conformity with the basic principles, to analyse the syllable structures of both in three different ways, depending upon which syllable the intervocalic consonants were assigned to. Firstly, we could suppose a division such as [hon][est] and [pet][rol]. Secondly we could suppose a division such as [ho][nest] and [pe][trol]. And thirdly we could suppose a division such as [ho[n]est] and [pe[t]rol]. The first division illustrates the *Principle of Maximal Codas*, for what happens there is that as many intervocalic consonants as are permitted by the basic syllable templates are assigned to the coda (rhyme) of the first syllable. Thus, in the case of *honest* the intervocalic /n/ is assigned to the first syllable and in the case of *petrol* /t/ is assigned to the first syllable – but not /r/, since that would give an unacceptable rhyme (/r/ has a higher sonority value than /t/). The second division illustrates the *Principle of Maximal Onsets*, for there the reverse happens, and consonants are assigned wherever possible to the onset of the second syllable. The third division illustrates the *Principle of Maximal Codas and Maximal Onsets*, since there intervocalic consonants are assigned both to the coda of the first syllable and the onset of the second syllable, provided that the syllable templates are not violated. These three divisions can be represented graphically, as in (2.32):

(2.32) a.

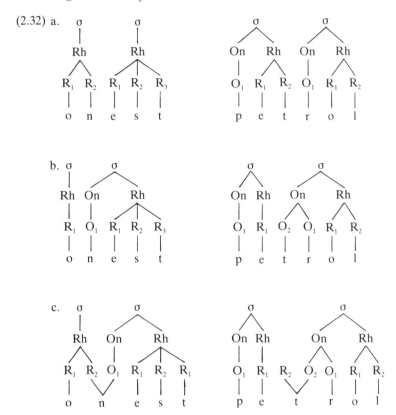

As we shall see from the discussion below, of these possibilities only the second and the third appear to be serious candidates, and indeed linguists have been divided on the issue of which is preferable. One paper which argues for the third analysis is Anderson & Jones (1974). We shall, however, follow both Kahn (1976) and Selkirk (1982) in assuming that underlying syllable division is made on the Principle of Maximal Onsets, that is to say, that intervocalic consonants are maximally assigned to the onsets of syllables in conformity with the basic principles of syllable construction in the language. We thus assume trees of the type represented in (2.32b).

Even if we make this assumption, it would appear that there is more to be done. For instance, it is all very well to assume that, say, the /n/ of *honest* should be assigned to the second syllable. But speakers cannot be so sure that the /n/ is unambiguously a member of the second syllable only. Surely the third analysis is preferable? One way round this problem would be to accept the Principle of Maximal Onsets in the underlying syllabification of the language, and then have a rule which, wherever possible according to rules of syllable structure, makes intervocalic consonants members of both syllables, or, to use the technical term, *ambisyllabic*. Such a rule of ambisyllabicity might look like (2.33):

(2.33)
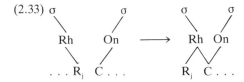

In this statement R_j must be interpreted as meaning the last rhyme segment (which, in practice, because of the Principle of Maximal Onsets, will be no greater than R_3).

Q. The assumption of the Principle of Maximal Onsets together with the rule of ambisyllabicity in (2.33) is in fact no more than a complex way of accepting the Principle of Maximal Codas and Maximal Onsets. It looks, therefore, as if we have made the wrong assumption. Consider therefore the following pairs of words: *petrol*, *patrol*; *aspidistra*, *asparagus*. Is there any reason for supposing that the syllabification of intervocalic consonants might be different between the members of each pair, and is there any way in which the rule of ambisyllabicity might be amended to cope with such a difference? Finally, does this avoid the criticism which we have just made of the account immediately above?

A. Looking at *petrol* and *patrol* first, it would appear that there is indeed a difference in syllabification, for it seems pretty clear that although it may be difficult to decide which syllable the /t/ in *petrol* belongs to, it is much easier to decide that the /t/ in *patrol* only belongs to the second syllable (we shall see later that there is good phonetic evidence for making such a claim, aside from what might be rather hazy and prejudiced intuitions). Similarly, in the case of *aspi(distra)* the /s/ (at least, see further below) appears to be connected to the first syllable, whereas in *aspa(ragus)* such a connection is far less obvious.

Determining the reason why this might be so – and let us assume that we have given a correct description – is perhaps less easy, until we consider what at first sight might appear to be an unrelated factor. This factor is the question of stress. Note that in *petrol* and *aspidistra* the first syllable is stressed, whereas in *patrol* and *asparagus* the first syllable is unstressed. Both Kahn (1976: 47–8) and Selkirk (1982: 366) argue that the crucial feature is the stressless character of the second syllable, but it may well be preferable to state that it is the stressed character of the first syllable that is crucial – see here Fallows (1981). The reason for this goes back to the structure of stressed and stressless syllables. In unstressed syllables, amongst other features, there will only be an obligation for one mora to be present, that is to say, one crucial difference between a stressed and an unstressed syllable will be that whereas a stressed syllable must contain either a long vowel (or diphthong) or short vowel plus a consonant, an unstressed syllable need only contain a short vowel or syllabic consonant, e.g. the second syllables of *happy* and *bottle*.

Consider in this light the cases of *petrol* and *patrol*. Apparently, these will have the structures in (2.34a and b) respectively by the Principle of Maximal Onsets:

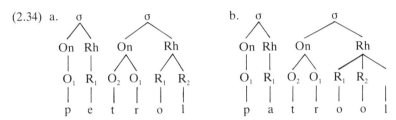

Let us indeed assume that this is the case initially. Then, however, rules of stress assignment will take place. However they are formulated, the consequence will be that the initial syllable of *petrol* will be [+stress] or its equivalent and the initial syllable of *patrol* will be [−stress] or its equivalent. At that point what we should note is that the syllable structure of (2.34a) for *petrol* violates the syllable structure template because that syllable is stressed yet contains in its rhyme only a short vowel. There is no corresponding problem with *patrol*. It should be clear, therefore, that the /t/ must indeed be re-syllabified so that it becomes ambisyllabic, for only then will the syllable structure template be obeyed. Unfortunately we cannot assume that the process of ambisyllabification is purely a redundancy rule, for if that were the case, then although, for example, the /n/ of *honour* would become ambisyllabic, the /n/ of *loner* would not, since there is a long vowel (or diphthong) in the first syllable of that word. Nevertheless, it seems proper that we should create a rule of ambisyllabification which pays attention to the demands of conformity to the syllable structure template, and therefore we propose that it should have the following form:

(2.35) *Ambisyllabification*

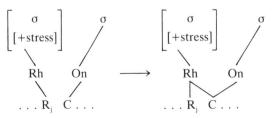

There are several points to be noted about this rule, which differs somewhat from the presentations in Kahn (1976) and Selkirk (1982). Firstly, the rule as stated allows only one consonant to be made ambisyllabic: this is a question to which we shall return shortly. Secondly, the rule as stated must be optional, to allow both for variations in syllabification according to rate of speech and in other phenomena such as aspiration of stops, which again we shall be considering shortly. But, for instance, Selkirk (1982) has to have two forms of her equivalent rule because in cases such as *petrol* and *honour* the change is obligatory. This can in part be handled by the claim that the output after ambisyllabification must conform to the syllable structure templates, and this of course ensures that in such cases the rule is obligatory. Unfortunately, the matter is not quite as simple as that. It seems more probable that ambisyllabicity occurs obligatorily if the first syllable is both stressed and contains an empty coda (this, by the way, is an argument for the retention of the nucleus and coda as constituents of the syllable).

Let us leave that point there, however, for what we should now like to do is give a brief demonstration of the superiority of a syllable-based approach over a purely segmental approach in dealing with some matters which appear to be purely a matter of segmental phonology. In fact, we simply wish to take one example, which concerns the aspiration of voiceless stops.

In most dialects of English (including standard British and standard American English) the voiceless stops /p, t, k/ are aspirated (to [pʰ, tʰ, kʰ]) under a variety of circumstances. The most usual circumstance is initially in a word, e.g. *pan, tan, can* = [pʰæn, tʰæn, kʰæn]. However, the same applies whenever these words precede a stressed vowel, provided that they are not immediately preceded by /s/: thus *repair* = [rəpʰeə] but *despair* = [dəspeə]. Devoicing of the following segment, which may be regarded as an equivalent of aspiration, also occurs if the liquids /l, r/ intervene before the stressed vowel: e.g. *please, apply, applicant* all show devoicing of /l/. For further details of these processes see Gimson (1980: 153–4).

Q. It is possible to state the following segmental rules for aspiration/devoicing:

(a) $\begin{bmatrix} + \text{stop} \\ -\text{voic} \end{bmatrix} \longrightarrow [+\text{asp}]$

(b) $\begin{bmatrix} +\text{son} \\ +\text{cons} \end{bmatrix} \longrightarrow [-\text{voic}]$

These will, respectively, aspirate voiceless stops and devoice liquids and pre-vocalic glides. Can you state the environments in which each will occur?

A.   Working within a segmental theory the statement of the environments is at best clumsy and at worst extremely difficult. Take the simpler case of aspiration of voiceless stops. We have already noted that it takes place initially before a vowel, that is: / # ——— [V]. It also takes place before any stressed vowel, provided that the stop is not preceded by /s/, that is: / X ——— [V, +stress], where X ≠ /s/. If we then consider the devoicing of liquids and glides, we find that this occurs whenever they are preceded by a voiceless stop and followed by a vowel, provided that the stop is not preceded by /s/, as in *respray*, where there is no aspiration. That gives the environment: /X [+stop, −voic] ——— [V]. Obviously it is possible to combine these environments, but we should be uncomfortable at attempting such a clearly awkward manoeuvre. Furthermore, we have already suggested that aspiration of voiceless stops and devoicing of sonorants are essentially the same process. Therefore it would be simpler if we brought them together. This can be done by assuming that the initial change is one that makes all relevant voiceless stops aspirated, including those before sonorants, and then invoking a further rule to devoice sonorants after voiceless aspirated stops. You should be able to observe quite quickly that this makes the process yet more complex and unwieldy.

On the other hand, a syllable-based description makes the question of stating the environments for the change very simple. All that we need state is that any voiceless stop followed by a vowel or sonorant plus vowel is aspirated provided that it is syllable-initial (there will be a further qualification below). Note that if we do that, then a whole range of examples are accounted for. Thus *pan* contrasts with *span*, because only the first has syllable-initial /p/. The same is true of the pair *repair* and *despair*. It will also be the case that we predict aspiration, and hence devoicing of /l/, in both *please* and *apply*.

Q.   Before we go on to consider cases such as *applicant*, which at first sight appear to cause no problems, we have to note words where a voiceless stop, although immediately followed by a vowel, does not aspirate. Typical examples are: *happen, motor, ticket*. Can you think of a reason why aspiration does not occur in such words?

A.   There is, of course, a segmentally based explanation, which is that the immediately following vowel is not stressed. But this has a corollary, namely that the preceding vowel is stressed. Recall, therefore, our rule of ambisyllabification (2.35). What this rule does is make the initial consonant of an onset ambisyllabic if the preceding syllable is stressed (in conformity with the syllable templates of the language). Thus the /p, t, k/

of *happen*, *motor*, *ticket* will be made ambisyllabic. On the other hand, all the other examples we discussed immediately above, i.e. *pan*, *repair*, *please*, *apply* will not be ambisyllabic – obviously in the case of *pan* and *please*, and because the preceding syllable is [−stress] in *repair* and *apply*. Note that examples where the voiceless stop is ambisyllabic, e.g. *ticket*, do not show aspiration, whereas examples where the voiceless stop is syllable-initial but not ambisyllabic, e.g. *repair*, do show aspiration. Kahn (1976: 74) suggests that this allows us to refine our statement of the environment in which aspiration takes place so that it states that aspiration of voiceless stops takes place only if those stops are syllable-initial but are not syllable-final after the operation of ambisyllabification. We can therefore restate our rule of aspiration as follows:

(2.36) *Aspiration*

$$\begin{bmatrix} + \text{ stop} \\ -\text{voic} \end{bmatrix} \longrightarrow [+\text{asp}] \ / \ \begin{bmatrix} \overline{} \\ +\text{SI} \\ -\text{SF} \end{bmatrix} [+\text{son}]$$

where SI = syllable-initial and SF = syllable-final.

Q.   This accounts for a large number of the potential examples, but problems occur specifically with the set of examples where a sonorant intervenes between the voiceless stop and the following vowel. Specific examples include: with aspiration, *apply*, *replace*, *actress*, *applicant*; and without aspiration, *destroy*, *displace*, *mistress*, *district*. Attempt to work out, firstly, which of these examples will be correctly predicted by our rules, and, secondly, how the rules might be amended in order to make correct predictions for all of them.

A.   The rules of ambisyllabification and aspiration as formulated above will correctly predict aspiration of the voiceless stop in the cases of *apply* and *replace*. The reason for this is that the first syllable is [−stress] and therefore the voiceless stop does not become ambisyllabic. Hence aspiration is free to take place. On the other hand, in *destroy* and *displace* there is no question of ambisyllabicity, since again the first syllable is [−stress]. Why, then, is there no aspiration? The reason, of course, is that according to the Principle of Maximal Onsets the /s/ is the first member of the onset of the second syllable rather than being the final (and only) member of the coda of the first syllable. Thus the /t/ and the /p/ are not syllable-initial (just as they would not be in *span* or *Stan*), and therefore aspiration does not take place. Thus these four words have their aspiration, or lack of aspiration, correctly predicted by the above rules.

Consider now, however, *actress* and *applicant*. We said above that ambisyllabification occurs when the preceding syllable is [+stress] and that the process of ambisyllabification affects the first consonant of the onset of the second syllable. In these cases, therefore, the following change should take place:

(2.37)

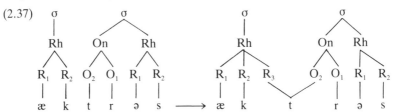

That is to say, the /t/ of *actress* (and the /p/ of *applicant*) should become ambisyllabic. If that happens, then the structural description for aspiration is no longer met, because although the /t/ will still be syllable-initial, it will now also be syllable-final. On the other hand, if we compare *mistress* and *district*, there is no problem. Here ambisyllabicity would apply to /s/ and hence the following /t/ would not be syllable-initial, since /s/ remains a member of the same syllable as the /t/, despite its additional membership of the preceding syllable. Therefore the /t/ will remain unaspirated. The problematic examples, therefore, are the type exemplified by *actress* and *applicant*.

A hint of the possible solution to these problem cases comes in the shape of the devoicing of the sonorant which we referred to above. The fact that in cases such as *actress* (and also in other, less controversial, cases such as *please*) the phonological aspiration of the voiceless stop is realised phonetically by devoicing of the following sonorant suggests very strongly an intimate relationship between the stop and the sonorant. This can be handled in terms of ambisyllabicity by claiming that this process involves the ambisyllabification of one constituent rather than one segment, the constituent concerned being the syllabic onset. Thus the structural change would be:

(2.38)

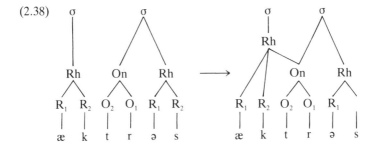

In (2.38), although the /t/ remains syllable-initial it does not become syllable-final since it persists in a tautosyllabic relationship with the following /r/. This solution does, however, have one problem, for, as you may have noted, the SSG is broken. (Note, by the way, that such an ambisyllabification process will never violate other template considerations; since the onset which is ambisyllabified has to be treated as a single constituent, not as two segments.) One way to avoid this problem of the contravention of the SSG is to suggest that in consideration of the sonority sequencing generalisation only the leftmost segment of the onset constituent is to be counted and any segment to the right of that is to be ignored. As we shall see in chapter 3, this is tantamount to claiming that all but the leftmost segment is 'extrametrical'. At the moment, it has to be admitted, this procedure seems to have been produced out of a magician's hat, but once you have read the sections on extrametricality later in the book you may find it interesting to return to this discussion and reconsider the viability of the proposal. Instead of taking up this suggestion we could retain the provision that only one segment·can be made ambisyllabic. Under these circumstances *actress* (and other parallel forms) will fail to become ambisyllabic, since the onset contains more than one segment. Therefore /t/ will remain syllable-initial and non-syllable-final and will be able to undergo aspiration.

At this point, where we have hinted at one of the more exciting recent developments in metrical phonology, namely the concept of extrametricality, we shall end this chapter. By no stretch of the imagination could we be thought to have given a full account of English syllable structure. We hope that we have demonstrated that it is necessary to invoke the concept of a hierarchically-organised syllable structure in order to provide adequate phonological descriptions even of apparently purely segmental phenomena. Yet to some extent it is true that even the cruder details of syllable structure remain to be worked out. In this connection it is worth pointing out not only that Kahn (1976) and Selkirk (1982) give accounts of the process of ambisyllabification (Kahn) or resyllabification (Selkirk) which are different from one another, but also that the account which we have given here is different from both these accounts. It is obvious both that a syllable-based description is useful and that much more work needs to be done. However, we hope and believe that we have outlined sufficient of the basic material here to permit you to understand and develop a syllable-based account of stress phenomena. For, as we shall see in the next and subsequent chapters, not only do metrical phonologists attempt an approach to stress which is radically different from that presented in chapter 1, but they also accept that the syllable, and a syllable which is hierarchically organised in the kind of way we have presented above, is crucial to a proper description of the stress patterns of English.

Notes and further reading

2.1 A good general description of the structure of English syllables which is not theoretically oriented is to be found in Gimson (1980: 237–53). The fullest statement of the possible monosyllabic structures of English in a form reasonably compatible with our outline above is to be found in Fudge (1969). For an introduction to syllable-based descriptions within the theory of metrical phonology, see the early work in Kiparsky (1979) and Selkirk (1982), although these are by now somewhat out of date (see the notes to §2.4 below). Kahn (1976) presents the first, and still authoritative, presentation of a description of English syllables within the framework of autosegmental phonology, for which Clements & Keyser (1983) provide an excellent update. Dependency phonologists have also written extensively on the syllable, and the starting-point here must be Anderson & Jones (1974); see also Jones (1976). An interesting series of articles which expand the metrical approach to syllable structure primarily in languages other than English are Ingria (1980), Leben (1980) and Prince (1980). Van der Hulst & Smith (1982) provide a very useful comparative overview of metrical and autosegmental theories. For dependency phonology, Durand (1986), although principally written within that framework, should provide useful points of comparison between all three theories.

2.2 A useful survey of attempts to correlate sonority and syllable structure, and also to relate both these to a wider range of phonological phenomena, is to be found in Bell & Hooper (1978). Of recent work on the sonority hierarchy and its relation to syllables, Vennemann (1972) and Hooper (1976: especially part II) provide important accounts within a linear framework, whilst Selkirk (1984a) provides the most recent nonlinear account.

2.3 This section follows the general principles of Selkirk (1984a), although it differs in some details. It is worth noting that the account here is intended to be largely neutral between metrical and autosegmental theories.

Some linguists still hold to the view that nucleus and coda are separate constituents; see here the discussion of Hayes (1982) in chapter 3 of this volume. It would be wrong to suppose that this debate has been settled.

For the status of long vowels and diphthongs, see the discussion in Lass (1984: §§10.3.2–3).

2.4 Selkirk (1984a) considers in some detail a possible template for English rhymes and should therefore be read in conjunction with this section.

Although nasals are by (2.16) excluded from the O_1 position, this may well be incorrect, given words such as *snow*. We would remedy this by amending (2.16.iv) to read $O_1 \geq 5$. In that case, *bnik*, etc. which demonstrate the unacceptability of sequences such as /bn–/, would have to be handled by some kind of collocational restriction – see Fudge (1969).

For the history of /j/–dropping see Wells (1982: 206–8, 247–8).

Essay and discussion topics

1. We have pointed out that there is a much more restricted distribution of syllable types in English than the syllable template permits. Using Gimson (1980) and Fudge (1969) as reference works and guides, consider some of the further restrictions on English syllable types and how you might incorporate such restrictions into the theory we have outlined in this chapter.

2. We have noted, but not seriously discussed, the fact that the rules governing stress assignment in English provide strong evidence in favour of a syllable-based description. Now go back over the rules we outlined in chapter 1, especially the English Stress Rule, and evaluate the possibility and the desirability of replacing that segmentally based version of the ESR by a syllable-based version.

3. Can you think of any other reasons for supposing that the syllable is a necessary part of the phonological description of English or of any other one language with which you are reasonably well acquainted?

4. We noted that the account we gave of aspiration of voiceless stops is different from that of both Kahn (1976) and Selkirk (1982). Compare and evaluate the merits of these three descriptions of the process.

5. There appear currently to be three competing theories of syllable structure: metrical, autosegmental and dependency. Compare and evaluate the merits of any two of these theories.

3   *Metrical phonology: the basic concepts*

3.1   *Introduction*

In chapter 1 we discussed the Sound Pattern of English (*SPE*)-based approach to stress. As we saw, this approach treated stress as a property of individual segments. Furthermore, assignment of stress was determined by sequences of particular segments. Nevertheless, we noted there that stress is commonly regarded as a suprasegmental phenomenon. In chapter 2 we were able to see that it is preferable to consider phonological strings as not merely linear sequences, but as having hierarchical organisation (based on the syllable). The major achievement of metrical phonology has been to extend such a hierarchically based analysis to stress. The first major work in this area was a paper by Liberman & Prince (1977) (henceforth LP), and it is to this paper that we look first. Let us start, therefore, by considering LP's criticisms of the earlier approach.

LP (262–3) suggest that the *SPE*-based theory of stress has seven special properties which distinguish it from the rest of generative phonological theory. As they say, this does not necessarily mean that the theory is incorrect. Nevertheless, it would clearly be advantageous if a theory of stress could be discovered which was not so radically out of line with the remainder of the phonological theory or which demonstrated that stress assignment had certain special properties which entailed an account of stress radically different from accounts of other phonological phenomena. Although not all these seven special properties are equally telling, it is worth noting what they all are (for fuller details see LP: 262–3):

(i)   The stress feature is *n*-ary.

(ii)   Non-primary values of stress are defined only syntagmatically.

(iii)   The distinction among various levels of stress has little or no *local* [LP's emphasis: RMH/CBM] import.

(iv)   It is only stress and stress-related phenomena which provide good evidence for the cyclic application of phonological rules.

(v)   Stress rules cause a widespread pattern of change.

(vi)   The point where a stress-assignment rule applies may be indefinitely far away from some other term which is necessary to define its environment.

(vii)   Only stress rules make use of the convention of disjunctive ordering.

There seem to be two crucial points at issue, namely the *n*-ary nature of the stress feature and the widespread pattern of change caused by the stress rules. Both lead to a single vital conclusion.

The problem with the stress feature being *n*-ary (or multi-valued) is not that simple fact. After all, it can reasonably be argued that vowel height, for example, is a single *n*-ary feature, rather than a complex of binary features such as [high] and [low] (or [high] and [mid]). The same, indeed, may be true of several other phonological features. The problem, rather, is what meaning it might be possible to attach to, say, [4stress], for, in LP's words, there is little or no 'local' import to such values; that is to say, if a particular vowel is marked [4stress] this does not specify a particular phonetic value for that vowel in terms of stress. If we take the phrase *sad plight* in isolation, with its 2 1 stress pattern, and then the same phrase in the sentence *My friend can't help being shocked at anyone who would fail to consider his sad plight*, where it has an 8 1 pattern, it is legitimate to ask what is meant by the different stress patterns. For it is abundantly clear that it cannot be the case that *sad* is twice as weakly stressed as *plight* in the first case, but eight times as weakly stressed as *plight* in the second case. Nor is the first example of *sad* four times more strongly stressed than the second example of *sad*. Indeed, none of the above makes any sense at all. Nor would anything like it. The point is, rather, that the *SPE*-type stress assignment rules produce a *relative ordering* within any given string. Thus in the phrase *sad plight*, *sad* is said to have the second strongest stress, whereas in the longer sentence *sad* is said to have the eighth strongest stress. In effect what this is telling us is that stress assignment rules operate relationally, despite the fact that they assume the guise of 'ordinary' phonological rules which operate in absolute terms.

This point is so important that it is worth repeating it, especially in view of the fact that *SPE*-type treatments have consistently obscured it. A typical instance here is the case of *blackboard*, with its alleged 1 3 pattern in isolation. What could that pattern possibly mean? Clearly, if the stress assignment rules do produce a relative ordering, than all that can be meant is that *board* is the third strongest stress in a phrase where only two elements are stressed – which is plainly nonsense. Thus the pattern can only be interpreted as having some absolute value (and hence a local phonetic correlate). But the example of *sad plight* shows that this is equally nonsensical. No doubt the 1 3 pattern is borrowed from a theory such as that of Trager & Smith (1951), where four taxonomic phonemic levels of stress are assumed, each with a local phonetic correlate (see here the notes to chapter 1.2). The point of this is that where two incompatible approaches to stress, such as the Trager–Smith analysis and the *SPE* analysis, are combined, they lead to conclusions which are meaningless. And the incompatibility can only derive from one (that of Trager & Smith) being a paradigmatic approach, and the other (the *SPE* analysis) being a syntagmatic approach.

As a link to the other crucial issue, consider again the phrase *sad plight*. A further criticism of the assignment of the contour 8 1 to that phrase when situated in the sentence discussed above is that the stress assignment rules are producing too many stress values. This can be more obviously demonstrated by the fact that there is no theoretical objection, indeed it is entailed by the theory, to the production of stress contours such as 16 1, or 29 1 (or whatever) for that phrase, according to context, since it is the syntactic complexity of the context which alone controls the number of distinctive stress levels. But no one, surely, would wish to claim that native speakers recognise an indefinitely large number of stress levels. What has happened is that the stress assignment rules are over-articulate: they produce more stress values than anyone would desire, more stress values than could possibly be significant. Why might this be so? The answer lies in the fact that the only constraint which operates to limit the widespread pattern of changes induced by the Stress Subordination Convention is the length of the syntactic string involved. Therefore, within any given string there can be indefinitely many vowels which have been assigned some value for the feature [stress], and hence there can be an indefinite degree of stress subordination. Relative stress values are relative to every other vowel in the string.

The fundamental insight of the work by LP, and one which presents a radical solution to these problems, is that a more adequate analysis of stress should look at the relative prominence of syntactic and morpho-logical constituents rather than the (quasi-) paradigmatic assignment of absolute stress values to vowels. Although in later developments of this theory the central role of syntax has been questioned, as we shall see in later chapters, this insight was essential to the development of the theory of metrical phonology. The central tenet of metrical phonology is indeed that the crucial factor in understanding stress patterns is that they reflect, to some extent at least, relations of prominence between constituents.

3.2   *The basis of metrical theory*

LP suggest, therefore, that what we must do (for the moment we shall restrict ourselves to above the level of the word) is build *metrical trees* which reflect the syntactic structure. Thus for the phrases *black board* and *John left* we can build metrical trees of the following shape:

(3.1) a.   b.

black board   John   left

Similarly, for the compounds *blackboard* and *stress-shift* we can build trees of essentially the same shape:

(3.2) a.   b.

black board   stress – shift

Q.   To show the relative prominence of each constituent in a metrical tree we label each node either *s* or *w*, where *s* means 'stronger than' and *w* means 'weaker than'. Take the four trees above and label the constituents appropriately. Also, consider what is meant by the phrases 'stronger than' and 'weaker than'. More specifically, 'than' what?

A.   You should have obtained the following results, assuming that the basic insights of the NSR and the CSR hold:

(3.3) a.   b.

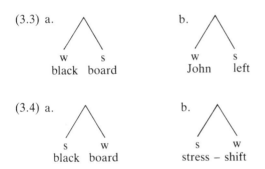

    w   s   w   s
black board   John   left

(3.4) a.   b.

    s   w   s   w
black board   stress – shift

Since these metrical trees are intended to express the relative strength of constituents, it follows that the relations hold between sister constituents, so that if some constituent is marked *s* this means that it is stronger than, i.e. it has greater prominence than, its sister constituent. Conversely, if some constituent is marked *w* this means that it is weaker than, i.e. it has less prominence than, its sister constituent. Thus stress assignment in metrical phonology is a matter of denoting the relative prominence of sister constituents. Therefore the labelling of the nodes as *s* or *w* is wholly dependent upon the existence of sister nodes and has no meaning independent of such a relationship between nodes. This has an important implication. Since in metrical phonology the relationships which are defined can only be those of stronger than or weaker than, it follows that the metrical trees which are constructed must always and only be binary-branching. Furthermore, the sister nodes must be in the relation [w s] or [s w], since [s s] and [w w] would be meaningless (it cannot be the case, for example, that each node is stronger than its sister). Equally, a node cannot stand on its own in either the configuration [w] or the configuration [s], since a sister node is required in order to make sense of the syntagmatic concepts 'weaker than' and 'stronger than'. Thus the only possible metrical tree structures are those in (3.5), whilst (3.6) shows a sample of illegal tree structures:

(3.5)

(3.6)

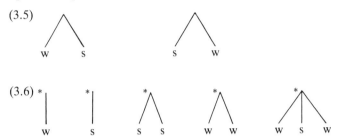

Q. Attempt now to draw metrical trees for the phrases *dew-covered lawn* and *coffee-table book*, where *dew-covered* and *coffee-table* are both compounds. Your trees should respect the insights of the CSR and the NSR, but ignore the internal structure of simple words.

A. Since the syntactic bracketing of *dew-covered lawn* is [[[dew] [covered]] [lawn]], and similarly for *coffee-table book*, and since metrical trees tend to reflect syntactic structure, you should have drawn the following trees:

(3.7)

(3.8)

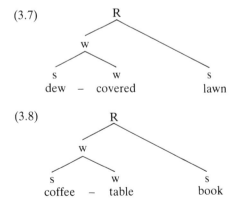

Before we go on to discuss the actual process of labelling nodes, which so far has been done, as it were, by magic, it is worth considering what trees such as (3.7) and (3.8) are telling us. The symbol R, by the way, is a simple way of annotating the root or topmost node of the tree: it tells us that it, R, dominates a constituent (a phrase in the case above). We use it here merely because it is frequently employed. But there is no absolute need for such an annotation, and we shall often ignore it.

If we take example (3.7), the tree gives us the following information. It tells us that of the sister constituents *dew* and *covered* the former is more prominent than the latter, and it also tells us that of the sister constituents *dew-covered* and *lawn*, the latter is more prominent than the former. It does not, however, tell us anything about the relationship between, say, *covered* and *lawn*. Indeed it could not possibly do so, because *covered* and *lawn* are not sister constituents. In this way, therefore, the criticism levelled at the *SPE* approach, that it produces statements about relative levels of stress between vowels which do not have any significant relationship holding between them, is elegantly overcome. For example, if we take once more the case of *sad plight*, you may now be able to observe that this theory of relative prominence will only relate the prominence of *sad* to *plight* (showing that *sad* is weaker than *plight*), and *sad* will never stand in any kind of relationship to any other item, even in the sentence which we used at the beginning of the chapter. The reason why the *SPE* analysis gave patterns such as 8 1 was that there were no constraints on relating the vowel of *sad* to any other vowel in the sentence. Indeed, in the case of *dew-covered lawn* the *SPE* analysis would have given a stress pattern 2 3 1, and thus claimed a relation between *covered* and *lawn* which does not exist, or which does not exist crucially, in the syntax of the phrase. On the other hand, metrical trees are inherently constrained, and this prevents the statement of non-crucial relationships.

But even if you are willing to accept the claims made by metrical trees as we have described them, you may have noticed a problem. For surely, even if it is the case that there is no relation between *covered* and *lawn* (but only between *covered* and *dew* and between *dew-covered* and *lawn*), we should nevertheless want to claim that there is a relation of relative prominence between *dew* and *lawn*. At the moment that does not appear to be possible. There is, however, a simple and natural solution. What we have to say is that for any pair of sister constituents, the constituent which is marked *s* is the *head* of the constituent which immediately dominates them. Thus, in the case of *dew-covered*, *dew* is the metrical, but not necessarily the syntactic, head of the constituent which immediately dominates them. Then, since the constituents *dew-covered* and *lawn* are in a [w s] relationship, this should be interpreted as a statement of the relative prominence of the heads of the constituents, that is, that *lawn* is stronger than *dew*. Exactly the same holds in the phrase *coffee-table book*. In the case of *sad plight*, *sad* will always be weaker than *plight* (by the NSR), and hence *plight* will be defined as the head of the constituent. From this it follows that *sad* will only stand in a relation of prominence to *plight*, regardless of the structure of the remainder of the sentence. On the other hand *plight* will stand in a relation of prominence to other constituents of the sentence.

It is not only the case that the above statement of prominence relations is intuitively more satisfying than the *SPE* one. It is also the case that defining such relationships, i.e. the correct labelling of nodes, is much simpler within metrical theory. As LP (257) point out, within this theory the NSR and the CSR are simply stated, as follows:

(3.9) For any pair of sister nodes $[N_1 \, N_2]$, then:
   (a) NSR: If $[N_1 \, N_2]_P$ where P is a phrasal category, then N_2 is strong.
   (b) CSR: If $[N_1 \, N_2]_L$ where L is a lexical category, then N_2 is strong if and only if (iff) N_2 branches.

There is no need for further specification, since if one node is marked strong then it follows that the other is weak, and vice versa.

Q. You should check for yourself that the statements in (3.9) will indeed produce the labelling of the trees in (3.7) and (3.8) which we earlier assumed. Then consider the following compound (taken from LP): *law degree requirement changes*. You should assume that this compound has the following syntactic structure: [[[[law] [degree]] [requirement]] [changes]] ('changes in the law degree requirement'). Attempt to draw a correctly labelled tree for this nominal compound. Then attempt to do the same for *labour union strike committee chairman*, where we leave you to ascertain the correct parsing yourself.

A. For the compound *law degree requirement changes* you should have drawn the following tree:

(3.10)

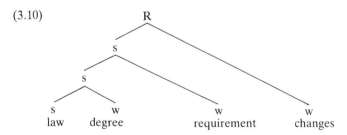

The basic structure of the tree is determined by the syntactic parsing. First of all *law* and *degree* are taken as sisters, i.e.:

(3.11)

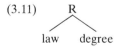

Then *law degree* and *requirement* are similarly taken as sisters, which gives:

(3.12)

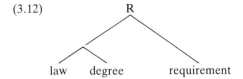

Finally the tree is completed by making *changes* a sister of *law degree requirement*. Then it is a matter of defining relative prominence. Since in each case we are dealing with a compound (noun), the CSR is the relevant rule. This states that N_2 is strong iff it branches. But in every case N_2 is non-branching, since it dominates only a single word (unlike N_1, which except in the case where it dominates only *law*, always dominates more than one word and is therefore branching). Thus N_2 is in every case weak, and correspondingly N_1 is in every case strong. Thus, for example, in *law degree*, *law* is the metrical head of the constituent, even although *degree* is the syntactic head.

The other example, *labour union strike committee chairman*, although also a compound, is more complex, and it is essential to obtain the correct syntactic parsing. Here we want to suggest that the constituent structure of this compound is one where *labour* and *union* are compounded together, *strike* and *committee* are compounded together, then these two compounds are compounded together before, finally, *labour union strike committee* is compounded with the lexical word (not a compound) *chairman*. This is by no means uncontroversial, although it follows the suggestions of LP, and we shall see in chapter 6 that there are alternative parsings for multiply embedded compounds. If we leave that point aside temporarily, however, the correct unlabelled tree structure, a faithful reflection of the syntax, is as follows:

(3.13)

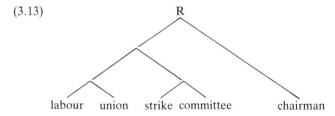

If we then apply the CSR to this unlabelled tree, we will find that *labour* and *union* will be marked as [s w], as will *strike* and *committee*, since the N_2 node in each pair of sisters is non-branching (they dominate *union* and *committee* respectively). When we consider the pair of nodes dominating *labour union* and *strike committee*, however, a different relationship emerges, since in this case N_2 is branching and is therefore to be marked as strong. Finally, the N₂ node dominating *chairman* is non-branching and therefore weak. Thus the following is the correctly labelled metrical tree:

(3.14)

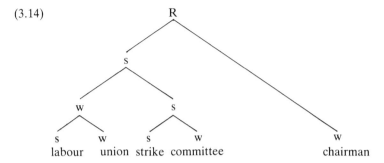

The element which is dominated only by *s*-nodes, here *strike*, is the most prominent element in the string, and this is usually referred to as the *Designated Terminal Element* or DTE.

As an aside more than anything else, it is perhaps worth pointing out that, to use LP's term (259), the trees we have constructed so far can be said to 'mimic' the numerical assignment of stress in the *SPE* analysis. What this means is that for all the trees so far we can reconstruct the numerical stress assignments given by the equivalent *SPE* rules by means of the following algorithm (LP: 259):

(3.15) If a terminal node *t* is labelled *w*, its stress number is equal to the number of nodes that dominate it, plus one. If a terminal node *t* is labelled *s*, its stress number is equal to the number of nodes that dominate the lowest *w* dominating *t*, plus one.

Thus, for example in the case of *coffee-table book*, this algorithm will derive the *SPE* contour 2 3 1, and for *labour union strike committee chairman* it will derive the *SPE* contour 3 4 1 4 2. If you like, you can check these for yourself, but the only consequence of this match (which, in fact, does not always exist: consider, for example, *a red book*, and see the discussion of *the fat cat*, below) is reassurance that the two types of analysis can convey some of the same information.

By and large, tree-building operations of the kind that we have been talking about so far are fairly close copies of the syntactic parsing, and the only difficulties that you will encounter involve a correct determination of the syntactic parsing (as in the example of *labour union strike committee chairman*). However, sometimes the syntactic trees and the metrical trees will not be identical – we have already seen that metrical and syntactic heads are not necessarily identical. Whereas metrical trees are strictly binary-branching, there is normally no such restriction on the trees constructed by phrase structure rules, nor is there any such restriction on the trees which are the output of transformational rules (if the grammar contains such rules – an irrelevant issue here). For example, it is commonly held that many noun phrases, such as *the fat cat*, have an internal structure approximately of the form Det+A+N, so that the NP node dominating this string is ternary-branching (it has three daughter nodes). What do we do in such cases?

The answer is that we must search for the rightmost element of each syntactic phrase and then work right-to-left along the string, creating pairs of constituents. Thus, in the case of *the fat cat* we must first of all pair *fat* with *cat* (*cat* being the rightmost element of the phrase), and then pair *the* with *fat cat*, to give the following structure:

(3.16)

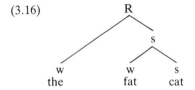

We find in (3.16) a metrical structure which is typical of all phrases, for the method for determining the structure of each and every phrase is identical. What we draw is a *right-branching tree*, i.e. a tree structure where only right sister nodes may branch (with, of course, the exception of the root node, where 'left' and 'right' are meaningless). As we shall see, it is entirely possible for a left-hand node to branch, but for the moment we take the view that this can occur only if one phrase is embedded within another.

Q. In order to make sure that you understand the method for producing metrical trees for phrases, construct the appropriate metrical trees for the following phrases and sentences: *John's big brother*; *Fred sold the book to Mary*; *My oldest friend threw the rather large stone across the river*. You should ignore the internal structure of polysyllabic words.

A. In all three cases we are dealing with phrases (or sentences), and therefore the NSR will apply, making N_2 strong. Thus, if we take *John's big brother*, you should find that you have drawn exactly the same tree for that phrase as for *the fat cat*, namely:

(3.17)

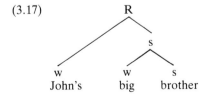

In principle, *Fred sold the book to Mary* has a tree structure similar to that of (3.17), since the tree is constructed by the same method. But if we consider the surface syntactic structure:

[s[NPFred] [VP[Vsold] [NPthe book] [PPto Mary]]]

we can see that in this case there are phrases embedded within larger phrases. This means that we must first draw partial trees for the embedded phrases, so that we get:

(3.18)

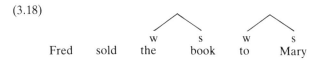

Next we build the tree structure further to get the partial tree for the VP, and this partial tree, since it must be right-branching, will be of the form:

(3.19)

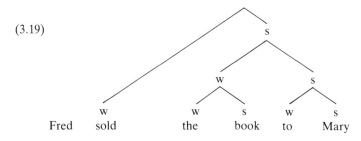

Finally, the two sister nodes NP and VP are joined together, giving:

(3.20)

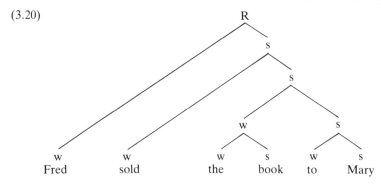

The tree of (3.20) apparently claims that *the book to Mary* is a constituent, which is syntactically unlikely. This, of course, is a product of the binary nature of metrical, as opposed to syntactic, trees, and is further proof that syntactic and metrical trees need not be identical in structure. Structure (3.20) also exemplifies the point that although metrical trees for phrases are fundamentally right-branching, the left-hand node will branch if one phrase is embedded within another. The same point, of course, applies *a fortiori* if some phrase contains a compound word.

The same method is again applied to derive the metrical structure of *My oldest friend threw the rather large stone across the river*. The points especially to note in this case are: (a) *rather large* is an adjective phrase embedded within a noun phrase, so that a subtree must be drawn for it before the tree for *the rather large stone* is drawn; (b) a tree must be drawn for *my oldest friend* before the subject NP and its sister VP are linked. The final result should be as follows:

(3.21)

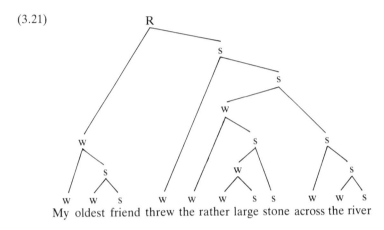

My oldest friend threw the rather large stone across the river

There are several problems associated with the trees that we have drawn so far, and one of them is worth considering immediately. If you compare the tree of (3.17) with that of (3.16), you will note that they ascribe the same level of prominence to *the* in *the fat cat* as to *John's* in *John's big brother*. But that is clearly incorrect: *John's* is more prominent in its phrase than *the* is in its phrase. Furthermore, if one tries to apply the algorithm of (3.15) to get *SPE*-type stress numbers, it will suggest that *the fat cat* and *John's big brother* both have the stress pattern 2 3 1. The *SPE* analysis would indeed give that as the stress pattern for the latter phrase, but, more reasonably, would give the stress pattern 0 2 1 for *the fat cat*. Whether or not the tree structure we have given for *John's big brother* is indeed the appropriate one is a question which we shall be discussing in later chapters, but whatever the answer to that, it should not disguise from us the fact that something has gone wrong with the tree for *the fat cat*.

What has gone wrong? The answer seems to lie in the fact that whereas *John's* is a lexical category word, *the* is not. It seems that we must reckon with the probability that lexical category words have a certain prosodic status, that is to say, that the category of word has, in the assignment of relative prominence, a particular role to play. Indeed, LP suggest that lexical category words have the role of occupying a particular *prosodic level*, which should be marked on trees. This prosodic level they call 'mot' (abbreviated by M), in order to distinguish it from whatever might be defined by the non-prosodic entity 'word'. The consequence of this is that in LP's model the appropriate trees for *the fat cat* and *John's big brother* will be (3.22) and (3.23) respectively, where (3.22) contains two prosodic words or mots and (3.23) contains three:

(3.22)

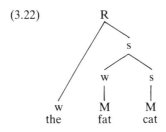

(3.23)

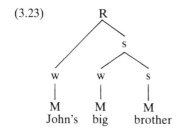

Note that if we modify the algorithm of (3.15) so that it applies only to syllables dominated by M, where all other syllables receive the numerical assignment [0stress], then the results produced will be in closer alignment with the *SPE* analysis.

Although the discussion above has something of an ad hoc air about it – it might well seem as if we had introduced the category mot solely in order to avoid one particular snag – there are other, independent, reasons for introducing the concept of prosodic level. To see one such reason consider again a compound such as *strike committee*. We have already claimed that the appropriate metrical structure for this compound is as follows:

(3.24)

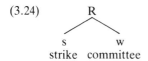

where the right-hand node is weak by virtue of the CSR, which says that N₂ is strong iff it branches. But we have already observed that both phrases and compounds have internal metrical structure. It would seem singularly unfortunate, under the circumstances, if words too did not have an internal metrical structure. For the moment let us simply assume that this is the case. If so, then it should be apparent that, whatever the precise internal structure of *committee* might be, the *w*-node which dominates it in (3.24) will be a branching node. It follows from this that a more appropriate representation of *strike committee* might be:

(3.25)

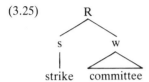

where the *w*-node is branching (although we have not filled in the details of internal structure). But in that case, according to the CSR, the right-hand node should be strong, since it branches. And this is incorrect. Let us, however, introduce again the prosodic level mot, as in (3.22) and (3.23). This will give us the tree structure:

(3.26)

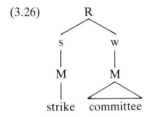

In that structure, the right-hand node is non-branching, and hence is correctly defined as *w*. In fact, we could also reformulate the CSR in the following way, to produce the desired results:

(3.27) *Compound Stress Rule*
If $[N_1 N_2]_L$ where L is a lexical category, then N_2 is strong iff it branches *at the same prosodic level.*

3.3   *Word-stress*

We shall return to the question of prosodic levels later. At the moment, however, it seems reasonable to accept LP's position and move on to a consideration of how the internal metrical structure of words might be organised. In their initial version of metrical phonology, LP suggest, in effect, that segmental versions of the English Stress Rule (ESR) and the Stress Retraction Rule (SRR) should be incorporated into the metrical analysis. The only major modification which LP make is that instead of treating stress as an *n*-ary feature, where rules such as the ESR assign [1stress], LP argue that stress should be taken as a binary feature, i.e. [±1stress], just like any other phonological feature, and that rules such as the ESR assign [+stress] to vowels, rather than [1stress], all vowels being underlyingly [−stress]. Here we might ask whether or not it is desirable that all vowels should be underlyingly [−stress]. Other phonological features are not always given a minus value in underlying representations, and this suggests, perhaps, that an oddity persists in LP's use of this feature. Nevertheless, it follows from the above that the apparatus of metrical phonology, as originally conceived, was intended to replace the Detail Rule, the CSR and the NSR of the *SPE*-type analysis, whilst leaving other rules largely untouched.

We should also note that LP more than once indicate that it would be preferable to reorganise such rules as the ESR so that they refer to syllables rather than segments. For the present, we shall not introduce any formal discussion of a syllable-based approach, but rather we shall make considerable use of an informal concept of the syllable. Therefore the following comments are necessary now. We wish to make the following assumptions. Firstly, the internal metrical structure of words is organised syllabically. Thus monosyllabic words such as *bad* have one metrical constituent, bisyllabic words such as *honest* have two metrical constituents, and so on. As we have already stated in chapter 1, this approach is consistent with the *SPE* approach (as adopted by LP). Secondly, the type of syllable-based description presented in the previous chapter is a necessary ingredient of a full metrical description.

For the discussion of the metrical structure of words, let us take as our first examples simple bisyllables such as *English* and *baroque*. The ESR as applied to these words in its new metrical form will give the patterns énglish, báròque (assuming that other relevant rules, such as Initial Destressing, are also invoked). The patterning of plus and minus values is exactly the same as the patterning of [1stress] and [0stress] before the application of the Detail Rule and other rules involving the Stress Subordination Convention (SSC). Metrical theory, as we have described it, dictates that the trees for these two words should be:

(3.28)

In this way the relative prominence of the two syllables (vowels) which is determined by the ESR is preserved in metrical tree structure.

Not all words (even bisyllabic ones) preserve this apparent identity between occurrences of metrically strong nodes and [+stress]. Consider, for example, the words *gymnast* and *thirteen*, in which both syllables receive the value [+stress] by virtue of the ESR and the SRR. Since the theory excludes tree structures where pairs of nodes are both marked *s*, it is clear that there cannot be a one-to-one relation between [+stress] and *s*. In fact, given what we have said so far, *gymnast* should have the structure of (3.29a), whilst *thirteen*, somewhat irregularly as we shall see, should have the structure of (3.29b):

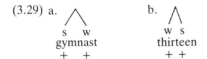

(3.29) a.
       s   w
    gymnast
    +   +

    b.
    w s
   thirteen
    + +

LP (265) suggest, nevertheless, that there is a correlation between values for the feature [±stress] and the labelling (*s*, *w*), which is as follows:

(3.30) If a vowel is *s*, then it is [+stress].
       Hence, if a vowel is [−stress], it is *w*.

This correlation will, for example, give only one possible metrical structure for a word such as *elephant*, where only the first vowel is [+stress]:

(3.31)

    s
  s w w
  elephant
  +− −

Q. Draw the appropriate metrical structures for the words *modest* and *careen*. Compare the structures of these two words with those of *gymnast* and *thirteen* and consider what difficulties the comparison presents and what conclusions might most profitably be drawn.

A. You should have drawn the following tree structures for *modest* and *careen*:

(3.32)
    s w
   modest
    + −

    w s
   careen
    − +

The problem here is that the tree structure for *modest* is identical to the tree structure for *gymnast*, and that the tree structure for *careen* is identical to the tree structure for *thirteen*. Yet it is clear that there is a difference in the stress specifications of *gymnast* and *modest*, and that the same difference, only realised in the opposite direction, is to be found between *thirteen* and *careen*. The only way to determine that from (3.32) and (3.29) is by considering the non-metrical information given there, namely that the second vowel of *gymnast* is [+stress] whereas the second vowel of *modest* is [−stress], and similarly, that the first vowel of *thirteen* is [+stress] whereas the first vowel of *careen* is [−stress].

LP do indeed claim that facts such as these show that the distinction marked by the feature [±stress] must be preserved within metrical theory. But this claim seems singularly unfortunate, in that it entails that information outside the metrical tree must be accessed in order to determine levels of relative prominence. The aim of metrical phonology (at least initially) was to encode all relevant information about prominence levels on the tree.

In later attempts to modify tree structure so that all necessary information is to be found in the tree, perhaps the most useful (re-)discovery in this connection has been that of the concept of the *stress foot*. In English, at least, a stress foot may provisionally be defined as a string containing as its first element a stressed syllable which is followed by zero or more unstressed syllables. We can take that convention (which will be fleshed out in more detail later) into the present theory without much difficulty, for, in the first instance, all that we have to do is to reinterpret the ESR and the SRR. It will no longer be the case that they assign [+stress] to certain vowels, as specified in the structural descriptions of the rule. Instead they will assign, according to their structural description, certain vowels, or, preferably, syllables, the property of being the *heads* of stress feet, as just defined. In other words, where the ESR and the SRR made certain vowels [+stress], this revised metrical version of these rules will make all and only all those syllables containing those 'certain vowels' the heads of stress feet. The consequence of this is that the metrical trees for *gymnast, modest, thirteen* and *careen* will be as in (3.33), where we use the symbol σ for syllable and, after Selkirk (1980), the symbol Σ for stress foot:

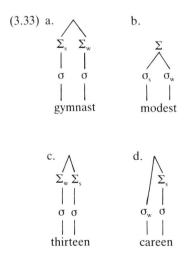

It should be noted here that the labelling of *s*- and *w*-nodes here is in fact identical to that used in (3.29) and (3.32). For the moment it is best to treat the introduction of foot and syllable labels as indeed no more than labelling. We shall shortly return to this point, but just now all you need note is that nothing that we have done violates the possibilities allowed to us by metrical theory (note here the introduction of the prosodic level mot). Thus the trees of (3.33) and the trees of (3.29) and (3.32) look at present as if they are no more than notational variants of one another. This, we shall shortly argue, is not entirely true.

Since we have defined a stress foot as a string of which the leftmost constituent is metrically strong (if you like, [+stress]) and all other constituents are metrically weak (if you like, [−stress]), the trees of (3.33b) and (3.33d) naturally follow. In (3.33b) the first syllable must be the head of the stress foot, since it is [+stress], and the second syllable will be a member of the same foot, since it is to its immediate right and is [−stress]. In (3.33d) the first syllable cannot be a member of the same foot as the second syllable, for the second syllable, being stressed, is the head of its foot and must therefore be the leftmost constituent of its foot. In other words stress feet are – and we apologise for the mixed metaphor – left-headed. In (3.33c), since there are two stressed syllables there must be two feet. The difference in relative prominence amongst these four words is, therefore, completely determinable from the revised tree structures which we have drawn for them.

The above discussion makes it look very much as if the stress foot is a prosodic level, as we have suggested might be the case for mot. This, a very real possibility, raises a number of complex issues which we would prefer not to go into in depth at present. Instead, some of these issues will be picked up and discussed in greater detail in later chapters. However, we must recognise that we are now dealing with a completely different concept of the ESR and the SRR from that presented in chapter 1, and, for that matter, in LP. It is, therefore, worth restating the presentation that we have just given. This restatement is not intended as definitive, as we shall see.

(i)   Stress assignment, rather, the levels of relative prominence, above the level of mot are determined by the metrical NSR and CSR (3.9a, b/3.27).

(ii)   Levels of relative prominence within the domain of mot are (in part) determined by the operation of the metrical equivalent of the ESR and the SSR, where the metrical equivalent of these rules have either the same structural description as in their segmental form or, more probably, a syllable-based equivalent.

(iii)   The metrical ESR and SRR are not, however, rules for assigning (binary or *n*-ary) value for some feature [stress]. Instead they are *foot-formation* rules. Wherever the structural description of the rules is met, then the appropriate syllable (vowel) is designated the head of a stress foot.

(iv) All stress feet are left-headed, i.e. all stress feet are left-branching binary structures where the leftmost syllable is marked *s*. Note that if a stress foot contains only one syllable, that syllable will not be marked *s* or *w*, since that would give an illegal non-binary structure. Of course the foot itself, even although only dominating one syllable, will be marked *s* or *w* by a rule yet to be considered.

3.4   *Stress relations within words*

Q. It can be observed that in (3.33) we have given all the possible metrical structures for bisyllabic lexical category words (mots). The principles outlined above can, of course, be extended to words of more than two syllables. Therefore, using these principles, redraw the tree of (3.31) for *elephant*, this time showing foot structure. Then draw similar trees for the following words: *acacia, America, asparagus, execute.*

A. The example *elephant* should pose no problems. In the segmental version of the ESR the only vowel which receives [+stress] is the first vowel. Therefore in the metrical version of the ESR the first syllable will become the head of a stress foot which contains two further syllables in a left-branching tree structure, thus:

(3.34)

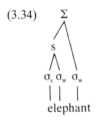

The example of *acacia* seems to show only one important difference, namely that it is the second syllable which is the head of the only stress foot (more trivially, there is only one further syllable to the right), and so too with *asparagus*, except that here, as in the case of *elephant*, there are two further syllables to the right of the head of the stress foot. If we ignore the initial syllable of each word for a moment, we obtain the following partial trees:

(3.35)

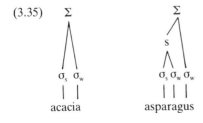

It looks as if what we should then do is simply adjoin the unstressed initial syllable of each word as a (weak) left sister of the foot node, which gives:

(3.36)

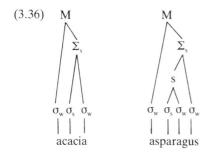

After all, in chapter 1 we observed that although the initial syllables of words such as these would, by the default version of the SRR, receive [1stress], i.e. [+stress], the rule of Initial Destressing would make these syllables unstressed, i.e. [−stress]. However, Zonneveld (1976) has demonstrated that Initial Destressing is sensitive to stress assignment rules, and that it occurs only if the immediately following vowel (in segmental terms) has the value of [1stress] after, at least, the application of the Detail Rule. Consider here the noun *adept* and the adjective *adept*. By the ESR, in LP's terms and thus using [±stress], both words will (because they are synchronically related – recall the discussion of *torment*, etc. in chapter 1) receive the following stress assignment: *adept*. Only in the case of the adjective is the initial syllable destressed. But the phonological structure of the two words is the same; it is necessary, therefore, firstly to apply the Detail Rule, which gives, for the noun and the adjective respectively, *adept* and *adept*. Then we can apply the rule of Initial Destressing (1.48), with the stipulation that the immediately following vowel must be [1stress]. Thus the initial syllable of the adjective will be destressed, but not the initial syllable of the noun.

As LP (283–91) point out, this can easily be converted to a metrical statement of Destressing. Two stipulations are required: firstly, Destressing should take place only after the construction of metrical trees; secondly, the syllable which follows the syllable to be destressed should not only be [+stress] but also metrically strong. Thus, given (3.37a) as the initial structure for the noun *adept* and (3.37b) as the initial structure for the adjective *adept*:

(3.37)

only the adjective will destress, because only there is the appropriate metrical structure for Destressing present. But this account is not entirely pleasing. Note that the procedure is somewhat complex. Firstly we have the assignment of values for [±stress]. Then trees are built up. Then, on the basis of tree structure, some values of the feature [±stress] are subject to change, whilst tree structure is maintained. Furthermore, under this account, it is entirely accidental that Destressing takes place after the building of metrical structure. It is perfectly compatible with this account that metrical structure would only have been built up after the operation of Destressing.

Q. Instead of the above account, however, we can provide an alternative formulation based on feet, which not only will solely use information in metrical trees and only affect tree structure, but also, as a consequence of this, necessarily refer to levels of relative prominence. Can you suggest what this foot-based rule of Destressing might look like?

A. The starting-point for any such rule must, of course, be tree structures incorporating feet. Thus we must start off with structures such as those in (3.38), which are similar to the earlier trees (3.36a, b) and (3.37a, b), except that here every syllable which would have received the value [+stress] by virtue of the ESR in LP's analysis must be designated as a foot, even if that syllable is initial and subject to Destressing. Thus we find the following trees:

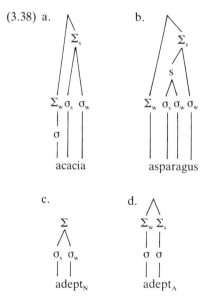

(3.38) a. acacia   b. asparagus   c. adept_N   d. adept_A

The foot-based rule of Destressing must then remove the property of being a foot from every initial syllable which is light (i.e. contains at most a short vowel followed by not more than one consonant – for the status of words such as *asparagus* see chapter 2) and which is immediately followed by a syllable which is the head of the next foot. In parenthesis we should note that Destressing also applies to certain Latinate or Romance prefixes, e.g. *ad-, con-, pre-, re*, even although they do not conform to the syllabic description. This, however, is not very important for our concerns, and it is sufficient here to label these prefixes, say, as [+Ro], to ensure that they, somewhat exceptionally, undergo the rule (see further LP: 284–8). The Destressing rule in foot terms has been expressed in slightly different ways by different writers (see, for example, Selkirk 1980: 584–6; 1982: 251–2), but the differences are insignificant. The simplest account assumes that all that happens is that a weak foot containing only one syllable, which must be either light or [+Ro], loses its foot status when it is immediately followed by another foot. In tree terms, that is:

(3.39) *Destressing (foot-based)*

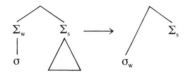

Conditions: σ is either light or [+Ro].

Trees (3.38a,b,d), but not (3.38c), will thus be transformed, giving the results of (3.40):

(3.40) a.

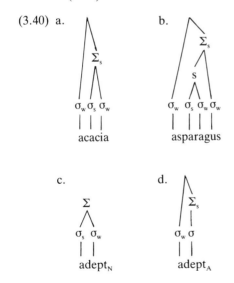

You may have noticed that Destressing as formulated above will not only apply initially but also anywhere that the specified tree structure is found.

This is indeed correct, but there are one or two more detailed specifications which must be made. We shall not discuss these here, but see instead Selkirk (1980: 590–2).

We hope that the preceding few pages will have convinced you of the superiority of a foot-based analysis over the presentation in LP which employs the binary feature [±stress]. More importantly for present purposes, however, you should note that in many respects the different analyses are fully compatible with one another: where we have designated feet on trees, LP mark the appropriate syllable (vowel) as [+stress]. Therefore it should not prove difficult to compare our foot-based analysis with the stress-based analysis of LP. We make this point here, because although we now wish to move on to another aspect of LP's original paper, we shall use foot-based trees in the following discussion, not the trees which LP employ.

Within the foot-based analysis which we have outlined, it is relatively straightforward to determine the relative prominence of the syllables within each foot. This is because each foot has a left-headed, i.e. left-strong, and left-branching tree structure. We could indeed, if we wished, stipulate that foot-internal structures are precise mirror images of phrase-internal structures. The latter are right-branching, as we have seen, and are right-strong by virtue of the NSR (for any pair of nodes $[N_1 \ N_2]_P$, N_2 is strong). We could therefore state that foot-internal structures are left-branching and that there is an equivalent of the NSR, namely a Foot Stress Rule or FSR, which states that for any pair of nodes $[N_1 \ N_2]_\Sigma$, N_1 is strong.

That is not difficult, but there still remains one major problem in determining the prominence relations within words. Although we have silently assumed that there must be some method of so doing, we have not yet seriously discussed the means by which the relative prominence of feet within words is determined. Note here, by the way, that this is the issue which LP (268) refer to as the consideration of what governs the labelling of 'higher-level nodes'. It is an additional advantage of the foot-based analysis that such higher-level nodes are now clearly definable as, in fact, foot nodes.

Q.   Draw trees for the pair of words *emigrate* and *emigration*, and also for the pair *reconcile* and *reconciliation*. Consider how the feet are linked together – this is problematic only in the case of *reconciliation* – and then label the feet as strong or weak in accordance with your intuitions about the relative prominence of the syllables. Can you determine any algorithm which would produce a labelling of the feet in accordance with your intuitions? It might be helpful here to think again about the labelling provisions of the NSR and the CSR.

A. If we consider firstly the case of *emigrate*, then by the ESR there are two feet whose heads are the first and third syllables (or, if you like, the first and third vowels are [+stress]). Exactly the same applies to the derived form *emigration*. Thus we can draw trees of the following form:

(3.41)

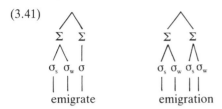

In the case of *reconcile* there are two feet, where the first and third syllables are the heads, and, following (3.41), this gives the tree structure:

(3.42)

In the case of *reconciliation*, however, there are three feet, whose heads are the first, third and fifth syllables. Initially this gives the structure of:

(3.43)

You will no doubt have noticed that in this last case there is a problem of how to link the feet together. The problem is exactly the same as that encountered when we attempted to draw binary-branching trees for phrases containing more than two syntactic constituents. Here too we appear to have a ternary structure, and, LP suggest, the answer is precisely the same. We must create a right-branching tree. For illustrative purposes, at least, we shall, following Selkirk (1980), label the node which dominates the two rightmost feet a *superfoot*, symbolized by Σ'. Thus we find:

(3.44)

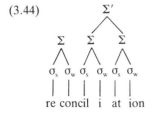

Thus we can see how word-internal trees are constructed for words containing more than one foot. The question remains, however, of how to label the feet appropriately. If your intuitions were correct, you should have labelled the feet as follows:

(3.45)

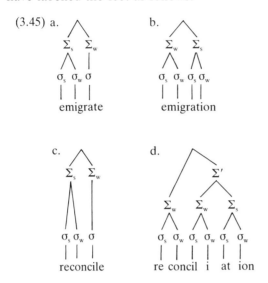

These trees tell us, correctly, that the most prominent syllable in each of these words is that indicated by the following small capitals: Emigrate, emiGRAtion, REconcile, reconciliAtion. It is possible to discern a regular patterning here: the strongest syllable in the word is the last syllable in the word which is (a) the head of a foot, and (b) has at least one other syllable to its right. This, of course, is exactly what the Detail Rule which we discussed in chapter 1 attempted to state in segmental terms, and, as LP (268) show, it is easily converted into a metrical statement, which in foot-based terms is as follows:

(3.46) *Word Rule*
For any pair of sister nodes $[N_1 \ N_2]_M$, N_2 is strong iff it branches.
Conditions: M is a mot
N_1, N_2 are feet or dominate feet.

The first condition should be transparent; the second condition ensures that the rule does not apply to foot-internal structures, although it will apply to superfeet-internal structures.

Q. In order to confirm that this Word Rule operates in the desired fashion and is a metrical parallel to the segmental Detail Rule, now draw trees for the following words which were discussed towards the end of chapter 1: *telephone, nightingale, tripartite, epicycloid, abracadabra, balalaika.*

A.   You should have drawn the following trees. If you have not, please go back over the last discussion and make sure that you understand the underlying principles of tree formation and *s/w* marking.

(3.47)

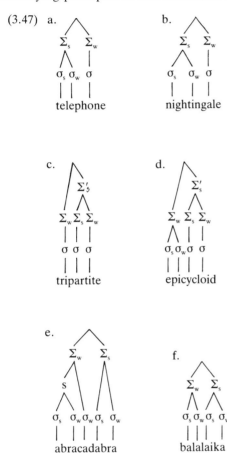

If you took the earlier hint, that it might be a good idea to think about the NSR and the CSR when considering the form of a rule to determine the relative prominence of word-internal feet, then you will no doubt have already discovered an interesting fact, namely that the CSR and the Word Rule are essentially the same: for any pair of nodes $[N_1 \ N_2]$, N_2 is strong iff it branches. This is really not all that remarkable, for, just as lexical words are (if they receive stress, that is) members of some lexical category (N, V or A), so too are compounds members of one or another of those same lexical categories. In essence the stress rules that we have been discussing all along have made one and only one distinction, which is whether they deal with a lexical category or a phrasal category. It is therefore a desirable feature of metrical phonology that it should be able to handle all cases of relative prominence above the foot level and below the phrase level by one and only one rule. Let us therefore combine the CSR and the Word Rule into a single rule, which LP (270) call the *Lexical Category Prominence Rule* or LCPR. Provisionally, and incompletely, we may state the LCPR as follows:

(3.48) *Lexical Category Prominence Rule (LCPR)*
For any pair of sister nodes $[N_1 \ N_2]_L$, N_2 is strong iff it branches.
Conditions: L is a lexical category.
N_1, N_2 are feet or dominate feet.
Branching must be at the same prosodic level, where mot (M) is a relevant prosodic level.

Unfortunately, although the LCPR works well for a great many English words, there remain a considerable number of exceptions. Fortunately these exceptions largely fall into a small set of internally regular subgroups. Therefore, let us now scan over these major exception types fairly quickly.

The first set of exceptions are words which have a monosyllabic suffix or quasi-suffix which nevertheless becomes the most prominent element of the word. A partial listing of these suffixes, together with some examples, is as follows:

(3.49) -ade   blockade, cascade, lemonade
        -air   affair, corsair, debonair
        -ane   mundane, pavane, ultramontane
        -ār   bizarre, cigar, guitar
        -ee   absentee, addressee, legatee
        -eer   chandelier, engineer, musketeer
        -elle   bagatelle, Courtelle, moselle
        -esce   acquiesce, effervesce, recrudesce
        -esque arabesque, grotesque, picturesque
        -ette   cigarette, kitchenette, novelette
        -ique   antique, bezique, unique
        -ise   chemise, expertise, valise
        -oo   bamboo, canoe, Kalamazoo
        -oon   baboon, pontoon, tycoon
        -Vche   cartouche, panache, pastiche

For a fuller, indeed comprehensive, list, see Fudge (1984: 40–1, 52ff).

There are several points to note here. Firstly, not all the above are suffixes; consider, for example, *bamboo*. But they all behave as if they were suffixes, hence the term 'quasi-suffix' used above. Secondly, the whole process is subject both to dialectal variation and lexical idiosyncrasy. Hence LP also cite forms in *-eau*, e.g. *flambeau, chateau, portmanteau, tableau,* which are indeed end-stressed in American English but are not so stressed in British English, where the most prominent syllable is the penultimate one. And we may also note and contrast examples such as *legatee,* which is end-stressed, and *employee,* which, in British English at least, is not regularly end-stressed. In this case we see considerable lexical idiosyncrasy, which appears to be related to the degree to which the word in question has been integrated within the native vocabulary.

Under these circumstances it seems entirely reasonable to assume that this set of exceptions should be marked in the lexicon. There are two fairly obvious ways of doing this. Firstly, we could mark all the relevant suffixes with some diacritic (LP use the diacritic [+F]); or, secondly, we could supply each word with a (partial) metrical foot structure in underlying representation, with the final foot marked as *s*. Since, as we have said, LP use the first alternative, and then add a further condition to the LCPR, we shall do the same here, but you might like to consider whether this is indeed the more appropriate way of handling the problem, which will be discussed again later in this chapter. The LCPR should then read as follows:

(3.50) *LCPR*
For any pair of sister nodes $[N_1 \ N_2]_L$ where L is a lexical category and N_1, N_2 are feet or dominate feet, then N_2 is strong iff one of the following conditions is met:
A. N_2 branches
B. N_2 is [+F].

The second set of exceptions relates to a discussion which we raised in chapter 1. There we noted that although nouns followed one version of the the ESR, verbs followed an abbreviated version of that same rule. Adjectives tended to vacillate between the nominal and verbal versions of the rule. Thus we found two primary categories of verbs: (i) those such as *practise, edit, elicit, astonish, swallow,* which had penultimate stress; (ii) those such as *torment, abstract, molest, allege, maintain,* which had final stress. Of course, by the ESR, the verbs of the second group will have [+stress] assigned to both vowels (i.e. both syllables will be the heads of feet). But clearly it is the case that it is the final syllable which is most prominent, and indeed, in cases such as *molest* and *allege* the initial syllable is subject to Destressing. It looks therefore as if the LCPR must be further modified to say that N_2 is strong if the constituent is verbal, or, taking adjectives such as *august* into account, non-nominal. In fact, we need only specify the constituents as [~n], as that feature was defined for the ESR

(1.57). It is worth noting here that examples in the first category above, e.g. *edit*, will not have their penultimate syllable destressed, since they are the heads of feet which contain another syllable.

Q.   Contrasting with examples such as *edit*, *swallow*, there are other bisyllabic (and polysyllabic) verbs which have a light final syllable which is nevertheless stressed. Examples of such verbs are: *emit*, *equip*, *permit*, *infer*. The same applies to nouns, where of course the final syllable may be heavy, although in such cases the final syllable, although [+stress] or the head of a foot, will not be metrically strong, since the constituent is a [+n]. Thus we find: *comment*, *insect*, *permit*, *prefect*, where although the second syllable is weaker than the first, it is nevertheless the head of a foot. Can you suggest any morphological reason why such exceptions occur?

A.   The answer appears to be that in each case we are dealing with words which consist of a prefix followed by a stem. We therefore have to impose a restriction on the ESR that on its first application it must not skip over the whole of a stem. Thus we have morphological structures such as *e+mit*, *e+quip*, *com+ment*, *in+sect*, and the first application of the ESR will produce a foot above the stem syllable. Following on from that, it is only necessary to apply the modification to the LCPR that we have just suggested, namely that N_2 is strong if the constituent is non-nominal or [~n]. It will then be possible to create the appropriate metrical structures for words such as *practise*, *astonish*, *swallow*, *torment*, *allege*, *maintain*, *emit*, *infer*, *insect*, *prefect*. Thus for *practise*, *maintain*, and *insect* we find the following trees. You should attempt to draw for yourself the trees for the remaining words which we have just cited:

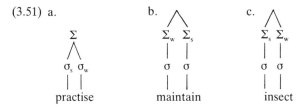

(3.51) a.   b.   c.

We cannot, however, preserve this modification to the LCPR just as it stands, for it makes a number of incorrect predictions. Consider the following pairs of words: *baptise*, *exorcise*, *rotate*, *delegate*, *pollute*, *execute*. The first member of each pair, as we have just predicted, receives end stress. But, contrary to our predictions, in the second member of each pair it is the first syllable which is most prominent. This quite regular patterning can be accommodated by stipulating that N_1 must be non-branching, for the final syllable is most prominent only when it is preceded by not more than one syllable. Oddly, however, there is a set of words which are all verbs and which violate this stipulation. Typical examples are: *intersect, intervene, supersede, supervene*. Contrast these with adjectives such as *circumspect, interstate* and *superstrate*. The question is why verbs such as *intervene* are end-stressed when the previous foot is disyllabic. Here again there is a morphological reason, for *inter-* and *super-* (also, for example, *circum-* in *circumvent*) are prefixes attached to some stem. We can therefore stipulate that for verbs, but not for adjectives, N_2 is strong provided that it immediately dominates a stem. This will then allow us the following statement of the LCPR:

(3.52) *LCPR*
For any pair of sister nodes $[N_1\ N_2]_L$ where L is a lexical category and N_1, N_2 are feet or dominate feet, then N_2 is strong iff one of the following conditions is met:
A. N_2 branches
B. N_2 is [+F]
C. L is [~n] (non-nominal) and N_1 does not branch
D. L is a verb and N_2 directly dominates the stem.

There are a fair number of exceptions even to this statement of the LCPR. For example, there are nouns such as *advance* and *delay* which nevertheless preserve the verbal prominence pattern. Then in American English, affixes such as *-ate* and *-ize* never receive prominence even if they are only preceded by a single syllable. Thus *baptize* and *rotate* are not end-stressed in American English – perhaps also in some dialects of British English. There are other examples where analogy seems to have overruled the regularities of the LCPR, so that, for example, *seventeen*, although it has a branching N_1, is end-stressed on the analogy of the other numerals from *thirteen* to *nineteen*, which go by condition C of the LCPR as we have stated it. Finally there are some odd nouns with a light initial syllable which receive end stress exceptionally, e.g. *attire, July, patrol*, contrasting with *rabbi, satire, essay*. It is possible to include most of these within the LCPR, and LP indeed do so. The first set of exceptions are diacritically marked and then fall under condition C above. The second set are handled by a further restriction on condition C. The third set are not considered. And the final set are handled by an entirely separate condition which LP label C. We should therefore point out that our conditions C and D reflect only condition D of LP's version of the LCPR.

It would be entirely possible to follow LP here and further modify the LCPR. However, we do not wish to do so. This is partly because we do not believe that it would be cost-effective – the complications involved in further modifications are considerable when weighed against the relatively small number of lexical items that each complication would handle. But it is also because we believe that it is extremely important that exceptions are recognised and that the issues involved in handling exceptions should be considered seriously. We shall, therefore, leave the LCPR as it stands. You might like to consider for yourself whether LP are right to find a subrule which will handle words such as *attire* but to ignore other examples, such as *seventeen*, of which they were doubtless aware. The general point remains, however, that the LCPR as it stands handles the vast majority of lexical items very adequately.

3.5   *Stress rules and the phonological cycle*

We now move on to an entirely different issue. You may recall that one of LP's objections to the Chomsky–Halle treatment of stress was that it required the cyclical operation of phonological rules. Now it is certainly quite clear that the Nuclear Stress Rule (NSR) as formulated in metrical terms destroys the need for any such cyclical operation. However, at lower levels the question of cyclicity remains an issue. And it is an issue when dealing with words of a type which we have so far not separately considered, namely words which are subject to processes of derivational morphology due to affixation. Very briefly, for otherwise this would lead us into a field with which we are not concerned, affixes in English are of two types: (i) stress-neutral; (ii) stress-shifting. Typical stress-neutral affixes include *-able*, *-age*, *-ed*, *-en*, *-ing*, *-ly*, *-ness*, for when these affixes are attached to lexical items the stress pattern of the item concerned is unaffected. Typical stress-shifting affixes, on the other hand, include *-al*, *-ar*, *-an*, *-ance*, *-ate*, *-ic*, *-ify*, *-ity*, *-ive*, *-ise*, *-ment*. Several recent treatments of such morphophonological issues have involved postulating various *levels* of morphophonology. Thus stress-shifting affixes are held to belong to level 1 whereas stress-neutral affixes are held to belong to some level later than level 1 (commonly level 2). Phonological or (properly) morphophonological rules are also assigned to levels, and the English Stress Rule is amongst those assigned to level 1. This means that only level 1 affixes can interact with a rule such as the ESR, and hence that affixes (and other morphophonological processes) at other levels are stress-neutral. We do not wish to go into the complexities of this interesting proposal here, for we wish only to point out that it is very possible to distinguish systematically between stress-shifting and stress-neutral affixes. Most of the work in this area, stemming from original proposals by Siegel (1974), has been conducted within the theory called Lexical Phonology (see 'Notes and further reading' at the end of this chapter). Here we shall simply maintain the distinction between stress-shifting and stress-neutral affixes.

In this context it is clear that the stress-neutral affixes are irrelevant. Metrical structure will be assigned by normal processes to a word such as *accomplish* (where prominence is on the second syllable) and then after stress has been so assigned the suffix *-ment* will be added without alteration of the metrical pattern. But what happens in other cases? Let us take as an example one that has been much discussed in the literature, namely the triple *sensation, sensational, sensationality*. Here, albeit reluctantly, LP are forced to accept a cyclical solution, although it might be termed a minimally cyclical solution, since it is almost equivalent to saying that the three words are completely separate items (but LP cannot say that because of other morphophonological rules such as so-called Velar Softening which relates the final /k/ of *electric* to the /s/ found in the same position when the suffix *-ity* is added to give *electricity*). What LP suggest is the following. First of all the root lexical item *sensation* is taken, to which the iterative ESR is applied. Then the suffix *-al* is added, and the ESR is re-applied. At least this is almost the case, but not quite; for first of all they invoke a principle of *Deforestation* (LP: 301):

> (3.53) Before applying any rules on a cycle, erase all prosodic structure in the domain of that cycle.

For LP, this allows the preservation of values for [±stress], but of course in terms of the account which we have presented nothing will remain after Deforestation, since all information in the trees, and that is the only information that we have, is erased by the process of Deforestation. Thus the building up of tree structure for a word such as *sensational* is an entirely fresh operation. After that is done, then the suffix *-ity* is added, and this entails once again the process of Deforestation and the re-application of the ESR. From this you will be able to see, we hope, why we term this a minimally cyclical solution.

   Q.   In order to see how the process we have just described works, you should now try to draw the appropriate metrical structures for each of the three words *sensation, sensational* and *sensationality*. Do any of the three trees which you construct pose any problems in terms of the relative prominences which they predict?
   A.   Let us take first of all *sensation*. By the ESR there are two feet, whose heads are the first and second syllables respectively. The second foot, N_2, is branching, and therefore will be labelled strong by the LCPR. Thus we have the following tree structure:

(3.54)
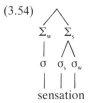

If that were the end of the derivation, then we would wish to apply the rule of Destressing (3.39), in order to defoot the Latinate prefix, but LP suggest that Destressing occurs only on the word cycle. This means that if we are dealing only with [sensation]$_N$ Destressing would take place, but that if we are dealing with, say, [[[sensation]al]ity]$_N$ then Destressing would not take place at this point in the derivation. Whether they are right or wrong, however, is not entirely relevant at present, since if we are dealing with the complex form the process of Deforestation will delete all metrical structure from earlier cycles and therefore it will be impossible to tell whether Destressing has taken place or not.

Let us now consider *sensational*. Assuming Deforestation, by which all the information in (3.54) is erased, we then re-apply the ESR, which will once more give two feet, in exactly the same structural positions as in *sensation*. Thus we have:

(3.55)

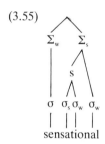

sensational

Once again, if that were the end of the derivation Destressing would apply, but otherwise it is irrelevant.

Therefore let us now move on to *sensationality*. Again Deforestation will erase all previously assigned structure and the ESR is free to apply iteratively over the whole constituent. In this case the first, second and fourth syllables will be heads of feet, and thus the following tree structure will result:

(3.56)

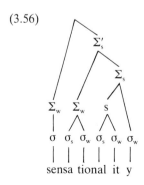

sensa tional it y

This tree can be objected to on two grounds: one morphological, the other phonological. Morphologically the tree is objectionable because it overrides morphological structure: [sensation] is no longer a structural unity. The same objection, as it happens, applies to (3.55), although there the phonological objection does not apply. The phonological difficulty with (3.56) is that it apparently fails to locate secondary stress. This is because there is no relation of relative prominence between the first and second syllables. Why? Because, as we suggested at the beginning of this chapter, *s/w* relations hold between heads, and therefore the *w*-marked syllable *sen-* is only marked by the tree as weaker than the head of its sister node, which is *-al*. In fact it can easily be argued that this failure was a product of LP's system which allowed information about relative prominence to be found outside the tree and in the values for the feature [±stress]. Within our version of the theory, the first syllable will be subject to Destressing and hence it will follow that it is weaker than the second syllable, which will remain the head of a foot. This phonological reason, therefore, is not compelling, as, for example, both Kiparsky (1979) and Giegerich (1985: 20) seem to think.

Nevertheless the combination of the morphological impasse and the temporary phonological misbehaviour (redeemed only by Destressing) suggests that something has gone wrong, and we must feel entitled to consider possible alternatives. In fact one has been proposed, largely independently, by Kiparsky (1979, 1982) and Hayes (1981, 1982). The basic principles and the initial argument are to be found in Kiparsky (1979), and it is that type of approach which we shall consider firstly, but then we wish to go on to outline the approach as developed in Hayes (1982), which seems to us a convincing and radical reformulation of the whole approach to word-stress within the metrical model.

Essentially Kiparsky (1979, 1982) proposes a strictly cyclical approach to the creation of metrical structure through the ESR, whether the latter is a foot-formation rule or a rule which assigns values for [±stress]. What we mean by saying that the assignment of metrical structure is strictly cyclic is the following. At each step of derivational morphology – insofar as that process is carried out at level 1; see our discussion of stress-shifting and stress-neutral affixes above – the ESR will apply regularly, but with one proviso, namely that existing metrical structure must be respected. This can be more formally stated as the *Strict Cycle Condition* (SCC), presented by Kiparsky (1982: 154).

(3.57) *Strict Cycle Condition (SCC)*
    (a) Cyclic rules apply only to derived representations.
    (b) Definition: A representation φ is *derived* with respect to rule R in
        cycle j iff φ meets the structural analysis of R by virtue of a

combination of morphemes introduced in cycle j or the application of a phonological rule in cycle j.

In effect, this means that on each new cycle the ESR will apply, but only to that part of the string which has been introduced on the new cycle. As we shall see, matters are slightly more complex than that; but let us first consider an example that is relatively straightforward, namely *standardisation*. In this case we shall be dealing with the following string: [[[standard]ise]ation]. On the first cycle we are concerned solely with the string within the innermost set of brackets. Application of the ESR as a foot-formation rule will give us the following:

(3.58)

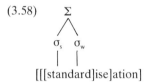

At the end of that cycle we can delete the innermost set of brackets and then re-apply the ESR, but given the SCC the foot-formation rule can now apply only to the material which has been introduced on the second cycle, namely *-ise*. Applying the ESR in this manner we then obtain:

(3.59)

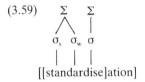

Since *standardise* is a word, to which the LCPR can apply, we must now indeed apply the LCPR, for not only is the ESR cyclic, but so also is the LCPR. This gives us:

(3.60)

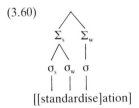

Note that in theory the LCPR should have applied at the end of the first cycle also, but since there was only one foot node there, the structural description of the rule was not met.

Again at the end of this cycle we must delete the innermost set of brackets, and the ESR will re-apply on the third cycle, this time to the newly-introduced material *-ation*. The result of this is the following:

(3.61)

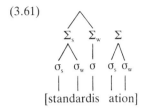

[standardis ation]

The LCPR then applies, to give the final structure:

(3.62)

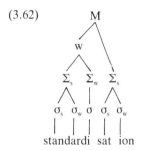

standardi sat ion

Q. In order to confirm your understanding of the principles of strict cyclicity, attempt to provide correct representations of the following words: *brilliantine, lemonade, ellipsoid, expensive.*

A. *Brilliantine* is exactly like *standardise*. On the first cycle (dealing with the string [brilliant]) a single foot is formed with the first syllable of the string as head, and then on the second cycle the ESR creates a second foot on *-ine*. Since this word is nominal and unaffected by any of the subconditions of the LCPR, the final metrical structure of the word will be:

(3.63)

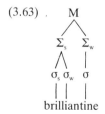

brilliantine

In the case of *lemonade* we start with a parallel structure, namely [[lemon]ade], and hence the final result might be expected to be the same. However, you should have recalled that the suffix *-ade* is marked as [+F], and hence the final tree should form a minimal contrast with that of (3.63), namely:

(3.64)

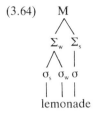

lemonade

Consider now the case of *ellipsoid*, which has the initial bracketing [[ellips]oid]. We must first of all apply the ESR to [ellips], and the normal operation of the ESR would give us a single foot with the first syllable as the head of the foot. In the accounts we have given so far of the ESR the only way to avoid this is to mark *ellipse* as [~n]. Using this convention we would then obtain the desired structure, namely:

(3.65)

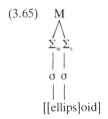

[[ellips]oid]

Although this gets us the correct result (subject to later Destressing, see below), it does so only in a most unsatisfactory manner. After all, it makes very little sense to label *ellipse* as [~n] when it is clearly nominal. We have, in doing so, merely disguised the fact that *ellipse* is lexically idiosyncratic, that *ellipse* disobeys the normal rules of English stress in an unsystematic manner – unlike, say, a verb such as *molest*, which follows the normal pattern for English verbs and thus can be quite rightly labelled [~n]. Kiparsky (1982: 164) therefore suggests that the kind of lexical idiosyncrasy exemplified by *ellipse* should be recognised in the lexicon, by providing the word with a lexical entry which includes a foot on the final syllable. Kiparsky is unclear on the problematic question of whether or not the whole word, or merely the final syllable, is provided with feet in the lexicon, but it seems likely that the second alternative is intended. Therefore, when [[ellips]oid] enters the first cycle it will already have been (lexically) provided with a partial foot structure which the ESR cannot erase. The reason for this is that the lexical provision of foot structure to *ellipse* is a special case of the more general rule of foot assignment, and there is a general condition, which Kiparsky (1982: 136) calls the *Elsewhere Condition*, which states that the special case has priority over the general case. We shall not pursue this matter further, however, but instead simply accept that the structure of (3.65) is that which obtains at the end of the first cycle (by provision B of the LCPR). Therefore the innermost set of brackets are erased and the ESR is once more free to apply, since derived material, i.e. *-oid*, has been introduced. By the ESR this will be assigned a foot, giving the structure of (3.66):

(3.66)

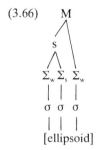

[ellipsoid]

Finally, by the rule of Destressing (3.39) the initial weak foot will lose its foot status in a fashion which should now be familiar.

The case of *expensive* also poses problems, but of a rather milder nature. Given the initial bracketing [[expens]ive], we shall obtain on the first cycle the following structure (note that provision C of the LCPR obtains):

(3.67)

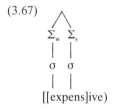

[[expens]ive)

The innermost set of brackets are then erased and the ESR is free to apply to the derived environment *-ive*. But it will only apply vacuously, since *-ive* will not be assigned a foot structure. A syllable such as this, which fails to be incorporated into the metrical structure, is called a *stray syllable*, and the usual approach is to claim that there is a rule of *Stray Syllable Adjunction* which will incorporate such a syllable into the final foot. Thus in this case, we have firstly:

(3.68)

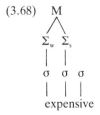

expensive

Then we apply Stray Syllable Adjunction to incorporate the final syllable into the final foot according to the canonical pattern:

(3.69)

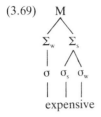

expensive

Destressing will, of course, deprive the initial syllable of its foot status.

Consider now an example such as *parental*. This will enter the first cycle with the bracketing [[parent]al]. By the ESR the following metrical structure will be assigned on the first cycle:

(3.70)

$$\Sigma$$

$$\sigma_s \, \sigma_w$$

[[parent]al]

The innermost set of brackets is then removed and the ESR is free to apply on the derived material. Now if we simply applied the ESR in the same restricted fashion as for *expensive*, we would end up with the clearly incorrect structure of (3.71).

(3.71)

parental

What has gone wrong?

The crucial difference between *expensive* and *parental* is that in the former case the stress pattern of the first cycle remains undisturbed by later cyclic applications of the ESR, whereas in the latter case it would appear that the stress pattern assigned by the first cycle is disturbed, since the second syllable of the word clearly must become the head of a foot. How can we account for this, given the SCC (3.57)? The answer appears to lie in a closer consideration of the ESR. Recall that the ESR, as we have formulated it, is a foot-formation rule. More particularly all that the ESR does is assign certain syllables the property of being the head of a foot. Syllables which are not designated as the heads of feet are then incorporated into feet by the provision that all feet are left-headed and left-branching.

If we adopt this account it is possible to see why *expensive* and *parental* should behave differently. After (3.67), the innermost set of brackets are removed from [expensive]. The ESR re-applies, but vacuously: it cannot remove the property of being the head of a foot from the penultimate syllable, since that property was assigned on a previous cycle. Therefore the final syllable of *expensive* is stray. Contrast now *parental*. In (3.70) we see the structure which is assigned on the first cycle. If we now erase the innermost set of brackets, then the ESR is indeed allowed to apply to the penultimate syllable, because on the first cycle that syllable was not assigned the property of being the head of a foot by the ESR. Thus this new application of the ESR does not undo the work of the first cycle, because it does not erase a foot created by the first cyclic application of the ESR. There is a crucial distinction to be made between the illegal deletion of earlier feet and the legal internal restructuring of feet, for the internal structure of feet is not a concern of the ESR *per se*. Thus the application of the ESR on the second cycle of the derivation of [[parent]al] results, as desired, in the following structure:

(3.72)

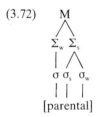

[parental]

Destressing will again give the desired final structure.

Q.   A pair of examples which usefully demonstrate the contrast which we have just been discussing are *falsify* and *solidify*. Show how the type of cyclic assignment given immediately above can adequately handle the differing prominence relations in these two words.

A.   Consider firstly the case of *falsify*, which in fact is not dissimilar to *expensive*. The correct morphological bracketing is [[fals]ify]. On the first cycle the ESR will create a monosyllabic foot, namely:

(3.73)

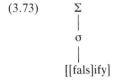

[[fals]ify]

The innermost set of brackets are then removed and the ESR is free, within the limits of strict cyclicity, to apply over the whole string. Proceeding from right-to-left, the ESR will first of all assign the property of being a foot head to the final syllable (since it contains a diphthong). The penultimate syllable, however, cannot be the head of a foot by the ESR, and since the ESR cannot erase existing feet, the work of the ESR is now complete. The penultimate syllable is then incorporated into the preceding foot by virtue of the condition that all feet are left-headed. Thus the following structure results:

(3.74)

$$M$$
$$\Sigma_s \; \Sigma_w$$
$$\sigma_s \; \sigma_w \; \sigma$$
$$\text{falsify}$$

The item *solidify*, on the other hand, is rather like *parental*. The correct bracketing is, of course, similar to that of *falsify*, namely [[solid]ify]. On the first cycle, therefore, the application of the ESR gives the following result:

(3.75)

$$\Sigma$$
$$\sigma_s \; \sigma_w$$
$$\text{[[solid]ify]}$$

When the innermost set of brackets has been erased the ESR is free to apply once more. As with *falsify*, the final syllable will be made into a foot head, but then the ESR will skip the penultimate syllable and be able to make the antepenultimate syllable the head of a further foot, since that process will not entail the erasure of feet assigned by earlier cycles. Thus we shall obtain:

(3.76)

$$\Sigma \quad \Sigma \quad \Sigma$$
$$\sigma \quad \sigma_s \; \sigma_w \; \sigma$$
$$\text{[so li di fy]}$$

Application of the LCPR gives (3.77). Note here that earlier cyclic applications of the LCPR cannot be violated, although in this particular example that condition, of strict cyclicity, is vacuous:

(3.77)

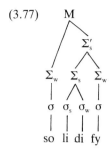

Destressing (3.39) will then apply, to deprive the initial syllable of its foot status, giving the final result:

(3.78)

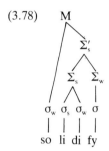

Q. You will recall that we started this discussion with the example *sensationality*, and we saw that the method of cyclical assignment of stress advocated by LP, in which all previous metrical structure is erased at each new cycle, produced the tree of (3.56), which is clearly unsatisfactory. Attempt now to provide a strictly cyclic derivation for this word and compare the final derived structure with that of (3.56).

A. The correct morphological bracketing of *sensationality* must be the same as assumed previously, namely [[[sensation]al]ity]. Furthermore, we can assume that the word is unmarked for feet in the lexicon. Therefore, we can assume that the word is unmarked for feet in the lexicon. Therefore, on the initial cycle we firstly apply the ESR to the string within the innermost set of brackets and then apply the LCPR, which gives the following result, parallel to (3.54):

(3.79)

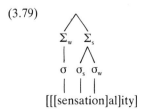

The innermost set of brackets is then deleted, and the ESR can then apply to the string [sensational]. If the ESR could erase feet, then it would erase the foot-head status of the antepenultimate syllable and then re-assign foot-head status to that syllable. However, this is no longer permitted, and therefore the ESR does not apply. Instead the final syllable is simply attached to the first foot to its left, giving (3.80) (application of the LCPR is here vacuous, as no new feet have been created). It is important to note that although (3.80) is parallel to (3.56), it is derived in a quite different way:

(3.80)

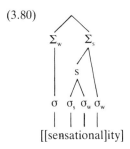

[[sensational]ity]

Again the innermost set of brackets is deleted, and we enter the third and final cycle. The ESR applies again, and this time that rule will firstly wish to assign foot status to the antepenultimate syllable. This is entirely legitimate within the cyclical operation, since it does not erase existing feet. Notice that further leftward iteration of the ESR is impossible without such erasure, and therefore it is blocked. The final application of the ESR, therefore, will give the tree structure of (3.81), where, however, the final cyclic application of the LCPR has not been shown:

(3.81)

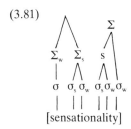

[sensationality]

Note then that the LCPR, since it too is strictly cyclic and cannot erase existing structure, will do no more than convert (3.81) into (3.82) – where we have re-inserted the internal bracketing of *sensationality* solely for ease of discussion below:

(3.82)

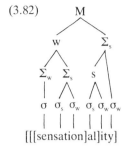

[[[sensation]al]ity]

Compare now the tree of (3.82) with that of (3.56), repeated here for convenience:

(3.56)

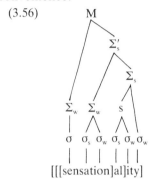

[[[sensation]al]ity]

It should be clear that (3.82), derived by the principles of strict cyclicity, is preferable to (3.56), derived by LP's cyclical process of Deforestation and full-blooded application of the ESR. Phonologically, if we ignore (although we may not be entitled to do so, see our discussion of (3.56) above) the process of Destressing, (3.82) captures the prominence relations between the first and second syllables of the word in a way that is simply not possible in (3.56): in (3.82) the second syllable is more prominent than the first. Morphologically, it should be clear that (3.82) is a distinct improvement over (3.56), for the metrical tree of (3.82), although it is not a complete reproduction of morphological structure, more closely resembles the original morphological structure: crucially, it treats *sensation-* as a word with an integrity of its own. Since we have already seen that metrical trees above the word level closely resemble syntactic structure, and since we have already observed that metrical theory assigns words a distinct prosodic level (mot), it is clearly desirable that below the word level metrical trees should as far as possible resemble original morphological structure. This is only possible within a strictly cyclical derivation. As Kiparsky (1982: 166) shows, such a system of stress assignment for English has other advantages too, and his comments are worth reading; but perhaps we can leave this point here, and simply agree that a strictly cyclical approach is preferable to that adopted by LP.

3.6   *Extrametricality*

Let us instead move on to a consideration of a further amendment to LP's original theory, an amendment which, we would wish to argue, provides a much simpler account of word-stress. It may even help to provide a much simpler account above the word level, but we shall not pursue that matter for the moment. This amendment has been proposed by Bruce Hayes, both in his doctoral thesis (Hayes 1981) and in an article 'Extrametricality and English stress' (Hayes 1982). Here we shall mainly follow the argument outlined in the latter, henceforth 'H'.

There are two points to note before we begin our discussion of Hayes' work proper. Firstly, H assumes as crucial a fully articulated theory of syllable structure of the type we discussed in the previous chapter. The syllable structure trees are grafted onto the metrical trees showing relative prominence in a quite straightforward and natural way (in practice this is rarely shown, for it is assumed that syllable structure trees are transparent and in no need of elucidation). Thus, if we take an example such as *designate* (/dezigneːt/), a full tree would look like (3.83):

(3.83)

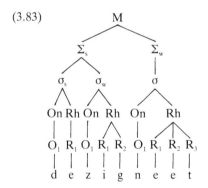

The second point to consider is purely notational. Taking (3.83), we would find that, following H, the full tree should be drawn as follows:

(3.84)

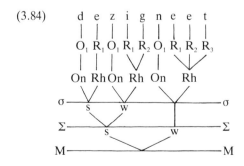

The obvious point to note here is that the trees are 'upside-down'. This is indeed normal practice in most recent work in metrical phonology, but it is introduced for purely practical reasons and makes absolutely no difference to what is being said (indeed LP themselves occasionally use such trees). Another point, although no more substantive, is perhaps slightly more interesting, for H no longer labels nodes as mots, feet and syllables. Instead, horizontal lines are used to indicate prosodic levels.

Q.   Once you have seen several of these trees you should find them as easy, if not easier, to interpret as the trees we have been using up to now. You may find it useful, therefore, to take some recent tree diagrams, such as (3.72, 3.74, 3.78 and 3.82), and redraw them according to the above conventions.

A.   You should have obtained the diagrams a, b, c and d (overleaf).

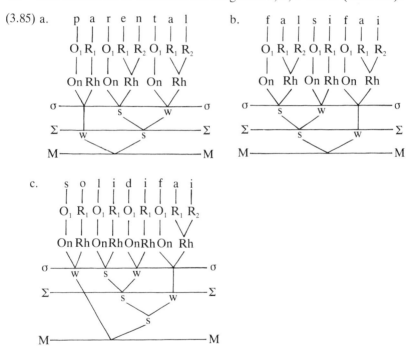

Note here that the first syllable, since it has been subject to Destressing, does not have foot status, and this can be determined uniquely from the diagram (the same, of course, should have been done in the case of *parental*, but Destressing was not shown in (3.72)). Since for H not all feet need be left-headed, his structure would be slightly different, with the first syllable being a (weak) member of the first foot, but we shall not pursue this problem here.

d.

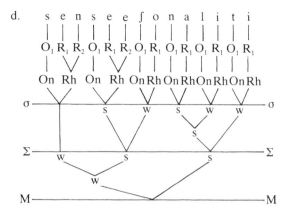

Of course to this tree the rule of Destressing must apply, whereupon we shall obtain a structure rather like that of (3.85c).

H usually does not show the branching below the syllable level, nor does he usually mark the levels as 'σ', 'Σ', 'M'; thus the tree for, say, *sensationality*, would regularly be presented in simplified form as (excluding the process of Destressing):

(3.86)   sensationality

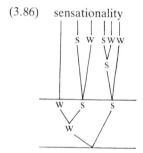

Having discussed these largely notational preliminaries, we can now move on to a consideration of the proposals which H makes. Consider firstly, therefore, the following examples of verbs and unsuffixed adjectives:

(3.87) (a)   (b)   (c)

     obéy   tormént   astónish

     políte   perháps   decrépit

     humáne   augúst   nórmal

     petíte   divért   consíder

We saw examples like these both in chapter 1 and earlier in this chapter: words such as these receive final stress if they end in a syllable containing either a long vowel, as in column (a), or a coda with at least two consonants, as in column (b). Otherwise, as in column (c), they receive penultimate stress. The fundamental insight of H is that stress assignment in such words can be handled extremely simply if we introduce the concept of *extrametricality*, a concept first used, although in a very restricted way, by LP (293).

The concept of extrametricality involves the claim that in some given string certain segments simply do not count for purposes of assigning metrical structure. That is to say, if some segment is extrametrical, then the rules of stress assignment, e.g. the ESR, ignore that segment. H points out (228) that cases of extrametricality all appear to be confined to the following format:

(3.88) $X \longrightarrow [+\text{extrametrical}] / \underline{\hspace{1cm}}]_D$

where X is a single phonological constituent, such as segment or a rhyme (etc.) and where $[\ldots]_D$ is the domain in which the stress rules of the language apply. Thus the material marked as extrametrical must be a single unvarying unit, and extrametricality may only be assigned at the right edge of stress domains. This latter point seems to be true for English, although Hayes (1981: 71–2) discusses a case in Winnebago, a North American Indian language, where extrametricality seems to apply at the left edge of stress domains, and Halle (1985) has cited a number of similar cases. It may be that extrametricality in any given language can apply either at the left edge or the right edge (but not both?), quite possibly depending upon whether feet are left- or right-strong. Clearer, and more important, is the point that extrametricality seems certainly to be possible only at the edges of domains.

Let us now assume that there is in English a rule of *Consonant Extrametricality* which states that the final consonant in any word is extrametrical (and thus ignored in the assignment of stress). This rule would have the form (H: 238):

(3.89) *Consonant Extrametricality (CE)*

$[+\text{cons}] \longrightarrow [+\text{ex}] / \underline{\hspace{1cm}}]$ word

This is by no means an arbitrary rule, but follows from the principles of syllabification discussed in the previous chapter. You will recall from there the Principle of Maximal Onsets, which states that consonants are maximally assigned to onsets rather than codas. Now if we take an example such as *torment*, although it is clear that in isolation the final /nt/ are both in the coda of the second syllable, it is easily observed that under the right conditions the final /t/ would belong to the onset of the following syllable: consider here *tormenting*. As regards syllable structure, therefore, word-final consonants are in a position of instability, and it seems reasonable to infer that this leads to their status as extrametrical.

If we then reconsider the words of (3.87) with their final consonants marked as extrametrical by rule (3.89), we obtain the following (note that for simplicity we have changed to underlying phonemic representations):

(3.90) (a)   (b)   (c)

    obée   tɔrmént   astɔ́niʃ

    poláit   perhápš   dikrépit

    hjuumeyń   ɔɔgúst   nɔ́rmal

    petíit   daivért   kɔnsídet

Looking again at these words, we can see that stress appears to be assigned to the final syllable if, after the operation of rule (3.89), the final syllable contains either a long vowel or diphthong or a consonant in the coda. In other words, the final syllable has stress assigned to it if, and only if, it contains a branching rhyme. Otherwise, stress is assigned to the penultimate syllable. Note that this implies that stress assignment pays attention only to rhymes, not onsets. Therefore in assigning stress we operate only on what is called the *rhyme projection*, i.e. the elements of the string dominated by rhyme nodes, and that onsets are ignored. This suggests that we can reformulate the ESR in the following way (H: 238):

> (3.91) *English Stress Rule (provisional)*
> At the right edge of a word form a maximally binary foot on the rhyme projection using the template $X(x)$ – that is, the right node of a branching foot must dominate a non-branching rhyme. Label feet *s w*.

What exactly does this mean, for there are several statements incorporated in this one large statement? Firstly, it states that feet as assigned by the ESR contain no more than two syllables. Secondly, as we mentioned above, it states that for the purposes of the ESR only the rhyme of each syllable may be considered, where X stands for any rhyme and x stands for a non-branching rhyme. Thirdly, it states that feet are left-strong. Each of these seems plausible, and none is entirely new, but we shall see that each of them requires a little more elaboration in the following pages.

For H the ESR only applies at the right edge of domains, as can be seen. For stress assignment elsewhere in a word H uses a separate but very similar rule of *Strong Retraction*. As we shall see later, he does not need to have three types of retraction, as did LP and as we discussed in chapter 1, but in fact, as Kiparsky (1982) shows, if the principles of strict cyclicity are invoked there is not even a need to have a separate rule of Strong Retraction. Instead, we can have a single iterative rule of stress assignment, which has one condition on it, a condition requiring that at the right edge of domains a *w*-node must not branch. Although we shall not discuss this matter again, since it was fairly fully discussed earlier, the ESR and Strong Retraction can be collapsed into one, provided that the requirements that ESR can only operate in derived environments and that it must respect existing foot structures are maintained. This version of the ESR is as follows (see Kiparsky 1982: 166):

(3.92) *English Stress Rule (revised version)*
Going from right to left across the word, assign maximally binary and left-strong feet.
Condition: *w*-nodes may not branch in the environment / ———], i.e. at the right edges of words.

Q.   Attempt now to derive the metrical structure of the following words (you may, if you wish, ignore the presently irrelevant rule of Destressing), using the rule of Consonant Extrametricality (CE) and the version of the ESR given in (3.92): *obey, humane, torment, normal, decrepit.*
A.   Let us begin with *obey*, which has the representation /obeː/. The rule CE cannot apply since there is no final consonant. Nor it is possible to construct a binary foot on this word since the final rhyme is branching. Thus, on the first iteration of the ESR we must construct a non-branching foot over the final syllable (note that we have enclosed syllable onsets in brackets since they are irrelevant to the operation of the ESR):

(3.93) o(b)ee

Further iteration of the ESR will simply make the initial syllable the head of a further foot:

(3.94) o(b)ee

For the moment we shall assume that the LCPR works as in (3.52). We therefore obtain (by provision C of the LCPR and before the rule of Destressing) the following structure:

(3.95) o(b)ee

The rule of Destressing will deprive the initial syllable of its foot status, giving:

(3.96) o(b)ee

Consider now the form *humane*, which we shall assume has the underlying representation /hjuumeːn/. In this case CE will apply, to give /hjuumeen/, but the ESR will still make the final syllable the head of a foot since the rhyme branches. This, together with further iteration of the ESR, will give:

(3.97) hjuumeen

Application of the LCPR, again using provision C, will give the final structure:

(3.98) hjuumeen

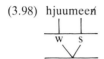

The case of *torment* is not radically different. Again CE will apply to give /tɔrment/, and again the final syllable remains branching at the rhyme. Therefore the final structure will be:

(3.99) tɔrment

In the case of *normal* CE, which gives /nɔrmal/, plays a crucial role, since the rhyme of the final syllable is no longer branching. Since the condition applied to the ESR above would no longer be violated by a single binary foot, such a foot is indeed created, to give:

(3.100) nɔrmal

Decrepit is rather like *normal*, for again CE giving /dikrepit/, stops the final syllable from having a branching rhyme. Hence the ESR creates a binary foot on the last two syllables, and then further iteration of the ESR places a foot on the initial syllable. Application of the LCPR then gives:

(3.101) dikrepit

The initial syllable is then destressed, presumably because it is a Latinate prefix and therefore [+Ro] (see the discussion of Destressing earlier in the chapter). This results in the final structure:

(3.102) dikrepit

Q. You may have observed that the ESR as formulated in (3.92) has a slightly different status from that which we had earlier suggested. We had suggested that the ESR was in fact a foot-formation rule which assigned particular syllables the property of being the heads of feet. There was then a further provision that all well-formed (polysyllabic) feet are left-branching and left-strong, i.e. there is a Foot Stress Rule (FSR) which states:

(3.103) *Foot Stress Rule (FSR)*
      For any pair of nodes $[N_1, N_2]_\Sigma$, N_1 is strong.

We have also noted that there is a rule of Stray Syllable Adjunction (SSA) which assigns syllables which are unattached to any foot to an immediately adjacent left foot. We can suppose, with H (235, 263), that in effect SSA is a well-formedness condition on tree structures which applies after each cyclical operation of the ESR, and that the result of SSA is determined by the FSR (3.103). Can you, therefore, suggest a reformulation of the ESR which is a foot-formation rule and which will combine with SSA and the FSR to provide the correct structures?

A. In this version of the ESR all that we are concerned with are syllables which receive foot status. All other syllables can be ignored. As always, we can propose that the rule operates iteratively from right to left, and therefore our initial concern must be with the rightmost syllable. The condition given under (3.92) must therefore be reformulated to state that the rightmost syllable acquires foot status if its rhyme branches (after the operation of CE). Then every second syllable receives foot status. Finally there must be a default condition stating that the leftmost syllable always receives foot status. This can be formally stated as follows:

(3.104) *English Stress Rule, foot-based (final version)*
      Proceeding from right to left from the edge of the domain and on the rhyme projection only:
      (i)   Assign the rightmost syllable foot status if it branches.

    (ii) Assign every second syllable (counting from the rightmost foot or the edge of the domain if there is no rightmost foot) foot status.

    (iii) Assign the leftmost syllable foot status.

Rule (3.104) is, of course, virtually identical to (3.92), but perhaps it has certain advantages. Firstly, the internal structure of feet is no longer determined by the ESR, but rather by general well-formedness conditions on such structure, as implemented by SSA and the FSR. This allows us to avoid a certain ambiguity in the operation of strict cyclicity. We have already noted that under strict cyclicity the ESR is not allowed to erase foot structure created by earlier applications of the ESR. What this in fact meant was that if an earlier application of the ESR had assigned some syllable the property of being the head of a foot, then that property had to be kept on later cycles. With (3.92), but not with (3.104), this point becomes moot, since later cycles are allowed to erase part of the existing foot structure provided that the heads of feet are not touched. With (3.104) no such problem arises, since internal foot structure is an issue separate from the ESR, one which arises through well-formedness conditions. Secondly, note that for H (and other writers) SSA is a rule which is in any case needed, so that our proposal does not involve any complication of the grammar. Indeed, SSA now has a much wider application. Thirdly, (3.104) pinpoints an interesting feature of the ESR, which is that it applies in a regular alternating fashion which can only be disrupted at the edge of a domain (either the right edge or the left edge). You may recall that we briefly discussed in chapter 1 the question of whether Long Retraction or Strong Retraction (which we also called Alternating Retraction) was the normal mode of retraction in English. At that point there was really no way of deciding. Now, however, it looks very much as if Strong Retraction is the norm. And as we shall see in later chapters, there is considerable evidence that the stress system of English is based on a foundation of alternation throughout.

    Although the above combination of CE and the ESR works very well for the assignment of stress in verbs, as soon as we turn to other parts of speech we encounter problems. Consider, therefore, the following nouns, taken from chapter 1, example (1.30).

(3.105)	(a)	(b)	(c)	(d)
	design	ellípsis	muséum	polýgamy
	ballóon	inspéctor	aróma	élephant
	cocáine	repúblic	flúid	précipice

Let us ignore for the moment the words in column (a). For the others the principle of stress assignment is well known: the penultimate syllable is stressed if it is heavy, i.e. has a branching rhyme, otherwise the antepenultimate syllable receives stress. In effect, these nouns behave in exactly the same way as verbs, except that the final rhyme is ignored. In other words, the final rhyme is extrametrical. We therefore need the following rule of *Noun Extrametricality (NE)*:

(3.106) Rhyme $\longrightarrow$ [+ex] / $\longrightarrow$]$_N$

We can then apply the following derivations, where, as we shall see, it is crucial that CE is ordered before NE – this might be a disadvantage, but it is scarcely important:

(3.107) propaganda   aroma   elephant

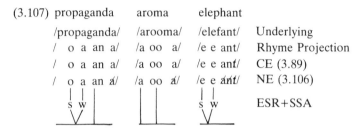

/propaganda/	/arooma/	/elefant/	Underlying
/ o a an a/	/a oo a/	/e e ant/	Rhyme Projection
/ o a an a/	/a oo a/	/e e ant/	CE (3.89)
/ o a an á/	/a oo á/	/e e ánt/	NE (3.106)
			ESR+SSA

One problem which now arises is that the proper application of the LCPR appears impossible. We shall look at the issue again soon, but first of all let us go back to the words of (3.105) column (a), words such as *design*. In such words the operation of NE appears to make impossible the proper assignment of stress, since the final syllable, which should be stressed, has been rendered extrametrical! The solution which H (239) adopts is a rule of Long Vowel Stressing which assigns foot status to final syllables containing a long vowel. This must occur before NE but does not interact with CE and therefore is crucially ordered only with respect to the former. It has to be admitted that this is a rather unsatisfactory solution: Long Vowel Stressing turns out to be the only rule in the phonological cycle other than the ESR which assigns foot status, and clearly, therefore, more work has to be done in order to see if there is some better solution (cf. here the alternative attempt discussed in chapter 5). The rule of *Long Vowel Stressing* can be stated as follows, assigning a foot to a word-final rhyme containing a long vowel:

(3.108) Rhyme $\longrightarrow$ Rhyme.../ $\longrightarrow$ #

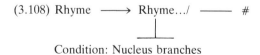

Condition: Nucleus branches

We should also at this stage discuss the evidence which exists for the ordering of CE and NE. Consider therefore a word such as *agenda*. Let us suppose that NE operates before CE. We would then get the following derivation:

(3.109) agenda

/adʒenda/	Underlying
/a en á/	Rhyme Projection
/a en á/	NE
/a eń á/	CE ˙

Since the final rhyme would no longer be branching, the ESR would simply assign foot status to the first syllable – which is incorrect. On the other hand, if CE precedes NE we obtain the following derivation, which, you will be able to observe, provides the desired input to the ESR:

(3.110)

/a en a/	Rhyme Projection
/a en a/	CE (vacuous)
/a en á/	NE

Another problem concerns nouns such as *gymnast*, *insect*, *proton*, etc., which have a foot on their final syllable. This type of truly exceptional behaviour (compare *modest*, *subject*, *helix*) is, H suggests, best handled by marking such words lexically with a word-final monosyllabic foot (compare here the discussion above of *ellipse*). H's suggestion seems entirely reasonable.

Q. Although it is by no means the case that we have now solved all the problems concerned with the operation of the ESR in nouns, as we shall see, it is perhaps worth going on now to a further consideration of adjectives. We have already seen that many adjectives, e.g. *polite*, *august*, *normal*, subject to the rule of CE, undergo the ESR quite regularly. There is, however, a further group of adjectives which, apparently, misbehave with respect to the ESR. For example, whilst *decrepit* has, as we have seen, penultimate stress, as the interaction of CE and the ESR predicts, *municipal* has antepenultimate stress. Further examples of such 'irregularity' are given in (3.11). Can you suggest any further extension of extrametricality, along the lines of NE but morphologically based, which would account for this?

(3.111)

municipal	adjectival	fraternal
tolerant	flamboyant	abundant
primitive	effusive	expensive

A. Since we have suggested that there is a morphological solution here, and since we have tabulated our examples in a very specific way, it is probably quite easy to see what the answer might be. For in all these examples the adjectives take a suffix (*-al*, *-ant*, *-ive*). If these suffixes are ignored, then the ESR will assign stress correctly. The rule which causes adjectival suffixes to be ignored is quite naturally called the rule of *Adjective Extrametricality* (AE); it can be stated as follows:

(3.112) $[X]_{\text{suffix}} \longrightarrow [+\text{ex}] / \text{———}]_{\text{Adj}}$

We can then provide the following sample derivations for *municipal*, *flamboyant* and *expensive*:

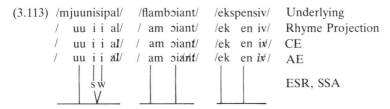

(3.113) /mjuunisipal/   /flambɔiant/   /ekspensiv/   Underlying
        / uu i i al/   / am ɔiant/   /ek en iv/   Rhyme Projection
        / uu i i al̸/   / am ɔiant̸/   /ek en i̸v̸/   CE
        / uu i i ál̸/   / am ɔián̸t̸/ /ek en i̸v̸/   AE
                                                         ESR, SSA

Leaving aside again the operation of the LCPR, this is clearly the desired result. Note also that *expensive*, rather like *agenda*, provides clear evidence that CE must precede AE. Before we move on from adjectival suffixes, however, it is worth noting that two suffixes, namely *-ic* and *-id*, do not undergo AE – H gives the examples *economic* and *intrepid*. We agree with him that these two suffixes do indeed have an exceptional status, and it is possible that nominal suffixes may need to be considered here too.

To sum up, therefore, we can see that this approach to stress assignment involves the marking of certain units as extrametrical before the application of the ESR, a foot-formation rule to which the SSA applies as a redundancy rule to ensure well-formed trees. Indeed, the SSA will apply at any stage in the derivation that it can. There is also an initial rule of Long Vowel Stressing. There are three rules of extrametricality (CE, NE, AE), where the first of these is ordered before the other two. Naturally NE and AE are not crucially ordered with respect to one another. Thus we have the following rules crucially ordered as below, together with the redundancy rule of Stray Syllable Adjunction:

(3.114) Long Vowel Stressing (3.108)
         Consonant Extrametricality (3.89)
         Noun Extrametricality (3.106), Adjective Extrametricality (3.112)
         English Stress Rule (3.104)

Despite the relative simplicity of the above account, there are still a great many problems left unresolved. We do not propose to go into all of them here: see instead the essay and discussion topics at the end of this chapter, where the most important omissions are introduced. Rather, we wish to concentrate on two issues: (i) what H describes as 'the fate of extrametricality markings'; (ii) the operation of the LCPR. Let us start with the first of these, where a suitable example is *medicinal*. This has the internal bracketing [[*medicin*]*al*], and therefore on the first cycle we should obtain the following derivation:

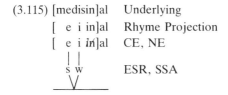

(3.115) [medisin]al   Underlying
       [e i in]al   Rhyme Projection
       [e i *in*]al   CE, NE
              s w   ESR, SSA

H in fact suggests a different structure, namely:

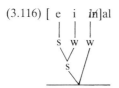

(3.116) [e i *in*]al
          s w w
              s

where, by SSA, extrametrical elements are adjoined to the left-adjacent foot in a manner which by now must be familiar to you. Or, at least, H appears to do this for the English examples which he discusses. At the beginning of the article, however, when discussing examples from Hopi and Latin, H does not permit nodes to dominate an extrametrical string. This turns out to be an issue of some importance, although we need not discuss it immediately. For the moment we shall assume that the tree which H prefers, i.e. (3.116), is correct. We shall, however, return to the issue later.

Of more immediate interest is the question of what happens on the next cycle (note that the LCPR will not apply to (3.116), which contains only a single foot). Suppose that we simply remove the innermost set of brackets. The AE will apply, to give:

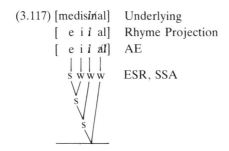

(3.117) [medis*in*al]   Underlying
       [e i *i* al]   Rhyme Projection
       [e i *i* *al*]   AE
          s w w w   ESR, SSA
              s
              s

There is, however, a very simple way of avoiding such an obviously incorrect derivation, namely, to claim that any element which is not at the right edge of a domain loses its extrametricality marking. H (270) suggests that this can be stated as a universal *Peripherality Condition* (PC), namely:

(3.118) $[X] \longrightarrow [-ex] / \text{———} Y]_D$

   where $Y \neq \emptyset$ and D is the domain of the stress rules

This condition would, of course, operate as a redundancy rule and thus come into play every time a set of brackets was deleted. Notice that if this condition is introduced the format for extrametricality rules specified in (3.88) is no longer necessary, since it states nothing that is not also stated by the PC. With the introduction of this condition the derivation of *medicinal* becomes as follows:

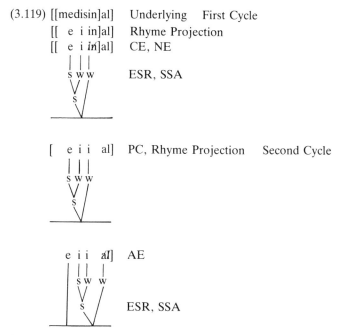

(3.119)   [[medisin]al]   Underlying   First Cycle
    [[e i in]al]   Rhyme Projection
    [[e i *iń*]al]   CE, NE

      s w w   ESR, SSA

    [e i i al]   PC, Rhyme Projection   Second Cycle

      s w w

    e i i *ál*]   AE

      s w w

       ESR, SSA

Then, as with so many other of the cases that we have looked at, all that we require is the correct operation of the LCPR. But it does seem very certain that extrametricality markings must be lost, by way of the PC, at the end of each cycle.

 Let us now move on to the question of the application of the LCPR. You will recall that after drawing the structures in (3.107, 3.113 and 3.119) we did not apply the LCPR. The reason for this is that H has suggested, albeit tentatively, that within a framework which uses extrametricality it might be possible to provide a simpler approach to the labelling of word trees than the LCPR allows. If you consider the words in the above examples, e.g. *propagánda, flambóyant, expénsive, medícinal*, it is, of course, possible to claim that in each the strongest syllable is so because, in terms of the LCPR, that syllable is N_2 and it branches. But notice another feature of those syllables: in each case they are the head of the rightmost foot in the string. What the LCPR states is that the rightmost foot in the string should be marked as strong iff it fulfils one of four conditions, i.e. it branches; it is [+F]; the word is non-nominal and N_1 does not branch; the word is a verb and N_2 dominates the stem.

H suggests that in a framework which uses extrametricality we need only state that N_2 is strong – without any conditions. How can that be? True enough, in some cases no difficulties arise. Thus where N_2 branches, as in all the examples cited above, N_2 will be strong either way. But consider the following minimal pair (cf. H: 271) *Théodòre* and *Thèodóra*:

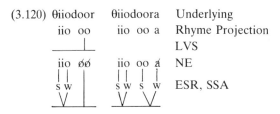

(3.120)

In the case of *Theodora* both the LCPR and H's rule (which he calls the Word Tree Construction Rule or WTCR) give the same answer, since N_2 branches; but in the case of *Theodore*, although the LCPR will give the desired answer, since N_2 does not branch and therefore N_1 is strong, the WTCR would seem to give the incorrect answer, namely that the final foot is strong. However, note that this final foot is extrametrical. Presumably, also, since LCPR is a cyclical rule (see the discussion of *sensationality* above), it must operate before brackets are removed and hence before the PC can apply. Suppose, therefore, the logical conclusion: word tree construction pays no attention to extrametrical segments. Thus in the case of *Theodore* the rightmost foot which the WTCR can see is the one whose head is the first syllable and therefore it is marked as strong.

Q. In fact the above account using the WTCR cannot be quite right. Why not?

A. If the final foot in *Theodore* is extrametrical and ignored by the WTCR, then the first foot cannot be labelled strong, since it has no sister. In order to get round this problem we have to propose that the WTCR gives the following structure:

(3.121)

Then the final set of brackets are erased and the final syllable is no longer extrametrical. Now, just as syllables which were unattached by the ESR are incorporated into feet by SSA, H suggests that unattached feet should be incorporated into word-level structures by a parallel rule of *Stray Foot Adjunction* (SFA). Thus (3.121) is converted into:

(3.122)

Several other problem types are capable of a simpler resolution under H's approach than under the LCPR. For example, words such as *balloon*, which under the LCPR account had to be labelled [+F] need only be labelled as [−ex] under this account. This will automatically provide the desired output. It might be argued that [−ex] is as much an arbitrary labelling as [+F], but this would be wrong, for whereas 'F' is some nonce coinage, [±ex] is a feature which, as we have seen, plays a crucial and well-defined role within the whole system. True, whether or not a word is marked as [−ex] is largely idiosyncratic, but that is reflected in the fact that such labelling will be part of each word's lexical entry (where appropriate), just as some words will be entered in the lexicon with a foot already assigned. It is important to distinguish between the arbitrary behaviour of certain lexical items and the introduction of an arbitrary feature.

Although this theory of extrametricality is as yet still in its infancy, it has been generally recognised as one of the more promising advances in the theory of metrical phonology. In the preceding pages we have not attempted to give a full account of the application of extrametricality to the stress system of English words (and we have totally ignored its possible applications above the word level). For a much fuller account you should read Hayes (1982). Instead, we should like to conclude this chapter by a consideration of one problem which faces H's theory, as exemplified by the question immediately below.

Q. In American English the pronunciation of the word *stalagmite* is *stalágmìte*, whereas in British English the pronunciation is *stálagmìte*. Determine firstly which pronunciation would be suggested by the rules discussed above and then consider how the rules might be amended in order to reflect the pronunciation in the other dialect.

A. The derivation you should have obtained is as follows:

(3.123) stalagmait   Underlying

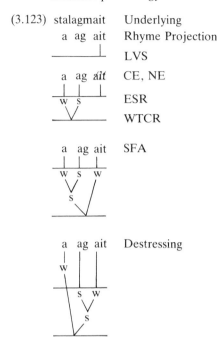

This, of course, reflects the American English pronunciation of the word, where the penultimate syllable is the strongest.

The only way to derive the British English pronunciation, it would appear, would be to make the word (or perhaps the (quasi-)suffix *-ite*) [−ex]. This would give us, before the operation of the WTCR, the following output:

(3.124) a ag ait

But then, if the WTCR were allowed to operate as H specifies, the wrong result would obtain, for it would mark the final syllable as strong, suggesting *stàlagmíte*. The only way to get to the correct answer would be to preserve the LCPR as it was formulated in (3.52).

We would like to conclude this chapter at this point, because this emphasises the fact that metrical phonology is by no means a fossilised dogma. Whether or not, for example, H's WTCR should replace the LCPR is a genuinely open question, which, as H (271) himself points out, needs much more research. And this is not the only problem which surrounds extrametricality. For example, are words which are marked as [−ex] nevertheless subject to CE? Is it the case that some suffixes (cf. the adjectival suffixes *-ic* and *-id*) are marked for [−ex] whilst others are marked for [+ex], and might this be a problem not just for adjectives but also for nouns (and verbs??)? Three question marks, perhaps, may suggest that much still remains to be done.

Notes and further reading

3.1 The first part of this chapter relies heavily on Liberman & Prince (1977), especially the first two sections of that paper, and it should be considered essential reading.

3.2 Again the initial part of this section closely follows Liberman & Prince (1977), especially section 2.1. For the adoption of an alternative foot-based analysis you should read Selkirk (1980).

3.3 For a foot-based rule of Destressing see Selkirk (1980). Liberman & Prince (1977: section 2.8) discuss the LCPR in some detail, but you should note that our statement of that rule differs from theirs, most notably in the statement of the conditions upon the rule.

3.5 Kiparsky (1979) first introduces the strictly cyclic approach to stress assignment into metrical phonology, and you should read this and compare it with the account in Liberman & Prince (1977: section 2.7). The later Kiparsky (1982) is rather more difficult but nevertheless important, especially in that it links up the cyclic metrical approach to the theory of lexical phonology. Further readings in lexical phonology are well covered in the bibliography to that article; see also Halle & Mohanan (1985) for a full-length treatment of segmental phonology within the theory of lexical phonology.

3.6 Hayes (1982) is a concise account of extrametricality and is essential reading. You might also like to look at Hayes (1981), upon which the later article is in part based.

Essay and discussion topics

1. Within the approach of LP one of the more difficult problems which they faced was the correct assignment of stress in words with the suffix *-atory*, e.g. *compensatory*, which in American English is pronounced as *compénsatory*. Give a full account of their treatment of this and other related issues and then consider either how such words would be handled within Hayes' theory or how LP might account for the British English pronunciation *còmpensátory*.

2. Give a full account of the environments in which Initial Destressing takes place and consider to what extent the outline of syllable structure theory given in chapter 2 adequately accounts for these environments.

3. In the account given above, when a foot is destressed initially it is not incorporated into the following foot but is an unfooted left sister of the next foot at the word level. In other accounts a destressed foot is incorporated into the immediately adjacent foot. Consider which account is preferable.

4. Liberman & Prince (1977) use an iterative ESR in which various words and affixes are labelled for Strong Retraction, Long Retraction and Weak Retraction. Hayes (1982) uses a non-iterative ESR and an iterative Stress

Retraction Rule which does not distinguish between various modes of Retraction. Kiparsky (1982) uses an iterative ESR which does not distinguish between various modes of retraction. Compare and contrast any two of these models.

5. Is Hayes' rule of Long Vowel Stressing either adequate or necessary? Can you suggest any alternative?

4 The phonology of rhythm (1): introduction to the metrical grid

4.1 Introduction

So far we have seen how metrical trees are constructed for words; typically, under LP's analysis, word-stress rules make reference to the feature [stress], whereas in later work appeal is made to a hierarchy of prosodic constituents – most important of which are the syllable and the (stress) foot – and this in turn leads to an enrichment of the tree representation. We also saw in chapter 3 how metrical trees were constructed for the representation of prominence relations within phrases; this higher-level organisation follows on quite naturally from the representation of word-stress itself, but one difference seemed to be that, in LP's analysis, higher-level tree structure was labelled solely according to the dictates of the LCPR, which guaranteed full and correct labelling of the entire tree. We have also seen something of the relationships and quasi-relationships that hold between stress patterns as defined on trees and the Nuclear and Compound Stress rules of the *SPE*-type phonological framework. The stress patterns of trees, for example, are always 'right-strong' at the phrase level; there is – as of course there ought to be – a basic similarity here between this characteristic of trees and *SPE*'s Nuclear Stress Rule, which (cyclically) assigned [1stress] to the rightmost relevant domain of the phrase. Thus, both an *SPE*-type and a metrical derivation for the phrase *many linguists*, although different in conception, appear to result in similar outputs:

(4.1) a.

    2   1
  many linguists

b.

In this chapter, however, we would like to address a suprasegmental feature of English that may not be handled adequately by tree structure alone. Recall that one of the arguments leading to the *SPE* account of stress and stress-related features was the observation that, under the terms of *SPE*'s linear analysis, 'relative prominence is preserved under embedding'. In effect, all this means is that the syntagmatic relationship that holds between *English* and *degree* in the phrase *English degree* is defined, given the cyclic application of rules which assign [*n* stress], as identical to the relationship that holds between the two words in a phrase such as *English degree blues*. In either case, *degree* will come out of the cycle carrying one less 'degree of stress' than *English*:

(4.2) a. English degree
        1   2   (by CSR)

  2b. English degree blues
        2   3   1   (by CSR and NSR, in that order)

Recall also that one of the arguments towards an arboreal, rather than a numerological, representation of stress was that the formalism employed to represent stress in tree diagrams *guarantees* that relative prominence will be preserved under embedding. As LP (258) write: '[Tree] theory . . . encodes relative prominence directly, as a local feature of constituent structure, and therefore the formalism itself does not force a cyclic procedure of rule application.' Thus the simplified tree diagrams for (4.2a, b) are, respectively:

(4.3) a.   b.

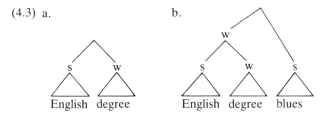

We do not need cyclic application of [1stress] and an over-articulated theory of stress numbering in order to preserve relative prominence under embedding; tree theory will itself preserve whatever stress relationships there are to preserve.

Q. Attempt now to construct trees of the simplified type (4.3a, b) – that is, trees which omit arboreal detail at the word level – for the following phrases: *English degree subsidiary*, *thirteen crazy tutors*, *Dundee marmalade factory*, and *understanding Ernie*.

A. Both the first and second examples are quite straightforward:

(4.4) a.

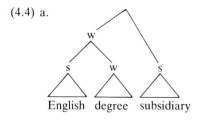

b.

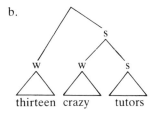

thirteen crazy tutors

The next example is ambiguous, since two trees can be drawn, i.e. one for [Dundee [marmalade factory]] ('marmalade factory in Dundee') and one for [[Dundee marmalade] factory]] ('factory which makes Dundee marmalade'). This, of course, is in full conformity with the syntactic ambiguity of the phrase. Respectively, then, the two trees are as follows:

c.

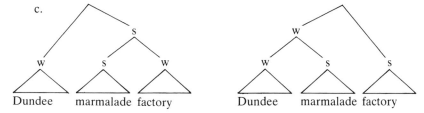

Dundee marmalade factory   Dundee marmalade factory

Our final example is more complex still; the word *understanding*, for instance, patterns under the LCPR as right-strong, yet one perceived prominence pattern of *understanding* in the phrase *understanding Ernie* is of the first syllable, *un-*, as stronger than the third syllable, *-stand-*. This suggests that two trees might be constructed for *understanding Ernie*, the first reflecting *understanding* as right-strong, as our word-stress rules will predict, the second reflecting the perception of *-stand-* as 'less stressed' than *un-*; this last tree is not predicted by the rules we have given so far:

d.

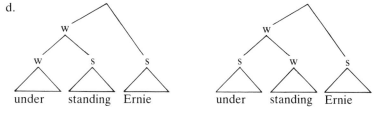

under standing Ernie   under standing Ernie

In the examples above, you may have noticed one or two anomalous features of the strings under consideration. In *understanding Ernie*, for example, is it true that 'relative prominence is preserved under embedding'? Clearly, there is a difficulty here, since we constructed two apparently plausible trees for the phrase, each of which reflected the relative prominence of the word *understanding* differently. And at the sub-word level, you may well have spotted (although this was not required in the exercise) that both *thirteen* and *Dundee* have the relative prominence pattern [w s] defined upon them when they are analysed in isolation; yet in our examples, embedded within phrases, the trees and sub-trees might well have taken the form:

(4.5) a.

b.

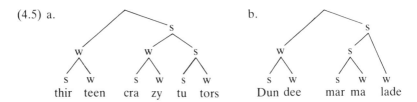

Given these observations, is it true to say that 'relative prominence is preserved under embedding'?

4.2   *Stress-shift*

We would like to suggest that there can be exceptions that do *not* prove the rule. As LP and others have observed, there are a significant number of words in English whose relative prominence is *not* preserved under embedding – whose stress pattern, that is, appears to 'shift' given the nature of the surrounding linguistic environment. Consider the numeral adjectives *thirteen, fourteen, fifteen* etc. The citation stress pattern for such words is [w s]; it is also true to say that the stress patterns of these same words remains [w s] in the phrases *nearly thirteen, just thirteen* – as predicted by the LCPR's higher-level arborisation. (Although the adjectives in question are 'lexical words', and are as such nominally entitled to undergo that subrule of the LCPR which assigns *s* to the leftmost node (syllable) since the right sister does not branch, recall that such words undergo subrule C of the LCPR, a subrule which allows us to define [w s] upon such words – see again chapter 3, page 91.)

However, *thirteen, fourteen* etc. appear to have a changed pattern of prominence when they occur with a (head) noun – specifically, with a monosyllabic head noun, or with a head noun that carries stress on its first syllable – as in the phrases *thirteen men, fourteen trout, fifteen tutors*. Notably, this changed pattern of prominence is not predicted (or handled at all) by *SPE* stress rules; nor is it predicted by the rules of tree formation as we have given them.

Q.   Remembering the two trees we constructed in our analysis of *understanding Ernie*, consider how you would construct trees to capture the observation that the relative prominence of words such as *thirteen*, *pontoon* is not preserved under embedding. Construct word-level and phrase-level trees for the phrases *thirteen men, pontoon bridge*.

A. You should have constructed trees as in (4.6) and (4.7):

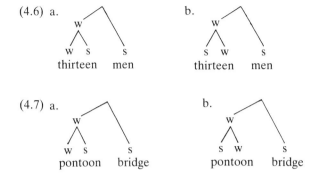

(4.6) a.

w
w s   s
thirteen men

b.

w
s w   s
thirteen men

(4.7) a.

w
w s   s
pontoon bridge

b.

w
s w   s
pontoon bridge

We could, of course, simply leave our metrical model there, suggesting a long list of exceptions to the rule that relative prominence is preserved under embedding. But since metrical phonology aspires to an exceptionless formal account of stress-related phenomena it would be better if we could somehow relate the trees (4.6a, 4.7a) to the trees (4.6b, 4.7b). Given the pervasive nature of the evidence, we might, for example, wish to suggest a formal operation on tree structure which would transform (4.6a, 4.7a) into their 'output' b-trees.

Q. Consider how you would formalise such a transformational rule.

A. We could say, for example, that:

(4.8)

w s $\longrightarrow$ s w

That is, informally, a string dominated by a pair of sister nodes whose configuration is [w s] is structurally transformed into a string dominated by a pair of sister nodes whose configuration is [s w]. This would allow us to suggest the following:

(4.9)

w s   s w
thirteen $\longrightarrow$ thirteen

But such a rule is problematic. As it stands, it is manifestly too strong, since it is so unconstrained that it makes the claim that *all* [w s] structures reconfigure as [s w]. Surely, this is incorrect. As LP might put it, as English speakers we do not pursue 'unbridled . . . trochaic fluency' (LP: 319). An unconstrained rule such as (4.8) would allow us, for example, to construct a tree such as (4.10) for the phrase *thirteen men*:

(4.10)

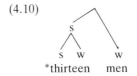

*thirteen   men

However, we know independently that such a tree is ill-formed, since phrasal collocations are always, simply by the NSR, right-strong (that is, always ultimately dominated by a [w s] configuration at a higher level in the tree). Therefore, rather than continue with formalising such a problematic transformation at this stage – although we shall have more to say along these lines later – let us simply observe that what we need to account for in our paradigm phrase *thirteen men* is the fact that just the stress pattern of *thirteen* alters under embedding. But using the tree to specify *how* this local change takes place is problematic. LP, and many, but not all, other metrical phonologists have postulated a further new way in which information concerning stress patterns is presented. This device is the *metrical grid*.

4.3   *The metrical grid*

Suppose that the syllables of *thirteen men* are represented not only arboreally but also in terms of metrical (grid) *levels*, as in (4.11a–c).

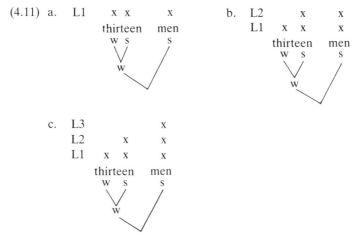

In (4.11a) each syllable – each terminal node of the tree – is assigned a position on what is called a *metrical grid*. This is the bottom level (L1) of the grid. L1 simply aligns the terminal nodes of the tree one-to-one with grid positions. However, we also need to reflect the relative strength of those syllables in the grid. To do this, we make reference to the labelling of the tree, and construct a second level (L2) on the grid. In (4.11b), the 'strong' (terminally *s*) syllables of the tree are defined on the grid as having more metrical strength than the 'weak' (terminally *w*) syllables; therefore *-teen* and *men* are grid-marked on L2, whereas *thir-*, as a *w* syllable, is not. In (4.11c), continuing the principle 'strong is stronger than weak', *men* gets a grid mark on L3 since it is defined on the tree as having more strength than *-teen*. The item *men* is given the strongest stress of the phrase in that it is uniquely and solely dominated by *s*, and we mark this relative strength as the solitary topmost *x* in (4.11c). The grid of (4.11c) is complete, in that it is minimally configured: it reflects the information contained in the tree and nothing else.

Q. Making reference to (4.11), construct trees and grids for the phrases *pontoon bridge, antique chair* in their citation forms, that is, before any transformation of the type discussed above has applied.

A. You should have trees and grids as follows:

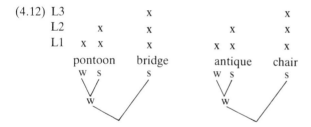

(4.12)

Since we have claimed that the metrical grid represents information concerning stress in a 'new way', we need now to interpret the grid's 'novelty'. Let us therefore look in more detail at grid *levels*.

In examples (4.11) and (4.12) we can say that in each complete grid the marks on level 2 are *adjacent*. We mark such adjacency in (4.13):

(4.13) L3   x
       L2   x ------x
       L1   x   x   x

The grid marks indicated stand next to each other in their respective columns, and of course, they appear at the same level. Moreover, the same grid marks correspond directly to entries at the next lower grid level. Now, however, consider a grid which reflects a different tree structure:

(4.14)

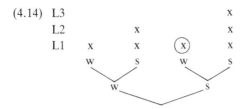

The marks on L2 are still defined as 'adjacent', since there are no grid marks between them at that level. However, the difference between (4.13) and (4.14) is essentially that, while the L2 grid marks in (4.13) correspond directly to adjacent grid marks below them, in (4.14) there is an intervening grid mark on L1 between the adjacent marks on L2; this grid mark is the circled *x* on L1 of (4.14). As we will see below, it is important for the theory of trees and grids that the *x*'s on L2 in (4.13) appear at the same level and have no intervening grid mark below them on the next lower level. A structure such as (4.14) can be defined as typically *alternating*, since higher grid columns occur at every other syllable: there are peaks of prominence bounded by troughs of L1 grid marks. We cannot describe (4.13) as alternating, however, since there is no intervening grid mark on L1 – the next grid level down from the grid level on which adjacency is defined. Following LP, we can call the non-alternating adjacency of grid elements on L2 in (4.13) a 'stress clash' or – more correctly in terms of the formalism we are presenting here – a 'grid clash'. Moreover, since one of the objects in setting up a metrical grid is to account, in a principled way, for the observation that relative prominence in certain words and phrases is sometimes 'variable', we may propose that such a grid clash *triggers* or motivates the reversal of nodes $\overset{\frown}{w\,s} \longrightarrow \overset{\frown}{s\,w}$ suggested in our preliminary discussion above.

4.4   *Iambic Reversal*

In (4.15a, b), we see the operation of what is known as *Iambic Reversal*. You will also see the terms *Rhythm Rule* and *Thirteen Men Rule* applied to this operation. Here, wherever possible, we use the term Iambic Reversal (or informally, *Reversal*) with relevance to this distinctive 'switching' of *w/s* nodes.) What seems significant in the light of work we present later is that the output of the Reversal rule is defined as an alternating [s w s] pattern; we shall see that there are other transformations that lead to an alternating output. In this sense, it may be that there is a quite general 'Rhythm Rule' of English, of which Reversal, and certain of the transformations we present later, form subparts.

(4.15) a.   b.

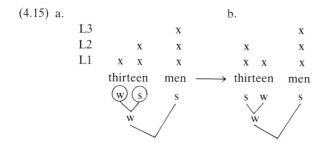

In (4.15b), the relevant (circled) nodes have been reversed, and the grid reconfigured in terms of the levels outlined in the discussion of (4.11). Since *thir-* is now stronger than *-teen*, it is this initial syllable that receives the grid mark on L2. Although in (4.15b) grid elements on L2 are still *adjacent* (since nothing on L2 stands directly between them), the overall grid structure is *alternating*, since the grid mark on *-teen*, L1, blocks 'grid clash' as we have defined it – compare (4.14). It is essential to note that on every occasion that a tree is reconfigured in conformity with the provisions of Iambic Reversal, then a new grid must be constructed for the new tree.

It seems, then, as if Iambic Reversal might account for our example *thirteen men* in a relatively interesting way. Notice that the structural change triggered by the grid clash in (4.15a) affects just the syllables of *thirteen*, since this is the only domain on which Iambic Reversal might apply without affecting prominence at the phrase level – see (4.10) if you need clarification here.

Before going any further in our discussion of Iambic Reversal, it might help if we clarify the meaning of such terms as *adjacent*, *alternating*, and *clashing*. LP (314) write:

Elements are metrically *adjacent* if they are on the same level and no other elements of that level intervene between them; adjacent elements are metrically *alternating* if, in the next lower level, the elements corresponding to them (if any) are not adjacent; adjacent elements are metrically *clashing* if their counterparts one level down are adjacent [our italics: RMH/CBM].

To recapitulate, L2 grid marks in (4.15a, b) are adjacent since there are no other elements on that grid level interposing between them; in (4.15b), however, the L2 marks, although still adjacent, are alternating since their counterparts one level down are *not* adjacent; and in (4.15a), L2 grid marks are clashing since their counterparts on L1 *are* adjacent. If you are still unsure on these points, you might like to check on how Iambic Reversal applies to the examples *pontoon bridge*, *antique chair*.

Typically then, a grid clash of the kind we have been discussing is essentially a matter of *level* – which nicely reflects the fact that LP define the grid as an ordered hierarchy of such levels. In effect, since the grid clash is defined in terms of level(s) rather than in the tree structure itself, Iambic Reversal is operative even when syllables intervene between the relevant (clashing) grid columns, as in (4.16).

(4.16)   a.   b.

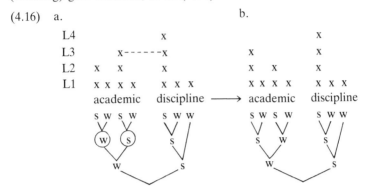

The clash defined on L3 of (4.16a) is the trigger for reversal of the circled nodes within the trees of (4.16). Operation of Iambic Reversal leads to the neatly alternating structure seen in (4.16b). You may have noticed, however, that Reversal is not *obligatory*. It is still quite possible to say:

(4.16)   c.   d.

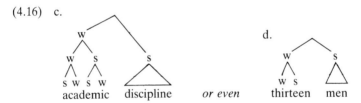

But there is nothing to say that Reversal *is* obligatory. As LP (320) state, '. . . the Rhythm Rule [that is, Iambic Reversal: RMH/CBM] appears to be more or less optional, in degrees ranging from "strongly preferred" to "quite unlikely" '. However, by using grid structure as a trigger for Iambic Reversal, it is possible to regard the grid and the configurations defined upon it as providing '. . . a clear and useful characterisation of some of the factors that influence how speakers of English choose to employ the optional stress-retraction process that we have formalized as the rule of Iambic Reversal' (LP: 321). We shall discuss the 'optionality' of Reversal later in this chapter, and investigate whether the likelihood of Iambic Reversal applying can be related to 'preferred grid configurations'. As a first attempt in this direction, we ask you to complete the following before reading further.

Q.   In (i)–(v) we have constructed the 'untransformed' grids for the phrases *Dundee marmalade*, *the plot thickens*, *Tennessee Williams* (where

Williams is taken to be disyllabic), *intersecting structures*, and *good-looking tutor*. Match each phrase to its relevant grid (you will need to draw the correct tree first) and then show how operation of Reversal (where applicable) creates the required non-clashing output pattern.

```
(i)                      (ii)          x        (iii)
        x                     x   x
      x   x               x   x   x                    x
    x   x   x   x       x   x   x   x   x            x   x
                                                   x   x   x   x   x
```

```
(iv)                        (v)            x
        x                         x        x
    x       x                 x   x        x
  x   x   x   x   x         x   x   x   x   x   x
```

A.   *Dundee marmalade* is matched by grid (iii); Reversal takes place in the usual way to give (4.17a):

(4.17) a.

The plot thickens is matched by grid (i); but it seems as if Reversal is inapplicable here:

(4.17) b.

Here, in (4.17b), although a clash is defined in terms of our earlier remarks, Iambic Reversal is blocked. It seems absurd to give *the* a greater metrical strength than *plot*. In fact we might choose to formalise a constraint on Iambic Reversal which would disallow the transformed configuration above. Although we discuss constraints on Iambic Reversal towards the end of this chapter, consider, as a preliminary, how you would formalise such a constraint. (You might like to consider the above example along with, for example, *obese tutor, maroon sweater*.)

Tennessee Williams is matched by grid (ii); Reversal takes place as indicated (4.17c):

(4.17) c.

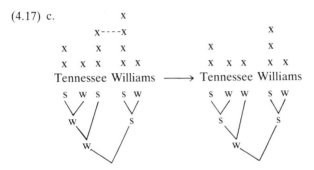

The phrase *intersecting structures* is matched by grid (v); Reversal takes place as indicated:

(4.17) d.

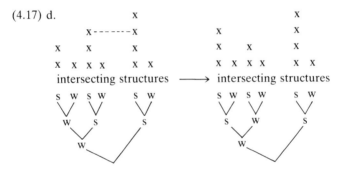

And *good-looking tutor* is matched by grid (iv) to give (4.17e):

(4.17) e.

```
                    x
            x       x
      x   x  x   x x
      good-looking tutor  ⟶  ??
      w   s  w   s w
           \/    \/
           s     s
        w_____/
```

Interestingly, the minimal grid for the phrase *good-looking tutor* will not trigger operation of Iambic Reversal, since there are no clashing elements present: the grid marks corresponding to *look-* and *tu-* are suitably adjacent but their counterparts on the bottom level (the next level down) are not. But is it not inconsistent to suppose that *intersecting structures* and *Tennessee Williams* undergo Reversal, while *good-looking tutor* doesn't? In fact this apparent exception gives rise to a controversial principle of some generality. As LP (322) write, the descriptive difficulty with the analysis of *good-looking*:

seems to be that the initial monosyllabic word . . . in cases like *good-looking* is not being given its proper 'weight'. It seems wrong to give a lexical entry (albeit monosyllabic) no greater representation in the metrical grid than a pretonic initial syllable would receive.

(And see here our comments on *the fat cat* and *John's big brother* in chapter 3.) LP go on to suggest that the grid column over *good-*, and this applies to similar cases such as *hot-headed (lover)*, *well-funded (project)* for example, should be made one level higher. If as a consequence of this (rather arbitrary) manoeuvre the overall grid scansion is then adjusted in accordance with the principle 'strong is stronger than weak', as it must be if *look-* is to remain underlyingly stronger than *good-*, then a new grid pattern will result, namely (4.18a), one in which a clash is defined. Pressure for Reversal to apply will now be essentially the same as that in, for example, *intersecting structures*:

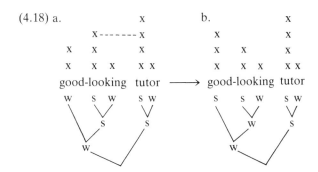

But, as you may have noticed, the output of (4.18) is questionable (as is the entire operation stemming from the 'strengthening' of the grid column over *good-*): the grid of (4.18b), for example, still contains a 'grid clash' as we have defined it – although there is no tree domain on which Iambic Reversal might operate. However, as we shall say more about grid scansion later, we shall for the moment leave the problem stemming from grid marking of lexical monosyllables posed but unresolved.

So far we have discussed and exemplified the operation of Iambic Reversal informally. Before moving on, let us pause for a brief summary in which we will discuss (and, in one instance, develop) metrical theory in a rather more formal way.

(i) Inherent properties of the metrical grid

The grid is essentially a device from which it is possible to read patterns of syllabic prominence. Such prominence – we will not call it 'stress' – is presented graphically in grid columns. In addition, the grid illustrates syllabic adjacencies, which are presented within the rows of each grid. Given that a fairly specific set of rules governs how any one grid is constructed, and constrains its well-formedness, we see that the grid is an 'ordered set of levels'. In order to illustrate this, we may use a musical analogy. Prince (1983: 20), for example, writes that 'The metrical grid comes out of the description of musical rhythm.' This is not too surprising since, in music as in the rather more unruly material of speech, what are indicated on the grid are those intensities or pulses which are 'intrinsically stronger than others'. Further, '[t]he stronger grid positions are those that have entries at [a] higher level' (Prince *ibid.*) By now, this should be self-evident. A little more difficult is Liberman's comment that the grid can be thought of as a 'hierarchy of intersecting periodicities'. We have already suggested that the grid is (contains) a hierarchy – an 'ordered set of levels' – but Liberman's comment suggests that the grid can also be envisaged as a device which marks a *rate of repetition*. In the following, for example, level 1 elements occur six times, level 2 elements three times, and level 3 elements twice:

```
(4.19)                        x
                       x      x
          x            x      x
     x    x    x   x   x      x
     the waste remains and kills
```

This repetition of elements may be termed *periodicity*. If you were to tap out the phrase *the waste remains and kills*, you might make your taps coincide with the six syllables marked on L1, or you could choose to tap three times coincident with those syllables marked on L2, and so on in other, similar and longer phrases. Although we shall return to this point, for the moment it is sufficient to have noted Prince's remark that the grid 'does aspire to the state of music'. Indeed, he goes on (1983: 21):

. . . this rhythmicity provides a fundamental motivation for the construct. When infelicities in grid form appear in the normal course of linguistic concatenation, it is often the case that various steps are taken to remedy them. A clear example of this is the Reversal rule of English, which readjusts certain otherwise expected patterns of prominence when they would result in a non-alternating or 'clashing' grid.

We discuss this issue further with respect to 'grid-phonology' in chapter 5.

(ii) The grid, Reversal, and tree structure

In our discussion of Iambic Reversal, we saw *why* a grid was needed and *how* grid configuration motivated a change in tree structure. LP (311) put this 'why and how' as follows:

[We] need an account of linguistic rhythm in terms of which the appropriate stress configurations are marked as 'clashing', thus producing a *pressure* for change. Second, we need a specification of the circumstances in which a given language grants *permission* for such a change to occur.

Let us develop this a little further. It is clear from our examples that while the pressure for change rests within the grid, permission for structural change resides in the tree structure. Since our proposed change w͡s ⟶ s͡w was – as we saw – somewhat problematic (although this is indeed what happens locally, triggered by clashing grid configurations), we follow Kiparsky (1979; see also Prince 1983: 31ff for discussion) in requiring that the *minimal* tree structure that would grant permission for Reversal to apply is as follows:

(4.20)

(See Kiparsky 1979: 424; Prince 1983: 31; see also Selkirk 1984: 177–8 for some further comments. You might also like to look now, briefly, at the remarks on this structure in chapter 6.)

In all the examples of Reversal we have looked at so far, this tree structure occurs. In a sense, we could regard the rightmost *s* of (4.20) as a tree specification of pressure for change. Although we shall see that the restrictive tree in (4.20) may arguably be *too* restrictive, especially when we come to consider iterative Reversals within phrases, for the present we shall assume that (4.20) provides a fairly adequate characterisation of the domain relevant to Reversal.

(iii) On grid construction

As we have stated, the grid is constructed from its lowest level upwards. Firstly, a row of placeholders maps the terminal syllables of the tree onto a grid level (L1) which LP have called the grid's 'terminal set'. Secondly, the relationship 'strong is stronger than weak' – a relationship which is defined on the tree – is mapped onto the columns of the grid. That is, the relative strength of each grid column should be congruent with the arboreally-given relative strength of the syllables to which they correspond. LP (316; see also Prince 1983: 23) enshrine this simple principle in their Relative Prominence Projection Rule (RPPR):

In any constituent on which the strong-weak relation is defined, the designated terminal element of its strong sub-constituent is metrically stronger than the designated terminal element of its weak sub-constituent.

The RPPR thus given is interpreted as a well-formedness condition on grid construction, and, being a well-formedness condition, is applicable whenever necessary. Typically, therefore, the RPPR will require that new grids above L1 be constructed after any structural changes have taken place, as we have seen already.

What the RPPR does is construct minimal grids, that is, grids which have less structure than any other (grid) interpretation of each tree. In (4.21), for instance, the grids are minimally well-formed:

(4.21) a.   b.

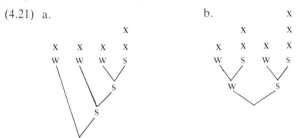

What is apparent here is that the RPPR, as Prince (1983: 23–4) points out, only 'establishes a partial ordering among terminals. In particular, the RPPR never relates terminals that are immediately dominated by *w* (and, conversely, always relates terminals immediately dominated by *s*)'. See here the discussion in chapter 3 where we pointed out that *w/s* relations are established between metrical heads. However, although Prince notes that 'the RPPR is the weakest theory of tree interpretation consistent with the intuitive sense of "s" and "w" ' and goes on to point out that 'Were it any weaker, some *s/w* relations would go unenforced . . .' (1983: 24), the RPPR brings with it (as you might have guessed from the preceding paragraph) rather specific problems of interpretation. We look at these problems a little later, but you might try formulating these problems for yourself in a provisional way. Now, however, we must return to the problem we left 'posed but unresolved' before starting on this overview.

4.5   *Constraints on Reversal*

In our earlier treatment of Iambic Reversal, we noted one apparent difficulty, that posed by application of Reversal in the phrase *good-looking tutor*. Our difficulty was created by the fact that the minimal grid (4.17e) did not give sufficient 'weight' to the lexical monosyllable *good-*. An apparently ad hoc solution was found in (4.18), where it was suggested that the grid column over *good-* should be reinforced on a second level, with the rest of the grid being adjusted in accordance with the RPPR. The same solution would seem to apply to all lexical monosyllables (that is, crudely speaking, those monosyllables belonging to the lexical categories N, V, A), which otherwise would only be marked at level 1 on the grid.

Q.   Construct trees and grids for the phrases *well-structured theorem, hard-boiled egg.*
A.   Your trees and grids should look like (4.22a, b):

(4.22) a.

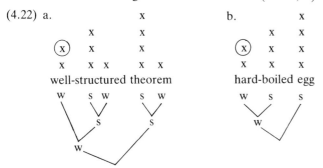

Both (4.22a) and (4.22b) allow operation of Iambic Reversal. However, our problem is that we now have *two* apparently well-formed grids for each phrase containing a lexical monosyllable, one where additional grid-marking has been assigned to lexical monosyllables otherwise marked only at L1, the other where no such additional grid marks have been assigned (for the circled grid marks in (4.22a, b) are due to additional marking of *well-* and *hard-*; see (4.17e) and (4.18)). This plurality of interpretation is allowed under the RPPR; there is no reason, in fact, for it to be disallowed, since the RPPR essentially only interprets *s* in the relationship *s > w*.

Q.   Construct untransformed trees and grids for the phrases *anti-Marxist broadside, pretonic lengthening.*
A.   Your trees and grids should look like (4.23a, b):

(4.23) a.

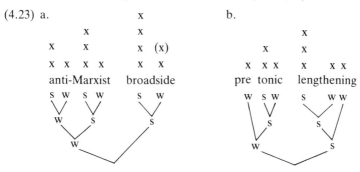

(4.23a) apparently undergoes Reversal; (4.23b) apparently does not. (A clash is defined in (4.23a), but not in (4.23b), where it might be expected between *to-* and *leng-*.) Relating these structures to our examples of (4.22), let us suggest provisionally that Reversal can only apply to a grid structure of type (4.24):

(4.24)

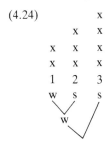

where element 1 and its relevant grid column mark a syllable that is a *stress foot*. This stress foot might be a syllable (such as *thir-* in *thirteen*, *bam-* in *bamboo*, etc.), an affix which is a morpheme of a certain class (such as *pre-* in *pretonic*), or a word (such as *good-*, *well-*). In fact we can posit a fairly strong principle of grid construction by saying that *stress feet are always grid-marked*. This leads us to the following underlying analyses:

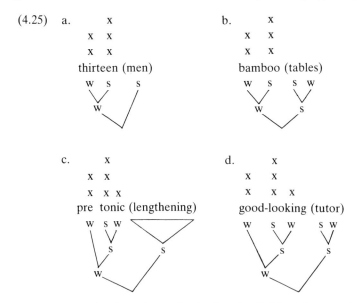

Our generalisation about the 'upbeat' syllable (element 1 of (4.24)) is therefore that the grid marks phonological structure above the syllable in a fairly explicit way. Prince (1983) in fact goes further, suggesting that the grid's markings correspond to a hierarchy of units *syllable*, *foot*, *word* and *phrase*, each being marked on a given level (or contiguous levels) of the grid. Prince's suggestion seems rather neat, and we shall return to it again in chapter 5 (where we shall also review Selkirk's rethinking of the role these structures have to play in metrical description). For the present, it seems as if we can (temporarily) escape from the difficulties posed by the example *good-looking tutor*. Furthermore, the constraint on Reversal seen in (4.24) applies conversely; Reversal can *never* operate when element 1 of (4.24) is a 'stressless' syllable (typically, the reduced vowel schwa heard in *maroon* and in some speakers' pronunciation of *obese* – recall *maroon sweater, obese tutor*). Now, earlier in this chapter we asked you to consider how you would formalise such a constraint on Iambic Reversal; it might be done as follows:

(4.26)

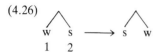

where element 1 is not a stressless syllable

This condition is sufficient to disallow, for example:

Q. But consider such examples as *antique dealer, Chinese expert* ('expert in the Chinese language'), which do not violate the constraint of (4.26). Can you work out why such forms appear *not* to undergo Reversal?

A. The answer lies not only in the underlying tree pattern for such phrases – which in itself is sufficient to prohibit Reversal – but also in the immovability of the main stress of the phrase or compound to which Reversal might apply. Thus, in *antique dealer* the tree/grid pattern is as follows:

Even though a clash is defined on the above grid, Reversal will not apply. The relevant permissory tree structure is unavailable and, as we have seen, Reversal is prohibited from moving the strongest stress of its phrase. (You should check this for yourself on examples of other compounds and NPs; see also our remarks on this compound in chapter 5.) So we may reformulate (4.26), taking this apparent second constraint on Iambic Reversal into account:

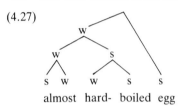

(i) where element 1 is not a stressless syllable
(ii) where 2 is not the strongest element of its phrase.

4.6   *Iterative Reversals*

To conclude this chapter, we focus attention on an example given in Hayes (1984), namely, the phrase *almost hard-boiled egg*.

Q.   Construct the metrical tree for *almost hard-boiled egg*.
A.   The tree should look like (4.27):

(4.27)

```
              ┌──────────────┐
          w ──┤              │
       ┌──────┤              │
    w ─┤       s             │
  ┌────┤    ┌─────┐          │
  s    w    w     s          s
almost hard- boiled egg
```

This analysis mirrors the syntactic labelling [[almost hard-boiled] egg] where *almost hard-boiled* is an 'adjective phrase'. (Interestingly, had the bracketing been [[almost hard] [boiled egg]] the metrical tree would have looked quite different; in this sense, as we have remarked before, metrical structure is to a greater or lesser extent dependent on syntactic structure.)

Q.   Now, bearing in mind that *hard-* is a lexical monosyllable (like *good-* in *good-looking*), construct a grid for (4.27).
A.   The grid should look like (4.28):

(4.28)
```
                          x
                     x    x
    x      x    x    x
    x  x   x    x    x
almost hard- boiled egg
```

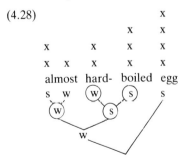

The grid of (4.28) is apparently well-formed under the convention that allots extra grid-strength to *hard-*, and under the RPPR. Moreover, despite the fact that there are two sets of nodes configured in the characteristic [w s (s)] fashion – the upper and lower pairs of circled nodes – only one pair of nodes is, under our analysis, susceptible to Iambic Reversal. Recall (4.20). This stipulated that the minimal tree structure on which Reversal could operate was, subject to the constraints we have discussed, the following:

Should we wish to perform Iambic Reversal on (4.28) on the lower terminal nodes in the first instance, that is, on the nodes dominating *hard-boiled*, then we are unable to do so since the structural requirements of (4.20) are not met. Therefore we are obliged to look for a domain on which (4.20) *is* defined. We find it at the next level up in the tree, on the nodes dominating the adjective phrase *almost hard-boiled*. The tree configuration fulfils the requirements of (4.20) exactly. However, the second constraint on Iambic Reversal (4.26) stipulated that:

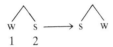

'where 2 is not the strongest element of its phrase'. It might be thought that the string under consideration *does* fall under our constraint, since *-boiled* is the 'strongest stress' of the adjective phrase. Does this disallow Iambic Reversal? Nominally, at least, this might be the case. However, look again at the tree diagram which states the domain of the rule's application. Since we are forced to perform the first iteration of Reversal on the *upper* set of nodes, the domain is defined as having *egg* as its strongest rightmost constituent. We might wish to argue, then, that the second constraint on Reversal does not apply when Reversal is performed on a 'higher level' set of nodes where the rightmost *s* is the 'strongest constituent' of the entire phrase under consideration. In addition, of course, the rightmost *s* we wish to reverse is here non-terminal; it cannot be said to directly and solely dominate the 'strongest stress of the phrase'. (We discuss this argument further in chapter 6.)

Selkirk (1984b: 177–9) notes a similar 'pseudo-problem'. She suggests that Kiparsky's (1979) tree-based formulation of the Rhythm Rule (Reversal), which gives as a description of relevant domain the structure (4.20), is 'too restrictive, not allowing for instances of stress shift that do in fact occur'. This certainly seems to be the case with (4.20) in an iterative, lower-level Reversal in *almost hard-boiled egg*. Notice too that this issue is not a problem in LP's treatment of Reversal: their proposed change w͡ s ⟶ s͡ w takes place wherever a grid clash necessitates it. However, it is possible to reformulate (4.20) as something like (4.20′), which will indeed allow iterative lower-level Reversal(s) to take place since it is less restrictive than (4.20) itself:

(4.20′)

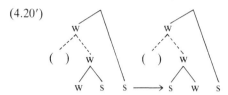

Selkirk's counterexamples are formed by such structures as *rather lily-white hands*, *slightly underripe pear* (among others). But, since these examples have the syntactic structure [[W [X Y]] [Z]] they have a citation metrical pattern defined upon them which is essentially the same as that defined upon *almost hard-boiled egg*. This metrical fact of life should allow reversal of upper metrical nodes in the first instance, as in:

(a)

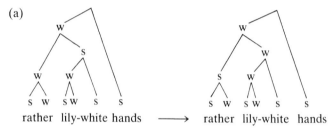

rather lily-white hands   ⟶   rather lily-white hands

It is on a second pass through Reversal that the nodes dominating *lily-white* are switched. This gives us the output patterns:

(b)

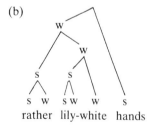

rather lily-white hands

and similarly:

(c)

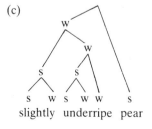

slightly underripe pear

These output patterns – fairly directly corresponding to the output pattern of *almost hard-boiled egg* – seem to us to be essentially well-formed; and indeed Selkirk (1984b: 179) gives similar grid output patterns as 'alternative pronunciations' of such phrases. The fact that Kiparsky's tree formulation of Iambic Reversal (4.20 cf. 4.20′) does not allow reversal of lower-level nodes in the first instance does not, in itself, constitute an argument against such a formulation. We cannot, therefore, totally agree with Selkirk when she writes (1984b: 178), 'Kiparsky's formulation must be incorrect.'

Accordingly, then, we will assume that the first pass through Reversal in our example *almost hard-boiled egg* takes place as follows:

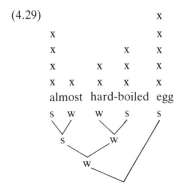

(4.29)

Again, a new grid has been constructed under the requirements of the RPPR. But there is still a relevant lower domain on which Reversal can apply, a domain which appears as if it should fulfil (4.20).

Q. Go through the final iteration of Iambic Reversal in the phrase *almost hard-boiled egg* for yourself, constructing the output tree and grid.
A. The output tree and grid should be constructed as follows:

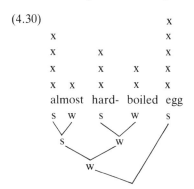

(4.30)

The final result, (4.30), although still containing a nominal clash, lacks the requisite tree structure on which any further rhythmically motivated operations might apply, and is therefore immutable. To introduce a further notion at this point, we might say that the grid of (4.30) is *eurhythmic*, and is therefore not simply structurally unavoidable but actually desirable.

4.7   Eurhythmy

The notion of *eurhythmy* has been discussed in Prince (1983 – who appeals to the notion of 'perfect grid') and, in rather more detail, in Hayes (1983, 1984). Also, the idea of 'ideal grid configuration' (or 'euphony') – which, in Selkirk's terms, makes reference to grid level(s) as well as grid spacing – operates in the (grid-based) word-stress rules given in Prince (1983) and Selkirk (1984b). All these writers make the claim that eurhythmy operates in English phonology in order that a preferred periodicity results in the string under review. Not that this is in any sense a new idea; we saw at the beginning of chapter 1, for example, that stresses tended to fall at equal intervals in English utterances. But the notion of eurhythmy is distinct from – or perhaps, forms an aspect of – isochrony; it implies a more specific tendency in English, that is, a tendency towards a particular spacing of stressed syllables, rather than a 'general tendency' (see Selkirk 1984b: 38ff for discussion). Again, this 'particular spacing' is a characteristic that has not gone unnoticed; as early as 1905, Jespersen noted:

Rhythm undoubtedly plays a great part in ordinary language, apart from poetry and artistic (or artificial) prose. It may not always be easy to demonstrate this; but in combinations of a monosyllable and a disyllable by means of *and* the short word is in many set phrases placed first in order to make the rhythm into the regular ˈaa ˈaa instead of ˈaaa ˈa (ˈ before the *a* denotes the strongly stressed syllable). Thus we say 'bread and butter', not 'butter and bread'; further: bread and water, milk and water, cup and saucer, wind and weather, head and shoulders, by fits and snatches, from top to bottom, rough and ready, rough and tumble, free and easy, dark and dreary, high and mighty, up and doing. It is probable that rhythm has also played a great part in determining the order of words in other fixed groups of greater complexity (1905/1952: 220–1).

However, as Prince notes (1983: 22), eurhythmy can be thought of specifically in terms of the grid by defining it as 'preferred grid configuration'. Hayes gives more detail relevant to our concerns in this chapter; Reversal, he writes (1984: 45),

. . . applies more readily when as a result the text receives a more highly valued rhythmic structure. The value of a rhythmic structure is computed from the grid by a set of rules I will call *rules of eurhythmy* . . . [A] reasonable hypothesis would be that the eurhythmy rules require equal spacing of grid marks at all levels . . . In particular, eurhythmy requires a *particular spacing of marks* to be found at some level of the grid.

Recall that in our discussion of *thirteen men* we called the output a 'typically alternating' structure. *Alternation* is indeed an extremely important notion, and one which has been developed in the recent literature of metrical phonology; Selkirk (1984b: 12ff) goes so far as to postulate the existence of something like a *Principle of Rhythmic Alternation* (PRA), a principle which constitutes (she suggests) a strong hypothesis concerning the nature of (universal) rhythmic structure. Moreover, she defines her rules of *grid euphony* as rules whose role 'is to ensure that the grid is truly rhythmic, to make it conform as closely as possible with the PRA' (1984b: 20). Here we examine alternation in the light of Hayes' (1984) paper, where he describes the output grids of *thirteen men*, *antique chair* etc. as 'highly valued' eurhythmically since they exhibit grid structures that are divided evenly by a mark on a lower level of the grid. Since the output grids are highly valued eurhythmically, Iambic Reversal, Hayes suggests, is extremely likely to apply. Nor does eurhythmy stop at alternation. Hayes proposes, for example, that 'A grid is eurhythmic when it contains a row whose marks are spaced close to four syllables apart' (Hayes 1984: 46). Thus, he argues, pressure for Iambic Reversal to apply in *Mississippi Mabel* is strong, since 'a quadrisyllabic interval is preferred to a disyllabic one'.

Q.   In order to make this last point clear, construct base and output trees and grids for the phrase *Mississippi Mabel*.

A.   Your trees and grids will look like those in (4.31):

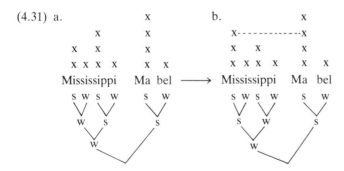

(4.31)

The dotted line on L3 of the grid for (4.31b) illustrates what Hayes calls 'the level of scansion' – the highest grid level where eurhythmy is relevant as a component of the phonology. Typically, this grid level is defined one level down from the level of the stress peak; in addition, the quadrisyllabic level is divided evenly by a grid mark on the next lower level. Thus, the output grid for *Mississippi Mabel* satisfies both the 'Disyllabic Rule' (DR) and the 'Quadrisyllabic Rule' (QR) of eurhythmy.

Clearly, our output for *almost hard-boiled egg* can be described – or perhaps 'eurhythmically evaluated' – in much the same terms:

```
(4.32)                  x
      x--------------------x
      x      x             x
      x      x      x      x
      x  x   x      x      x
      almost hard- boiled egg
```

The dotted line on L4 indicates the 'level of scansion' – one level down from the highest stress peak – and, under Hayes' Quadrisyllabic Rule, a grid is eurhythmic when it contains a row whose marks are spaced close to four syllables apart. Nor does it matter (under Hayes' terms) that the output grid (4.32) still contains a clash, since 'the level at which the clash occurs is not the level that is scanned' – i.e. the 'level of scansion' (Hayes 1984: 47). The notion of eurhythmy, then, appears to provide good reasons why certain strings are susceptible to operation of Iambic Reversal, while others (such as *Tennessee legislation*) are reluctant to undergo any changes motivated by rhythm. In short, eurhythmy offers an explanation of what has been called the 'optionality' of Iambic Reversal.

To make sure you have understood just how eurhythmy works, you might like to construct base and output trees and grids for the phrase *twenty-seven Mississippi legislators*. We give no direct answer to this question, but in case you experience difficulties, we refer you again to the discussion above, and to Hayes (1984).

Notwithstanding the fact that eurhythmy provides a set of fairly powerful explanatory hypotheses as to how grids may be interpreted, problems with grid scansion remain. Firstly, the notion of eurhythmy should not be accepted uncritically, particularly when it is allowed to license rather ad hoc operations on the grid. Hayes, for example, suggests that eurhythmy provides a supplementary principle of prosodic organisation in that it allows 'Beat Addition' when the result of Beat Addition is a eurhythmic grid. One of his examples is *Farrah Fawcett-Majors* (Hayes 1984: 46–8):

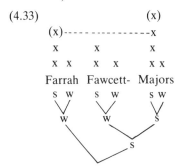

```
(4.33)                  (x)
        (x)--------------x
        x      x         x
        x  x   x   x     x  x
        Farrah Fawcett- Majors
```

Hayes proposes Beat Addition – which is realised as the bracketed extra grid mark on *Farrah*, with *Majors* adjusted in accordance with the RPPR – in order that the preferable interstress interval results. Here, as indicated on L3 of the grid of (4.33), it is a perfect four syllables. We shall discuss Hayes (1984) and a rethinking of structures such as (4.33) in rather more detail in the next chapters.

However, a two-fold problem lies in wait for structures such as (4.31), (4.32) and (4.33): the first part of the problem lies in the very concept of eurhythmy that is 'evaluating' the output grids of these examples; the second and related part of the problem lies in the power of the RPPR. We must discuss these issues now, if only to anticipate the further airing to be given to the problem later.

In effect, the concept of eurhythmy dictates what grid configurations are possible and preferable. It is thus an extremely strong concept, one that evaluates the result of application of metrical transformations such as Iambic Reversal. But it is not strictly true to say that eurhythmy is simply evaluative; it also has a bearing on how, in what order, metrical rules apply to tree structure, as rule-ordering is obviously relevant to what output structures are eventually arrived at. Consider again our paradigm example *almost hard-boiled egg*. In our work on this example, we assumed, provisionally, that iterative application of Reversal took place on a higher domain first, then proceeded to treat the terminals dominating *hard-boiled*. But there was nothing to absolutely *require* us to work in this way apart from the rather questionable SD of the Reversal rule (questionable because the second constraint on Reversal had to be somehow overcome in the case of *almost hard-boiled egg* and similarly structured phrases – recall the discussion and examples at (4.28ff.)). It is arguable, however, that eurhythmy does indeed oblige us to work in this way, simply because the output of the metrical rule(s) leads to a more eurhythmic grid. In a sense, then, where metrical derivation confronts the complexities of rule application, eurhythmy implies a methodology as well as providing an evaluation. Crudely put, it seems to be the case that 'you may apply . . . rules in any order and manner so long as the output is more eurhythmic than the input' (Dogil 1984: 293). Dogil goes so far as to call the notion of eurhythmy a 'conspiracy' and, certainly, if we regard the crude summary in the preceding sentence as correct, there seems to be some truth in the conspiracy charge. Further, Dogil writes:

Conspiracies are overpowerful devices which have been systematically avoided in generative grammar. . . . Especially suspect are those conspiracies the results of which are theoretically and empirically impeachable. . . [Eurhythmy: RMH/ CBM] decides whether a rule is applied or not. It also determines the manner in which a rule may be applied. One should expect such a powerful concept to follow from some very deeply seated and general properties of grammar. Hayes does not provide motivation of this sort. . . . [H]e does not claim that eurhythmy is an explanandum based on objective empirical judgements of the speakers. In many places . . . Hayes admits that empirical judgements vary, and he also concedes that the crucial data '. . . are of the kind only linguists ever say' . . . [In Hayes': RMH/CBM]] model linguistic structures and derivations are controlled by nonlinguistic constraints, the nature of which is unknown. The process of evaluation (eurhythmy) lies beyond grammar, so it may not be explained using linguistic methods. (Dogil 1984: 294–5)

Matters are further complicated by the second issue we noted above: the power of the RPPR. The RPPR, it will be recalled, simply enforces the rule 'strong is stronger than weak'. Anything in a (sub-)tree dominated by *s* will display additional grid marks to anything in a (sub-)tree dominated by *w*. This allowed us to construct 'minimal grids'. But the grids of our examples (4.22–33) are not so minimal, in that, in order to motivate and justify Reversal, we have used supplementary information concerning the string so that we might arrive at certain conclusions about grid phonology. In particular, we have added metrical strength to lexical monosyllables, and we have been justified in doing so by the RPPR, which only enforces 'strong is stronger than weak' and does not relate terminals that are immediately dominated by *w*. So the RPPR admits (4.33) as well-formed. In fact, under the RPPR, in a tree structured like (4.34) the relationship A to B goes unenforced (also, of course, B to C):

(4.34)

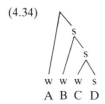

Similarly, as Giegerich (1985: 224) suggests, in the trees of (4.35), the RPPR interprets A:B and A:C, but it is too weak to interpret the relationship between B and C:

(4.35) a.   b. x   c. x
        x   x   x   x x
        x x x   x x x   x x x
        A B C   A B C   A B C
        s w w   s w w   s w w

All three interpretations of (4.35) are available under the RPPR; free variation is possible in the grid strength of syllables within any tree structure so long as the relationship *s* > *w* is enforced. This allowed us to construct (4.33) under the RPPR; it also allows us to construct:

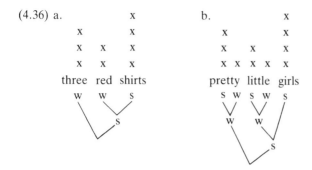

Both (4.36a) and (4.36b) are eurhythmic. But again, the RPPR also allows us to construct:

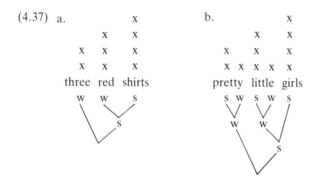

(4.37a) appears distinctly odd; (4.37b), as Giegerich has pointed out, indicates a grid pattern that reflects the syntactic structure [[pretty little] girls], i.e., girls that are 'pretty little' – an analysis for which the metrical tree should, surely, be rather different.

What this amounts to is a suggestion that an undesirable multiplicity of interpretations is available under the RPPR. Moreover, even if we allow eurhythmy to 'value' one particular interpretation over another, we are still left with a complex theoretical problem, since in order to construct well-formed 'eurhythmic' grids for phrases such as *hard-boiled egg*, we are forced to make use of the convention which strengthens lexical monosyllables. Of course, this can be accomplished under the RPPR, but we have already seen that the formulation of the RPPR itself is a difficulty. And if we do 'strengthen' lexical monosyllables in grid structure(s), we are making use of supplementary information that is not contained within the tree itself. As Giegerich has suggested, these difficulties ultimately lead to questioning exactly what it is that the grid *does*:

Giving the grid access to information that is not present in the tree has rather undesirable consequences concerning its status, for remember what the grid is meant to be in the first place: a device interpreting the metrical tree. It loses this status under LP's provision of metrical strength; it by-passes the tree in that it appeals to the (morpho-)syntax; it also shows up a shortcoming in LP's trees. Clearly, the prominence behaviour of lexical items ought to be analysed in the metrical tree. (1985: 229)

On the other hand, if it can be shown that the grid expresses phonological structures not readily interpretable from tree structure itself – if, for example, eurhythmy *is* best regarded as a grid-marked periodicity and can be shown (therefore) to be a structural component of grids themselves, or if the tree and its grid represent, as Hayes suggests (1984: 33), linguistic stress and rhythmic structure respectively – then there are good reasons for retaining the grid as an interpretative device, or even for widening the role the grid has to play in English suprasegmental phonology. As might be expected, the discrepancies in analysis which we have introduced have led to sharply divergent views on the status of trees and grids. We might call these views, roughly speaking, 'grid-only phonology' and 'tree-only phonology'. It is to these respective concepts that we turn in the following chapters.

Notes and further reading

4.1 The introduction follows *SPE* and LP (1977), especially the first section of the latter paper. You might also find it profitable to look at Langendoen (1975), who elaborates a theory of Readjustment rules based on *SPE*. Such Readjustment rules convert the syntactic string under consideration into parallel constituents which then enter the phonological component of the grammar, where the cycle then produces alternating stress numbers.

4.3 For an introduction to the metrical grid see LP: 311–23; this is absolutely essential reading. You might also like to look at Mark Liberman's (1975) Ph.D thesis, where the concept of 'metrical grid' got its first airing. Although this thesis is a fairly technical work, you will find pp. 70–89 and 262–300 particularly interesting. On further aspects of grid alignment and structure, you should look at Prince (1983), particularly pp. 19–46.

4.6 On iterative Reversals, and the problems stemming from them, see especially Kiparsky (1979), Selkirk (1984b), and Hayes (1984).

4.7 On eurhythmy and grid structure, you will find the paper by Hayes (1984: 33–69) readable and stimulating. The whole issue of eurhythmy is (re)considered in Selkirk (1984b). For some criticisms of grid theory, you should look at Giegerich (1985: 222–31). This reference also includes a useful discussion of Prince's (1983) 'grid-only' formulation of Reversal. For some trenchant criticisms of eurhythmy as a teleological notion, see Dogil (1984).

Essay and discussion topics

1. How are metrical trees related to grids? What problems, if any, do you observe in the matching process?
2. Eurhythmy is claimed to operate within certain 'target' phonological structures in English. How far is this true? Does eurhythmy appear to operate in other languages? (Use your own data as far as possible.)
3. Hayes (1984) suggests that the metrical tree and grid are related to 'linguistic stress' and 'rhythmic structure' respectively. To what extent does Hayes justify his suggestion? (You might like to look at the relevant section(s) of the following chapter here before answering this question.)
4. In LP's tree/grid model, the marking of lexical monosyllables on a minimal second grid level seems essentially arbitrary. Can you think of any more principled way in which prosodic constituents (such as the stress foot and, perhaps, the 'mot') might be reflected in metrical grids?
5. LP and Kiparsky give rather different structural descriptions to the Reversal rule – see again (4.20) and (4.20′), (4.24) and the discussion following. Which analysis is to be preferred, and why?
6. On the basis of your observations so far, would you agree with the assertion that 'trees are independently needed' in phonological structures of the kind we have been discussing?

5 The phonology of rhythm (2): 'grid-only' metrical phonology

5.1 Introduction

In the last chapter we looked at the construction of metrical grids, and saw they were required in order to trigger Iambic Reversal. We also looked at the rhythmicity which appeared to provide a fundamental motivation for constructing grids; the notion of eurhythmy can be regarded, perhaps, as one reflection of the quasi-musical properties inherent in each grid. However, we also saw that the operations motivated by clashing grids, and by Beat Addition on grid columns, were not without practical and theoretical problems. In this chapter we shall discuss a grid-based approach to higher-level phonological structure which attempts not only to handle these problems, but also to account for a wider range of data by broadening the role the grid has to play in metrical phonology. In addition, we shall consider a related approach which essentially continues the line of analysis introduced in chapter 4, but which refines the roles trees and grids have to play by relating them to different linguistic functions. As we shall see below and in chapter 6, what we are essentially concerned with is a type of classical problem in linguistics: there are in this case at least three descriptions (and this implies three methodologies, three theories) which compete for adequacy in the task of analysis.

Before we begin our review of grid-only phonology, let us specify again the problems outlined in chapter 4. Firstly, there was an apparent problem in the grid-marking of lexical monosyllables (recall *good-looking tutor*). It was suggested that the reinforcement of the relevant grid column by one mark in order to account for the metrical strength of such items was ad hoc in conception. Of course, it may well be the case that such an analysis is essentially correct – monosyllabic lexical items marked for stress (bearing the feature [stress], or better, specified as stress feet) should certainly contrast with unstressed, weak syllables – but at present we seem justified in searching for more principled alternatives in the grid-marking of such items. In particular, it seems as if giving up reference to the metrical organisation encoded in tree structure – which is essentially what a grid-reinforcement rule of this kind does – has dire theoretical consequences. We also introduced a doubt concerning tree structure, in that, for the purposes of grid-marking, strength relations in the (uniformly branching) *w*-labelled terminals of each tree had to be interpreted as equivalent underlyingly; this led to further problems in how grids themselves might be interpreted. Secondly, we looked at a related problem, that of the RPPR. We saw that the RPPR, although billed as the 'weakest theory of tree interpretation consistent with the intuitive sense of "s" and "w" ', was in fact an extremely strong convention in that it allowed free variation in grid strengths so long as overall *s/w* relations were maintained. This inevitably led to ambiguities and undesirably complicated analyses – recall the discussion of *pretty little girls*. Thirdly, we saw that there were niceties of constraint to be considered in the formulation of Iambic Reversal; and connected with formalising such constraints is the overall picture of Reversal as it is triggered by grid clashes. As Giegerich writes (1984: 21–2):

. . . not all structures that share these characteristics [i.e. structures which are marked as clashing on the grid: RMH/CBM] are equally likely to undergo reversal. The width of the clash seems to play a major part in the factors governing likelihood – *fourteen men* seems more likely to reverse than *anticommunist views* or even *anticommunist opinion*. This criterion might correlate in some way with differences in speech tempo. Another criterion is the familiarity of the words that are candidates for reversal: familiar ones will be more likely to undergo the rule than rare ones. And finally, the reluctance or willingness to apply the rule may in many instances be speaker-specific. For those reasons, I suspect that an attempt to provide formal criteria for an item's likelihood to undergo reversal might be doomed to failure . . .

But not all linguists appear to be as pessimistic. The notion of eurhythmy, for example, seems to provide some motivation for a formal set of criteria that might govern application of Reversal: items are more likely to reverse when the result is a eurhythmic grid. Yet this connects with the last point we wish to reiterate here. In chapter 4 we suggested that, despite its apparent explanatory adequacy as a component of English phonology, the notion of eurhythmy should not be accepted uncritically – especially if its role in phonology is 'teleological'. A teleology means that rules are goal-directed, yet it is far from clear that such an assumption is phonologically justified (to take but one example, English speakers do not have entirely 'clashless' speech). And turning to specifics, the rule of Beat Addition – crucial in the initial analysis of some eurhythmic structures – seemed problematic, largely because of the power of the RPPR. In the examples so far considered, all that Beat Addition appeared to do was to prefer one analysis out of those available, and for no particularly good empirical reason. Moreover, for Beat Addition to operate at all – and for eurhythmy to operate – in the structures we have so far examined, the analysis is forced to admit the problematic lexical monosyllable convention noted above. Essentially and, as it turns out, crucially for the description of tree and grid structures, what such an analysis does is give the grid access to information not contained in the metrical tree structure itself. For example, the grid has to 'know' that a particular item is a lexical monosyllable by reference to a separate set of rules that are quite possibly non-prosodic in nature (at least, this is the case in LP). We must surely ask for a more explicit account of the principles that might bear on the construction of each grid.

These problems are not trivial: they go right to the heart of phonological theory in that they force us to question the very concepts of 'tree' and 'grid', and they ask us to reconsider the representation of stress. Needless to say, such problems have not gone unnoticed. Research in these areas has led to the development of three rather divergent schools of thought. The first is represented by Prince (1983 – henceforth in references, P) and Selkirk (1984b). Both these phonologists advocate a grid-only approach to metrical structure, arguing that the grid is related to (although not, perhaps, crucially dependent on) morphosyntactic structure; that rhythmicity provides a fundamental clue to interpreting the grid; that the prominence relations expressed in tree structures may be better captured in grids alone; and that therefore, strictly speaking, tree structure is unnecessary. A second view, which we shall go on to consider later in this chapter, is that of Hayes (1983, 1984). Hayes argues (1984: 59) that trees and grids

. . . play sharply distinct roles in rhythmic phonology, being related, respectively, to stress and rhythmic structure . . . [T]rees and grids represent different things (stress and rhythm), have different functions, and obey different laws – hence, neither is dispensable.

The third view of metrical structure, which advocates a 'tree-only' phonology, as in Giegerich (1985), is considered in chapter 6. Now, however, we must begin to examine the first of these views: that of grid-only phonology.

5.2   Reconsidering grids

In the following, we shall concentrate on only two aspects of Prince (1983): his reinterpretation of grid strata, and his reformulation of Reversal in a grid-only operation known as *Move x*. P (24–31) first discusses the merits and demerits of the LCPR and the RPPR as they are given in LP's initial theory. The RPPR interprets the dictum '*s* is stronger than *w*'. There are various difficulties inherent in the formulation of the RPPR, chief of which is the observation that the RPPR only establishes a partial ordering among the terminal nodes of certain trees (P: 23). As we have noted, the RPPR will not relate sister terminals dominated by *w*. It is in fact crucial to the initial theory of tree/grid phonology that such a relationship should not be specified, since this allows 'readjustment' rules, cast as 'supplementary principles of prosodic realization' (P: 24), to operate on metrical structures. For example, the grids of (5.1) and (5.2) seem to be equally well-formed:

```
(5.1)               x
        x    x    x
        x    x    x
       ten green chairs
```

```
(5.2)               x
        x         x
        x    x    x
        x    x    x
       ten green chairs
```

We might wish to call the grid in (5.1) 'minimal' – it bears out the relations in a [w w s] tree without adding anything to such relations except 'lexical monosyllable strengthening'. The extra grid-strength on *ten* in (5.2), though, is a divergence from the minimal pattern. But (5.2) is perfectly plausible under the RPPR in a grid/tree model; it is also well-formed under the Disyllabic Rule of eurhythmy ('The domains delimited on the level of scansion should be divided evenly by a mark on the next lower grid level' – Hayes 1984: 48). Both (5.1) and (5.2), then – the first minimal, the second a readjusted surface structure – are well-formed. And there appears to be a good reason why the first of two or more underlying 'weak' syllables may become strengthened. For example, look at a [w w w s] tree such as the following:

(5.3)

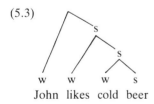

```
        w    w    w    s
       John likes cold beer
```

P writes (24) that the initial down beat (in this case, *John*)

. . . is often felt to be more strongly stressed than the others. . . . Divergences from the 'flattest' [=minimal: RMH/CBM] interpretation will arise from subtle variations of emphasis consistent with overall *s/w* structure. . . . This fact might be recorded as a supplementary principle of prosodic realisation, based on constituent structure and linear order, distinct from the primary interpretation of the stress pattern.

This 'supplementary principle', bearing on initial downbeats, might allow us to construct a grid such as (5.4), for example. Both (5.3) and (5.4) are, of course, quite consistent with the RPPR:

```
(5.4)                 x
        x             x
        x    x    x   x
        x    x    x   x
      John likes cold beer
```

But if this 'supplementary principle' is distinct from primary interpretation of the stress pattern, how far is it so? If the grid does not make direct reference to tree structure, what else is it referring to, and can it be shown that such reference is made in a principled way? And is there not a weakness in tree structure and the RPPR if a tree such as (5.3) does not reflect those fairly plausible strength relations seen in (5.4)?

Questions like these are countered in the first part of P's paper. He writes (24), for example, that grids of the form:

```
        x                          x
   x  x  x                    x  x  x  x
   x  x  x                    x  x  x  x
   x  y  z  (cf. (5.1), (5.2))  and  w  x  y  z  (cf. (5.4))
```

derive from the RPPR which, 'supplemented by a natural principle of minimality', picks out such grids as 'fundamental'. But the only way such a natural principle could be made formally explicit is to posit that, in a tree-grid model, (right-branching) terminals dominated by w are equal in metrical strength. Divergences from the minimal pattern must therefore be described as somehow extrinsic in character, making reference to a separate set of rhythmic principles. We have seen nothing yet, however, that would give us firm theoretical grounds for deciding what such a separate set of rhythmic principles might be. And, as it stands, the RPPR is so strong that it allows grid-strength to apply in free variation to any and every grid column dominated by a (right-branching) terminal w-node, so long as overall w/s relations are maintained. For Prince, however, the RPPR is 'the weakest theory of tree interpretation consistent with the intuitive sense of "s" and "w"', and – initially, at least – he assumes that the RPPR 'gives us the basis for an accurate account of syllabic stress patterns' (P: 24). There are good reasons, we think, for supposing that this particular claim is problematic. Prince himself goes on to summarise the problems inherent in formulation of the RPPR within a tree-grid model. The central observation is that fully constructed grids, such as (5.2) and (5.4), carry over relatively little of the information in their corresponding trees. In fact, if we think of minimal grids, we might be justified in thinking that strength-relations might be assigned rather better by a simple grid-only rule – a rule that must operate on terminals.

5.3   The End Rule

Q.   Consider structures such as the following:

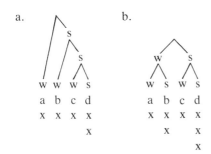

Look at the constituency that is indicated by trees (a) and (b). Then decide how you would formulate a grid-only rule that would assign the correct grid-strength to each terminal item.

A.   In the tree (a) above, [cd] is a constituent; so is [bcd], likewise [abcd]. In every case, [d] is the rightmost element of each constituent, and it is strong. In (b) above, [ab] and [cd] are (sub)constituents; [b] and [d] are rightmost in their constituents, and they are strong; in the constituent [abcd], [d] is rightmost, and it is strong. If we were to formulate a rule that would correctly assign prominence in a grid-only model, then we might wish to say something like the following: 'In any constituent C, the rightmost terminal is strongest' (P: 25). Essentially, what we are dealing with is the notion of 'headedness': we must simply mark the head of each constituent as strong on the corresponding grid, where that head is the rightmost element of C. As P points out, such a simple formulation will capture many of the phenomena that fall under the blanket-heading 'Nuclear Stress'; however complicated the branching pattern of a tree might be, provided it is labelled [w s] throughout, a grid-based 'rightmost prominent' rule (which we shall, following P, call the 'End Rule') will capture all the metrical strengths required. In (5.5), for example, minimal prominence is correctly assigned to the grid in terms of the End Rule ('rightmost terminal in constituent C is strongest'):

(5.5)

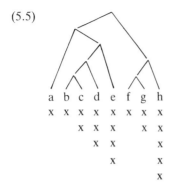

And you will notice that for any tree labelled [s w] throughout, a mirror-image of 'rightmost strongest' End Rule will apply:

(5.6)

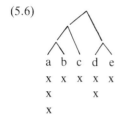

Q. It seems, then, as if the original function of the RPPR, that of assigning the appropriate strength-relations in the columns of each (underlying) grid, can be supplanted entirely by the rightmost/leftmost terminal End Rule, and this is what P suggests. Look again at (5.5–5.6), and recast the provisional formulation of the End Rule in grid-only terms.

A. A revised End Rule might run as follows: 'In a constituent C, the leftmost/rightmost terminal in C is associated with a stronger grid position than any other terminal in C.' A moment's reflection should convince you that such a rule will indeed construct the grids of (5.5–5.6). However, there are various theoretical assumptions concerning hierarchical metrical structure which seem to raise serious problems for the End Rule as given. There are in fact three very specific problems that we must now consider.

Q. Making reference to chapters 3 and 4 if necessary, try to decide what these problems are. How do they bear on the provisional formulation(s) of the End Rule?

A. *Problem A: word-stress in grid-only theory.* In chapter 3 we saw that the metrical theory of word-stress made apparently crucial reference to a hierarchy of prosodic constituents. Chief of these constituents were the syllable and the stress foot. We also saw that there was a superordinate unit, the 'prosodic word' or 'mot', which was also arguably a component of the metrical hierarchy. Yet consider such words as *representational*, *specificity*, *polyphiloprogenitive*. In a grid-only model, and before the End Rule has applied to project main word-stress, such words will have grid entries as follows – more or less along the lines of the analysis we introduced in preceding chapters:

(5.7) L2   x   x   x
       L1   x   x   x   x   x   x
            re pre sen ta tio nal

(5.8) L2   x   x
       L1   x   x   x   x   x
                 spe ci fi ci ty

(5.9) L2   x   x   x   x
       L1   x   x   x   x   x   x   x   x
            po ly phi lo pro ge ni tive

In (5.7–5.9), grid levels 1 and 2 in each case represent, roughly-speaking, the 'syllable–stress foot' hierarchy. But if we are now to consider projecting main word-stress, the End Rule in its present form makes reference to the rightmost *terminal* of each example (and let us assume that each example forms a 'word' constituent). Surely, this would be incorrect? How can the End Rule apply without reference to the kind of explicit hierarchical organisation found in metrical trees?

Problem B: the role of the LCPR. Consider the two trees (5.10, 5.11):

(5.10)

Manchester Housing Committee

(5.11)
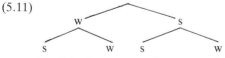
English degree attendance requirement

In each case, the rightmost compounds are labelled under the LCPR, which stipulates (among other things) 'Right node is strong if it branches'. Yet such higher-level metrical organisation is not represented, obviously enough, in the terminal strings of syllables in the metrical grid. Yet it is essentially terminals that the End Rule is concerned with; cast as a grid-only rule, it has no access to tree labelling. How, then, is it to interpret metrical structures that were previously interpreted under the branching-ness condition(s) of the LCPR?

Problem C: Reversal. As we saw in chapter 4, Iambic Reversal apparently makes crucial reference to tree structure. Furthermore, the Reversal rule has applied at those levels in the tree structure correspond-ing, roughly-speaking, to the metrical hierarchy of 'stress foot–word'. Yet the End Rule cannot make reference to tree structure; it can neither 'reverse' metrical structures nor specify where such an operation might take place. How, then, is a grid-only version of Iambic Reversal arrived at?

It is his answers to these specific problems that give Prince's work a strong claim on our attention, and we must look at these answers now in order to anticipate later work in this chapter. Let us turn first to Problem A, that posed by projection of main word-stress in the grid-only format.

Q. Look again at grids (5.7–5.9). Bearing in mind the fact that the End Rule (in its right-hand version) promotes the last element of a given constituent, and given the fact that the grid is an ordered hierarchy of metrical levels, perhaps it would be more adequate if we were to assume that the End Rule should promote the last element of a constituent where this element is at some particular level. Consider how you would reformulate the End Rule so that it would both express this relation, and lead to plausible analyses of (5.7–5.9).

A. The full and correct underlying versions of (5.7–5.9) are, let us assume, as follows:

```
(5.7′) L3          x
       L2    x   x   x
       L1    x  x x  x x  x
             representational

(5.8′) L3          x
       L2    x   x
       L1    x xx x x
             specificity

(5.9 ) L3              x
       L2    x    x    x x
       L1    x x  x x  x x xx
             polyphiloprogenitive
```

What seems to be apparent is that the End Rule must apply not to the rightmost element (in this case, syllable) of each (word) constituent, but to the rightmost entry at grid level 2. This assumption is of course consistent with what we have already seen is the hierarchical representation of stress;

if we assume, for example, that level 2 grid-marks in some way represent a syllable that is a stress foot, then what the End Rule has done in (5.7′–5.9′) is strengthen the rightmost level 2 entry – the (head of the) rightmost stress foot in each constituent. In (5.7′–5.9′) the rightmost entries at level 2 correspond to an 'end of the word' constituent: no other entries at that level stand between them and the word-end, and they are thus accessible to promotion by rule. There is a basic congruence between this type of analysis and the rules of word-stress we looked at in chapter 3: both analyses make reference to units such as first/last stress foot in each word. In terms of grid strata, though, we must now look at how the End Rule might be again reformulated so that it reflects main word-stress quite naturally. What we must do is ensure that the relationship between such main word-stress (those solitary grid-marks on level 3 in (5.7′–5.9′)) and the entries at the grid level immediately below it is specified as a well-formedness condition on grid structure. As a well-formedness condition, the rule will of course apply after each level of the grid has been constructed, up to and including a possible 'Phrase level'.

Q. The following is the version of the End Rule given in P (27):

Let p be the strongest grid position in a constituent C. There is a level $(n+1)$ such that (i) p is the only position in C with representation at level $(n+1)$, and (ii) other positions in C have representation at level n. The End Rule says: The entry for p at level n is the rightmost/leftmost entry at level n for C.

In order to interpret this new formulation of the rule correctly, construct grids for the words *mystification, paradigmatic, abracadabra* (you may like to contrast the grid-based projection of word-stress here with the kind of analysis given in chapter 3), and for the phrase *yellow peril*. Do you notice any problems connected with the grid-building process?

A. The End Rule will allow us to construct grids (5.12–5.15):

(5.12)
L3		x	entry p at level $(n + 1)$ (Wd level)
L2	x	x	stress foot (Σ) level (level n)
L1	x xx x x		syllable (σ) level

mystification

(5.13)
L3		x	entry p at level $(n + 1)$ (Wd level)
L2	x x x		Σ-level (level n)
L1	x x x x x		σ-level

paradigmatic

(5.14)
L3		x	entry p at level $(n + 1)$ (Wd level)
L2	x	x	Σ-level (level n)
L1	x x x x x		σ-level

abracadabra

```
(5.15)  L3              x    entry p at level (n + 1) (? Wd/Phr. level ?)
        L2   x          x    Σ-level (level n)
        L1   x  x    x  x    σ-level
             yellow  peril
```

In each case the End Rule guarantees that there will be one and only one main word- or phrase-stress, corresponding with and overtopping the last entry at level n in each constituent. But there are still various problems connected with (5.12–5.15). Notice that we have marked the various levels in each grid; this is not just a matter of clarification, but rather of giving a specific interpretation to the grid strata themselves. Indeed, P suggests that the prosodic categories – in his model, syllable, stress foot, (prosodic) word (mot), and phrase – should be used explicitly to name levels in the grid. Of course, this may not be wrong; such terms (with the exception of the term 'Phrase', which forms a category we have not yet discussed) are familiar to us from chapter 3, and it may well be desirable to incorporate them into the theory of grids if such a theory is to be descriptively adequate. But matters are not quite as simple as that. Firstly, a general problem: on what phonological grounds are grid levels held to correspond with prosodic categories? P (28), for example, writes that 'most of these level labels are not really primitives of grid theory, but are projected from syntactic (or phonosyntactic) structure. We are given independent definitions of syllable . . . , word, phrase; these determine the grid strata. Only Σ belongs entirely to prosody, though it might be thought of as grid structure between syllable and word.' The central problem is, however, that the relation of '(phono)syntactic surface structure' to prosodic categories is nowhere specified. For instance, in (5.15), if each grid is indeed level-specified for prosodic category, it would be entirely plausible to construct a grid such as (5.16):

```
(5.16)  L4              x    Phr. level
        L3   x          x    Wd level
        L2   x          x    Σ-level
        L1   x  x    x  x    σ-level
             yellow  peril
```

Yet what phonological advantages does (5.16) have over (5.15)? Is there not some duplication among the prosodic categories as they assign or correspond with the grid-strengths of particular syllables, and does this not lead to a certain arbitrariness in the analysis? To what extent are prosodic levels directly derived from morphosyntactic constituency, and is this question in fact well-conceived?

Take the example *polyphiloprogenitive*. It illustrates as well as any other example the fact that the correspondence between grid-level and prosodic category is obscure; and complicating matters further are what P (27) describes as supra-Σ/Wd prominence distinctions made on the grid 'due to rhythmic principles'. In the example *polyphiloprogenitive*, for instance, basic grid construction rules would allow us to construct (5.17):

(5.17) Wd   x
    Σ   x   x   x x
    σ   x x   x x   x x xx
          polyphiloprogenitive

Yet, just as we saw that initial downbeats in structures such as (5.3) might pattern as more prominent than other downbeats in any pre-head concatenation, so we might wish to say that a similar principle is at work in structures such as (5.17). We could plausibly assume, for example, that the initial Σ – specifically, the head of that Σ – receives an extra grid mark by the dictates of quite general rhythmic principles. But what happens then to the one-to-one correspondence between grid levels and prosodic categories? P's answer is to suggest that 'prosodic categories should label contiguous bands, not just single levels' (P: 27), as in example (5.18):

(5.18) Wd   x
    Σ   ⎰ x   x
         ⎱ x   x   x x
    σ   x x   x x   x x xx
            polyphiloprogenitive

However, what is not clear in this assumption of contiguity is exactly how many levels are occupied by each of the prosodic categories. Is it the case that contiguity extends to two levels maximally? Or more than two levels – depending on the morphological composition or, even, on the mere length of the constituent under consideration?

We shall leave the questions introduced in this brief discussion open, and return to them again later. For the moment, let us merely remark that the morphosyntactic/prosodic category-grid level thesis is something of a problem, and that a direct reflection of the problem is found when we come to consider Reversal, cast as a 'Movement' rule on the grid. For the present we shall simply assume with P that a prosodic hierarchy is represented in grid structure. It also seems to be the case that, despite the above doubts, the End Rule works unambiguously to locate primary word- and phrase-stress.

The End Rule, however, must act not only as constructive and interpretative, but also as functional in relating the prosodic levels within the hierarchy. For example, in the version of the End Rule given above, nothing was said about the variable level *n*, and this omission must be rectified if we are to formulate the End Rule adequately. This functional role of the End Rule is put as follows (P: 28):

In a constituent C, the leftmost/rightmost entry at level α corresponds to an entry at level β, where β is the next level up from α in the prosodic hierarchy and β is the prosodic category that the syntactic category C is related to.

A brief reconsideration of examples (5.12), (5.13) and (5.15) will illustrate how this functional role of the End Rule works to specify the relationship between grid levels:

```
(5.12')  Wd        x          level β; β related to syntactic category 'word'
         Σ    x    x          x is rightmost entry at level α
         σ    x xx x
              mystification
```

Example (5.13) patterns similarly:

```
(5.13')  Wd           x       level β; β related to syntactic category 'word'
         Σ    x   x   x        x is rightmost entry at level α
         σ    x x x   x x
              paradigmatic
```

```
(5.15')  Phr.         x       level β; β related to syntactic category 'phrase'
         Wd   x       x        x is rightmost entry at level α
         Σ    x       x
         σ    x x     x x
              yellow  peril
```

5.4   The End Rule, the LCPR, and extrametricality

Q.   Bearing in mind the explicit correspondence holding between grid levels and prosodic categories, construct the appropriate underlying grid for the phrase *Japanese screenprint*. What problems are raised by your analysis?

A.   We might wish to construct an underlying grid as follows:

```
(5.19)   Phr.            x
         Wd        x     x   x
         Σ    x    x     x   x
         σ    x x  x     x   x
              Japanese  screenprint
```

There is something odd, however, about the grid of (5.19): the grid-marking of *screenprint*. We have represented *screenprint* as a transparent compound consisting of two lexical words (monosyllables), and we have marked such items at the appropriate Wd level on the grid. The reason why such an analysis might be considered incorrect relates yet again to the stratification found in each grid. If we analyse *screenprint* as [[screen][print]]$_N$, it would surely be more correct to reflect this on the grid as:

```
Wd    x
Σ     x    x
σ     x    x
      [screenprint]N
```

After all, compounds are syntactically *words*, and we might wish to suggest that such items should culminate in an entry at the Wd level on the corresponding grid. Yet on what grounds do we ignore the syntactic labelling of innermost brackets, which seems to demand that such items be analysed as 'words'? The answer seems to be that if we analyse *screenprint* as in (5.19), with Wd grid-marking on each item of the compound, then under the functional formulation of the End Rule we will generate the wrong underlying pattern for the phrase:

```
(5.20) Phr.                  x    level β; β related to syntactic category 'phrase'
       Wd    x    x    x     x is rightmost entry at level α
       Σ     x  x   x    x
       σ     x x x    x    x
             *Japanese  screenprint
```

Constructing a deviant output, however, and arguing back from it to constitutive principles of analysis is like putting the cart before the horse. And a rather simpler analysis of compounds suggests itself.

Recall that in our introduction to this chapter we specified three problems bearing on the provisional formulation of a grid-only phonology. The first of these problems, Problem A, related to word-stress in grid-only theory, and we have already given this brief consideration. With (5.19) and (5.20), however, we move towards Problem B, that of reinterpreting the previous role of the LCPR within metrical theory. But as we saw at the end of chapter 3, it is quite possible that extrametricality may be able to supplant the LCPR. As you will remember from that discussion, the idea of extrametricality is roughly that certain segments (consonants) or syllables may be declared extrametrical when they occur at the edge – in English, the rightmost edge – of a domain (constituent); they will thereafter not be scanned in the accounting procedures that metrical stress rules depend on. In a tree such as (5.21a), for example, the final constituent is labelled by the LCPR; in (5.21b), the same result is achieved by declaring the final syllable extrametrical:

(5.21) a.   b.

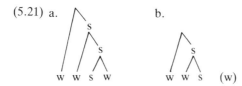

Q. The notion of extrametricality, though, is in no way crucially dependent on specific characteristics of tree form. In many ways it seems just as simple to formulate extrametricality in terms of grids. Attempt to formulate a grid-only rule that might account for extrametricality in a structure such as (5.21), and which will allow correct operation of the End Rule in that example and others.

A.   An extrametricality rule of this kind might be informally stated as follows: 'For any constituent in the right edge of a domain, the final (rightmost) element is to be regarded as extrametrical.' A simple formulation like this allows us to reconstruct (5.21) as follows:

(5.21) c.   [x [x [x x]]]
             A   B   C D

[CD] is the constituent on the right edge of domain [ABCD]; [D] is the rightmost grid element of this constituent, and is extrametrical, as is indicated by the parenthesised grid-mark in (d) below:

(5.21) d.   [x [x [x (x)]]]
             A   B   C   D

The End Rule, therefore, may make no reference to [D], but instead strengthens [C], as this is the rightmost entry at the appropriate level (level n or α) which the End Rule can 'see':

(5.21) e.   x
             [x [x [x (x)]]]
             A   B   C   D

If we assume that extrametricality operates as in (5.21c–e), then we can generate many word-stress patterns corresponding to those analyses given in chapter 3 (but see the further discussion of extrametricality later in this chapter). Consider, for example, words like *execute*, *Theodore*, *designate*. In each case, extrametricality will affect just the rightmost constituent (stress foot), and allow us to create primary word-stress on the initial syllable by operation of the End Rule (right-hand version):

(5.22) Wd   x   End Rule
       Σ   x (x)   Σ-extrametricality
       σ   x x x
             execute

Analyses of extrametricality in *Theodore* and *designate* fairly directly correspond to (5.22). Although there are still many complexities to be considered (How, for example, is extrametricality ordered with respect to other stress rules? Are grid-based word-stress rules cyclic?), we shall leave a fuller consideration until later. For the present, let us return to the issue we reintroduced with Problem B: that of the LCPR, and the correct grid-scansion of simple compounds such as *screenprint*. We have already seen that extrametricality will operate within grids to subsume at least some of the functions of the LCPR (as in 5.21a–e). What happens, though, if we allow compounds such as *screenprint* to fall under the rule expressed in (5.21)? Surely, the general extrametricality rule will parenthesise the rightmost element of each compound structure:

(5.23) Wd   x   x   (x)
     Σ   x x   x   x
     σ   x x x   x   x
        Japanese screenprint

If this is the case – and although he by no means makes this assumption consistently throughout his paper, P suggests it is (see his examples *labor union*, *labor union strike*, *labor union strike force*; P: 30) – then the Wd grid-mark on *-print* in (5.23) will be rendered extrametrical. Not only does this give a correct representation to the compound itself, but it also allows the End Rule (right-hand version) to operate at the Phr. level:

(5.24) Phr.   x
     Wd   x   x   (x)
     Σ   x x   x   x
     σ   x x x   x   x
        Japanese screenprint

However, although (5.24) allows us to escape from the difficulties outlined above, it is still unclear whether extrametricality ought to be allowed to operate on 'words': clearly, segments (consonants) and syllables can be straightforwardly considered extrametrical within the kind of word-stress analysis introduced in chapter 3; such a rendering is a considerable gain in elegance. Yet if extrametricality operates as in (5.23–24) on 'words' as well as on consonants and syllables, then what seems apparent is that the right-hand End Rule specifies both strongest phrase-stress ('Nuclear Stress') and those phenomena that have been considered under the heading 'Compound Stress'. Where extrametricality is the *modus operandi* of the End Rule, apparently both the Nuclear and Compound rules can be collapsed into one. This, if true, is a very striking result. We shall see shortly, however, that an alternative grid-only analysis is available which revises the notion of grid level(s) so that the End Rule itself becomes a questionable formulation.

5.5   *Reversal as Move x*

Leaving the issues raised by discussion of Problem B open, let us move on to discuss Problem C, reformulation of Reversal in a grid-only format. As we saw in chapter 4, in LP's initial theory tree structure defined the domain of Reversal, while the grid specified which elements at what level formed the relevant clashing items. In this analysis, the grid produced the pressure for change; the tree gave permission for Reversal to take place. It might be thought that putting tree structure to such use would constitute one of the more powerful arguments against grid-only phonology and for the retention of the kind of prosodic structure found in trees. For P, however, this is not so. P formulates a grid-only account of Reversal that makes crucial reference to clashing grid configurations at a certain level or levels before specifying what change takes place.

Q. Study the following underlying grids and attempt to work out a simple grid-based rule which will adjust clashing elements so that an alternating (non-clashing) grid is generated in each case.

```
a.                                    b.                              x
     Phr.              x                   Phr.          x    x
     Wd          x    x                    Wd       x    x    x
     Σ       x   x    x                    Σ        x    x    x
     σ       x   x    x                    σ        x    x    x   x
         fourteen  trout                       Hyde  Park  Corner
```

A. (5.25, 5.26) show what rule might produce the desired result:

```
(5.25)           x                 x
            x    x            x    x
        x   x    x        x   x    x
        x   x    x        x   x    x
        fourteen  trout  ⟶  fourteen  trout
```

```
(5.26)              x                    x
               x    x              x     x
         x     x    x        x     x     x
         x     x    x        x     x     x
         x     x    x   x    x     x     x   x
      Hyde  Park  Corner  ⟶  Hyde  Park  Corner
```

In each underlying grid there is a clash one level down from the highest (Phr.-level) grid peak. In each case, if we move the grid mark at the highest clashing level to the nearest leftward landing site on its own level, then this gives us the requisite alternating pattern. Note that each output above satisfies the Disyllabic Rule of eurhythmy; the fact that these output grids still contain what look like grid clashes is irrelevant, since these clashes do not occur on the level of scansion – one level below the rightmost grid peak. In any case, there are no other grid marks we are able to move leftwards; phrasal grid peaks are (at least in these examples) absolutely fixed.

P dubs this operation 'Move x'. He describes the procedure as follows:

> An entry at a certain level . . . is moved within its level away from a position of clash. Where does it move to? Evidently, to the first position it can legitimately occupy. Move x is a kind of minimal readjustment of grid configuration, and as such is a natural candidate to consider for the formal mechanism behind observed rhythmic adjustments. (P: 33)

Notice how the specifications given in P's description of the process, and in (5.25, 5.26), imply three important conditions on Move x. Firstly, x must move leftwards. Just as the arboreal account of Reversal in English readjusted an 'iambic' [w s] pattern, so Move x operates in an obligatory direction. There is no 'Trochaic Reversal' – or its grid-only equivalent – in English. Secondly, only one x may move at any one time. In some cases this prevents relocation of the main stress of a phrase (or compound), even where two continuous grid levels are associated with one prosodic category. For example, Move x cannot operate in the phrase *antique dealer*; in (5.27) we give P's analysis of the string; it may of course be the case that *antique dealer* is to be analysed along the lines we suggested in (5.23, 5.24).

```
(5.27) Phr.   x                      x
       Wd     x    x                  x          x
       Σ      x  x    x               x  x       x
       σ      x  x    x  x            x  x       x  x
              antique dealer  ─/→  antique dealer
```

(You should check your understanding of this by looking at other examples where Move x does not apply – try *defence budget*.) Thirdly, x must move within its own level to the nearest leftward landing site; this condition, like the preceding one, debars the construction of ill-formed grids that have gaps between levels. Consider, for example, the phrase *anti-communist rally*:

```
(5.28) a.  Phr.                 x                             x
           Wd      x            x              x              x
           Σ     x    x         x            x    x           x
           σ     x x x   x x    x x          x x x   x x      x x
                 anti-communist rally  ─/→  anti-communist rally
```

Move x should skip grid columns until it finds the nearest leftward landing site on its own level. The correct output of (5.28a) is, of course, the following:

```
(5.28) b.  Phr.                    x
           Wd    x                 x
           Σ     x    x            x
           σ     x  x  x     x x   x  x
                 anti-communist  rally
```

Q. Move x brings with it some familiar – and some not so familiar – problems. Thus it has been claimed in the literature (see Dogil 1984; Giegerich 1985) that despite the grid level/prosodic category equation made throughout P's work on grid theory in English, the lack of phonological structure in this model does not always allow for instances of Move x in structures where it might be expected to occur quite straightforwardly.

To make this last point clear, construct the correct underlying representation for the phrase *Japanese bamboo*, and then attempt operation of Move x.

A. The underlying grid is that of (5.29):

```
(5.29) Phr.                 x
       Wd        x          x
       Σ     x   x     x    x
       σ     x x x     x    x
             Japanese  bamboo
```

But in such a structure, as P himself observes, no clash is present. The expected clash, between *-nese* and *-boo*, is nullified by the presence of the Σ-level grid-mark on *bam-*. Therefore, no operation of Move x is possible. This is not the only example where Move x apparently does not occur where expected. In (5.30–5.32), for example, formal grid clash is not present, but it seems entirely plausible that such phrases are indeed structured on the surface as 'reversed' (we mark the 'expected clash' with a dotted line):

```
(5.30)                      x
                   x---------x                 x
           x      x  x       x          x      x
           x  x  x   x    x x x         x   x  x
           undersea  exploration  ⟶  ? (cf. undersea . . .)
```

(5.31)   x

```
          x- - - - - - - - - - - x           x
    x    x      x    x                x    x
    x   x x   x    x     x          x   x x   x
    absolutely   hard-boiled   ⎯⎯→  ? (cf. absolutely . . .)
```

(5.32)   x

```
          x- - - - - - - -• x              x
    x    x      x  x                 x    x
    x    x      x  x                 x    x
    unmarked antique   ⎯⎯→  ? (cf. unmarked . . .)
```

By way of contrast, notice how clearly a tree-analysis of such phrases would specify the domain of Reversal:

(5.30′)

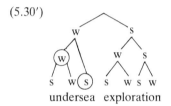

undersea exploration

(5.31′)

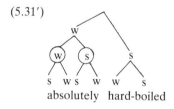

absolutely hard-boiled

(5.32′)

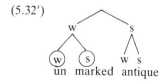

un marked antique

Examples (5.30–5.32), then, prove to be problems in the formulation of Move *x*, and ones to which P gives no direct answer. He writes (35) that 'Move *x* applies in a wider range of environments than we predict', and goes on to suggest tentatively that 'Perhaps "clash" ought to be characterized somewhat more broadly; or perhaps other conditions on eurhythmicity are having their effect . . .' Yet if the dictates of eurhythmy are allowed to license 'movement rules' on grids, rules that are not legitimised by a formal description of their preconditions, then this makes

Move *x* much less elegant than it first appears and, perhaps, dangerously teleological.

Q. Let us move on to discuss another related problem with Move *x*. Again, the problem apparently results from allowing the grid alone to represent metrical structure. As a preliminary, give a grid analysis of Move *x* in the phrase *one-nineteen Grey Street*.

A. Move *x* seems to work straightforwardly in this example:

```
(5.33)              x                             x
       ←------x     x              x              x
       x    x     x   (x)        x     x      x   (x)
       x    x x   x    x         x     x   x  x    x
       x    x x   x    x         x     x   x  x    x
       one-nineteen Grey (Street)  ⟶  one-nineteen Grey (Street)
```

But notice the representation given to *one* in (5.33). In the underlying structure, *one* is marked at the Wd level. This may of course turn out to be quite correct, but it is nevertheless arguable, as we saw from our discussion of LP's model, just what degree of strength lexical monosyllables receive. In LP's model such items were marked on the second level of the grid; this is essentially the convention adopted by, for example, Hayes (1983, 1984). In P's model, however, *one* receives an even greater degree of metrical strength. It should by now be clear to you that there is a great deal wrong with *both* these analyses. In (5.33), for example, notice what happens if we omit the Wd grid level:

```
(5.34)             x                            x
       ←---x       x              x             x
       x    x   x  x           x    x   x       x
       x    x   x  x           x    x   x       x
       one-nineteen Grey (Street)  ⟶  *one-nineteen Grey (Street)
```

Omission of the Wd level grid-marking (which is somewhat equivalent to assuming that *one* is a stress foot rather like *nine-*) leads to an ill-formed output. Moreover, we are still left with an awkward problem with (5.33) itself – another iteration through Move x is possible in that output structure:

```
(5.35)             x                            x
       x           x              x             x
       x   ←-----x x              x    x        x
       x   x   x   x              x    x   x    x
       x   x   x   x              x    x   x    x
       one-nineteen Grey (Street)  ⟶  *one-nineteen Grey (Street)
```

It seems clear that the output to (5.35) is ill-formed. Consider, for example, the evidence from such 'right-branching' modifiers as *well-maintained gardens, Red Chinese initiatives*. The underlying grid representations for these phrases are, respectively:

(5.36)
```
                 x                        x
    ←--------x    x          x            x
    x    x   x    x          x     x      x
    x  x x   x                x  x  x      x
    x  x x   x   x            x  x  x      x   x
    well-maintained gardens  ⟶  well-maintained gardens  ⟶  ?
```

(5.37)
```
                 x                        x
    ←-------x    x           x            x
    x   x   x    x           x     x      x
    x   x x  x (x)           x    x x     x  (x)
    x   x x  x x x x         x    x x     x x x x
    Red Chinese initiatives  ⟶  Red Chinese initiatives  ⟶  ?
```

Like (5.33), both (5.36) and (5.37) are configured as clashing underlyingly, and allow one iteration through Move *x*. Yet as P notes (36), such 'right-branching' modifiers in general inhibit further readjustment after only one iteration of the rule. Structures such as:

```
x                 x                  x
x    x            x    x             x    x
x    x   x        x    x x           x    x    x
x    x   x        x    x x           x    x    x
well-maintained . . .  Red Chinese . . .  and  one-nineteen . . .
```

are undesirable – consider the 'near minimal' contrast that holds, for example, between *No Propane Blues* and *No Cocaine Blues* (p. 37).

Q. What inhibits a second iteration through Move *x* in (5.35–5.37)? Consider the evidence from 'left-branching' structures such as *thirteen-twenty Grey Street* or, say, *Glasgow Park Central Metro Station*. Move *x* seems to work – up to a point – in these examples, and moreover it seems to work in a particular vertical plane. Can you generalise from the evidence provided about Move *x* in such examples and suggest a solution to the problem posed by (5.35–5.37)?

A. *thirteen-twenty Grey Street* patterns underlyingly as:

(5.38) a.
```
                x
          x     x
       x  x     x
     x x  x     x
     x x  x  x  x
     thirteen-twenty Grey (Street)
```

If Move x is now to derive a correct surface pattern, it must not only proceed from left-to-right but (more importantly, as we shall see) from bottom-to-top. If we were to proceed top-to-bottom, for example, we would derive:

(5.38) b.
```
                    x
        x           x
        x    x      x
    x   x    x      x
    x   x    x  x   x
```
*thirteen-twenty Grey (Street)

and no further iterations of Move x would be possible (the condition on Move x that stipulates that only one x may move at any one time prevents further movement). If we proceed left-to-right, bottom-to-top in (5.38a), though, what P aptly calls the 'self-feeding' character of Move x becomes apparent: after one iteration through Move x (on *thirteen*), the derived grid is that of (5.38c), and one higher application of the rule is required:

(5.38) c.
```
                  x                            x
   ←-------x      x            x               x
   x       x      x            x       x       x
   x  x    x      x            x  x    x       x
   x  x    x  x   x            x  x    x  x    x
```
thirteen-twenty Grey (Street)   ⟶   thirteen-twenty Grey (Street)

A similar process is apparent in the second example, *Glasgow Park Central Metro Station*. After two 'self-feeding' iterations through the rule, the surface pattern is that shown in (5.39):

(5.39)
```
                        x
    x                   x
    x           x       x
    x     x     x       x
    x     x     x       x
    x  x  x     x  x    x  x
```
Glasgow Park Central Metro (Station)

Notice that apparently a yet further iteration of Move x is possible – from *Central* to *Park*. In (5.39), however, we are dealing with a similar problem to that seen in (5.35–5.37): in each case let us provisionally suggest with P that since Move x proceeds obligatorily bottom-to-top, it is debarred from applying to lower levels once higher levels have been reached. In (5.36) and (5.37), for example, you will see that the first and only x to be shifted is the x at the Phr level; under the terms of our provisional solution, we are then prevented from applying Move x at any lower level. In (5.33), the same process is apparent – cf. (5.35) – and the same will of course apply to (5.39).

Is this provisional solution all we would like it to be? Is it always the case that Wd-level clashes are removed, then Phr.-level clashes, until no further upward iterations (or perhaps, 'cycles') of Move x are possible? Unfortunately not. Consider the phrase *dandruff shampoo research*. In the underlying patterning of the phrase, a Wd-level clash is unveiled; by strict bottom-to-top processing of Move x this clash should be alleviated. Yet this doesn't happen:

(5.40)

```
                      x
           x   x                  x
x          x   x                  x        x
x          x   x   x              x        x   x
x   x      x   x   x   x          x    x   x   x
dandruff shampoo research  ─/─→  *dandruff shampoo . . .
```

As an alternative, P suggests (38) that 'It is more illuminating to examine the relation between syntactic structure and the ease of moving x.'

Q. Consider again examples (5.33), (5.36) and (5.37). For each phrase, indicate how syntactic bracketing might be relevant to the possible application of Move x.

A. In each case a syntactic bracketing would run as follows:

[[A   B]   C]
  one-nineteen Grey . . .
  well-maintained . . .
  Red Chinese . . .

In the case of the syntactic constituent [AB], no clash is visible when that bracketed string is analysed in isolation; it is only when the head N is added that a clash becomes visible at the 'NP level'. Clash is only defined at this level, and this clash motivates Move x between B and A. Move x is 'unnatural', P claims, if it occurs entirely within B or A. Hence, Move x takes place naturally between *one* and *nineteen*, but is debarred from applying within *nineteen* – cf. (5.35) – and likewise for similarly-structured phrases. P chooses to formalise this syntactic bounding condition on Move x in terms of the subjacency defined within each grid. For example, in pre-Move x *one-nineteen Grey Street*, the pattern is that seen in (5.33), which we repeat below:

(5.33′)

```
                    x
           ⓧ        x
x          x̄        x
x    x     x        x
x    x     x        x
one-nineteen Grey (Street)
[[A      B    ]  C   ]
```

The circled x will move; shift between B and A, one level down from the motivating stress peak, is natural. The boxed x, however, two levels down from the motivating stress peak, will not move.

What is it that the bounding-subjacency condition on Move x achieves that a tree-formulation of Reversal (for example) cannot? Recall that a tree-theoretic account of Reversal makes reference to a superordinate

structure, as well as to the distinctive switching of s/w-nodes; the superordinate structure encodes the syntactic information given in the bounding/subjacency condition on Move x. In the paradigm example *one-nineteen Grey Street*, for example, a tree-theoretic account should only allow one iteration of Reversal:

(5.41)

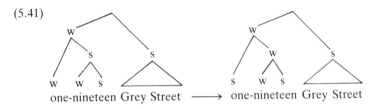

The output tree to (5.41) does not contain any environments that immediately or obviously satisfy the SD of Reversal: *nineteen* is dominated by two w's, and this should, surely, prevent further Reversal (even though a grid clash would still be defined for that output tree). But are matters as simple as this? Again we run into difficulties. The output tree of (5.41) corresponds to the output tree for *almost hard-boiled egg* after one iteration of Reversal (see again chapter 4). Yet we assumed in chapter 4 – and we will go on to assume in the following chapter – that two iterations of Reversal do indeed take place in this phrase, the second in a tree directly corresponding to the output tree of (5.41). It appears, then, that while tree theory does provide a convenient means of annotating phonosyntactic structure – and see again (4.20), (4.20′) – in this instance at least it gives no insight into how a bounding condition on Reversal/Move x might be characterised (and see the further discussion of tree structures and Reversal in chapter 6 here). But does grid theory do so much better?

Q. Give a grid-only analysis of the phrase *almost hard-boiled egg*. Does Move x apply? What problems do you encounter?

A. The grid pattern for the phrase is, we assume, as in (5.42a):

(5.42) a.

```
                    x
              x     x
x       x     x     x
x       x     x     x
x   x   x     x     x
```
almost hard-boiled egg

This grid makes the claim that *hard-*, as a lexical monosyllable within an 'end-stressed compound' (see chapter 6, under 'Further constraints on Reversal' for more discussion of this point), is marked on a third grid level corresponding with the prosodic category Wd. Yet such an analysis only allows one Move x, and that very dubious:

(5.42) b.

```
                    x
        x           x
x       x     x     x
x       x     x     x
x   x   x     x     x
```
*almost hard-boiled egg

(5.42b) reflects the syntactic structure [[almost hard] [boiled egg]]; it is not the pattern we would like to derive. Perhaps the nub of the problem is formed by the grid-marking we are allowing to compounds? Perhaps – and we have discussed this point briefly already – since compounds are 'words' syntactically, we ought to suggest that such items culminate in a Wd-level entry on the grid as it is built up from syntactic surface structure, as in (5.42c, d, e):

(5.42) c.

```
          x
      x   x
      x   x
```
[hard-boiled]

d.

```
                      x
      x               x
      x         x     x
      x   x     x     x
```
[almost [hard-boiled]]

e.

```
                      x
                x     x
      x         x     x
      x   x     x     x
      x   x     x     x
```
[[almost [hard-boiled] egg]]

(5.42e) appears to be a rather more plausible underlying pattern, but how does it fare in terms of Move x? Two self-feeding iterations of the rule seem possible – but notice that (5.42e) is all but identical to (5.33′). Since *hard-boiled* is now analysed as a 'word' (it is grid-equivalent to *nineteen* in

(33')) it has the same syntactic bracketing associated with it: [[A B]C]. Yet this bracketing, bearing on the applicability of Move x, only allows one iteration of Move x on a topmost grid level. In terms of the bounding/subjacency constraint on the rule, the boxed x over *boiled* in (5.43) is fixed (compare (5.43) with (5.33')):

(5.43)

```
                        x                      x
  <-------------x       x          x           x
  x            ☐x       x          x       x   x
  x        x   x        x          x       x   x
  x    x   x   x        x          x   x   x   x
  almost hard-boiled egg  ------>  almost hard-boiled egg
```

It seems, then, as if a grid-only account of rhythmic reshuffling runs into fairly intractable difficulties. The bounding/subjacency constraint on Move x appears to be inadequate; so does, for example, an ad hoc stipulation (P: 42) that Move x may act to alleviate grid clashes, but not to create others (consider again *one-nineteen . . . , dandruff shampoo . . .*). Such an account of Move x is also considerably less elegant than the tree-based account of Reversal, notwithstanding the problems which are implicit in that formulation too. It is apparent, though, that the difficulties we have encountered in trying to formalise a grid-only metrical theory stem from one central inadequacy: if we may put it this way, P's grids seem to hierarchise both too little and too much structure.

In the first place, it is debatable whether we should indeed give up the richness encoded in standard tree theory. We saw in chapter 3, for instance, that tree theory not only gave an adequate characterisation of what constituted syllables and stress feet, but also determined the boundaries of those constituents; P's grid-only theory does not do this. As Giegerich writes (1985: 235) '. . . stating the fact that a certain phonological unit has its prominence peak on, say, foot level doesn't mean that the boundaries of that foot have thereby been determined . . .' Matters are further complicated by the status of the constituent 'word'. In P's model, it is the only member of the prosodic hierarchy that is non-phonological in nature (neither is it given a phonological characterisa-tion in the kind of word-stress rules we looked at in chapter 3). This fact connects with what we have called the 'duplication' that arises in P's grid-only model. In turn, this connects with the supposition that P's grids hierarchise 'too much' structure, in that marking the prosodic categories explicitly and consistently leads to the inadequacies of Move x we have been discussing; it also leads to ambiguities in the grid analysis of compounds. Since these problems appear to be related – they all stem from rather basic grid-construction rules, and how we interpret such rules – it is both desirable and plausible to reconsider how grids may be aligned with the surface syntactic structures on which they seem, partly or wholly, to depend.

5.6 Grid theory revisited

Q. Look again at the beginning of this chapter. You will see that there we mentioned the rhythmicity which appears to provide a fundamental motivation for grid-theory. Can you make a provisional guess as to how grids might be reinterpreted in a revised grid-only model?

A. A reconsideration of this kind forms a large part of Selkirk (1984b; henceforth in this chapter, S). This work is the fullest treatment given so far to grid phonology. Particularly important for our purposes is S's distinction between rules that construct grids, aligning them with surface syntactic structures, and rules that interpret grids, manipulating underlying patterns so that rhythmically well-formed outputs are generated. S calls grid construction rules Text-to-Grid Alignment (TGA) rules: such rules construct a partial grid, making reference just to the internal composition of syllables and/or their position within specified syntactic domains. Grid interpretation rules, on the other hand, are properly 'phonological' – they do not apply necessarily in terms of surface syntax, but rather work to ensure that grids are well-formed in accordance with what S suggests is a general Principle of Rhythmical Alternation (PRA) operative on all levels of the grid. The PRA ensures that grid clashes, or grid lapses (long stretches of 'weak' grid positions) are alleviated by Movement, Addition, or even Deletion rules: both Beat Addition and Move x can be regarded as rules of this sort rather than as TGA rules – although Beat Addition, as we will see, operates both at the Wd level and at the Phr. level in the new model. Oversimplifying drastically, we might represent the process of phonological derivation as in (5.44):

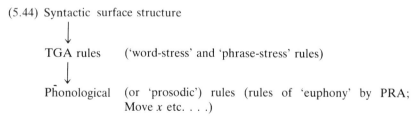

(5.44) Syntactic surface structure

TGA rules ('word-stress' and 'phrase-stress' rules)

Phonological (or 'prosodic') rules (rules of 'euphony' by PRA; Move x etc. . . . .)

There are other components of a potential model that must be included: what, for example, is the role of intonation within grid theory? And how far may juncture be represented on each grid? We will leave these questions for the moment, because we would like to continue a

consideration of how the grids in S's model are different from the grids of P's model. This means looking at S's TGA and euphony rules.
   Consider a grid such as (5.45):

```
(5.45)                                     x
                         x                 x
         x               x     x           x
         x     x         x     x           x
         x     x     x   x     x     x     x     x     x
```

Rather than interpret such a grid (or indeed, any grid) by making an explicit grid level: prosodic category equation, S views the grid as a truly rhythmical construct. The bottom row, the 'syllable level', of (5.45), for example, is in S's model seen as a grid level consisting of a row of *demibeats*; further, any grid marks on a second level or above may be referred to as *beats*. The distinction between beats and demibeats in some ways directly corresponds to the strong/weak, stressed/stressless distinction we have been making throughout: a beat (or demibeat) that does not correspond to a grid entry at a higher level may be referred to as a weak beat (or demibeat); beats (or demibeats) that do coincide with a beat on a higher metrical level may be referred to as strong beats (or demibeats) (see S: 11). Consequently, the notions 'stressed', 'stressless' and 'degree of stress' can be represented simply by the alignment of beats and demibeats on any metrical grid: a 'stressed syllable' will be aligned with a beat, an 'unstressed syllable' with a weak demibeat, and a syllable has 'more stress' than its neighbour if it has representation at a higher grid level.
   There seem to be several good reasons for reinterpreting grids in this way, as encoding a 'rhythmic theory of stress' (S: 19) rather than entries at certain specified prosodic-category levels; the first relates to the contrast that may be made between a grid-only and a tree theory of word-stress. In tree theory, word-stress rules typically make reference to both relational (*s/w* labelling) and non-relational (prosodic hierarchy) devices. They can in a sense be regarded as falling into two separate but related parts: that is, tree theory needs both labelling and the hierarchy if it is adequately to characterise patterns of stress. A grid, on the other hand and in S's view, gives a uniform representation to both relational and non-relational aspects of the stress patterns observable in words and phrases (S: 17): viewed as sequences of beats and demibeats, whose presence and character are crucially determined by the presence of others in the same grid, a grid rationalises the special properties that characterise word- and phrase-stress rules and treats them inclusively. Notably in this model, grid entries do not need to be equated with prosodic categories: stress patterns are represented just in terms of their grid alignment, and, as it turns out, the

assumption that grid entries correspond with certain specified category labels is positively wrong. We return to this point below.

There is a second reason, S suggests, for viewing the grid as encoding a 'rhythmic theory of stress'; in the revised model, grids give an insight into the notion of 'possible stress pattern for Language X'. The PRA, to take the clearest example, will operate at every level of each grid; it will ensure that alternation is indeed fundamental in English stress patterning. Yet, S argues, in tree theory this kind of organisation (which we will call, following chapter 4, a restrictive periodicity) is merely stipulated; it does not form a constitutive principle of analysis. (You may notice of course that just as eurhythmy may be operative at higher grid levels, so the higher-level nodes of trees might be regarded as conforming to a similar principle of maximal alternation. In what we have seen so far, eurhythmy is non-empirical in character and is thus just as much a 'stipulation' as the kind of preferred rhythmic structuring encoded in trees – see chapter 6 for further discussion.) S's point, however, is well taken: supplemented by the PRA, the grid will certainly represent a particular kind of periodicity as fundamental, and this cannot be overlooked.

A third reason for reinterpreting grids now suggests itself. S claims that revised grid theory need make no reference to the categories of the prosodic hierarchy. But how far is this true? It is indeed necessary, as we saw earlier, to re-assess the claims for the existence of suprasyllabic prosodic constituents. S writes (27), for example, that

. . . it is clear that some of the phonological phenomena that were thought to provide motivation for . . . higher units of structure are better explained in terms of the metrical grid alignment of the sentence. Some categories will disappear entirely from the prosodic structure repertoire; others will be given a much reduced role in phonological description, once the role of rhythmic structure in phonology is fully understood.

The problems with the prosodic hierarchy in P's model seem to centre largely around the role which categories such as the stress foot (Σ) and the prosodic word (Wd) play in that grid-only model. What becomes of these categories in S's model? The answer, apparently, is that if we regard the grid as an alignment of syllables at a certain level or levels, then the need for such categories simply evaporates. On Σ, for example, S (31) writes that

. . . there is relatively little evidence that the foot itself serves as a domain for phonological rules. Most alleged foot-sensitive rules can be easily and with no loss of generalisation recast as rules sensitive to the stressed/stressless distinction [for example, rules governing the allophonic variation of voiceless stops in English – see S: 421, fn.38; see this volume, chapters 2 and 6: RMH/CBM]. In the present theory such rules would be recast as rules sensitive to the metrical grid alignment of syllables. We hypothesize, therefore, that there is no prosodic constituent *foot*.

And what happens to the prosodic word? This constituent too apparently plays no part in S's model. This leads us to discussion of possibly one of the more interesting of S's proposals.

Following Liberman (1975), S suggests that the metrical grid alignment of an utterance is more than the sum of those beats and demibeats that translate syllables; in particular, syntactic juncture may be represented on the grid in terms of silent grid positions, themselves underlying demibeats, which intervene between the grid representations independently given to lexical words. Although we shall discuss this matter further, for the present just note that it is arguably the case that silent demibeats occur at the end of the word, the end of a branching constituent, and at the end of a daughter of any sentence node (S: 184). Thus, for example, the grid representation of *Louise laughed* is roughly as in (5.46):

```
(5.46)                    x
              x           x
            x x           x
            x x   x   x   x   x       x   x . . .
            Louise        laughed . . .
```

If this is the case, then the need for the prosodic constituent 'word' disappears: we do not need 'word' to specify main word-stress, since this will simply be an independently given TGA definition of a syllable 'at-a-certain-level' (where that alignment is established within a domain characterised in syntactic terms – S: 30); neither do we need the word to express notions such as 'word-initial/ -internal/ -final', since these notions are expressed in terms of grid adjacency: silent demibeats never occur word-internally, therefore syllables in the same word are strictly grid-adjacent; moreover, 'word-initial' and 'word-final' can be seen as synonymous with 'lack of grid-adjacency to what precedes' and 'lack of grid-adjacency to what follows' (S: 30). If this hypothesis proves correct, then of course the prosodic word does not need to figure as a constituent in the revised grid model.

What of the other putative prosodic constituents, such as the 'phonological phrase' and the 'intonational phrase'? In the case of the former constituent, it appears that phonological rules need make no necessary reference to such a supra-word unit. We could assume that a movement rule like Move *x* took the 'phonological phrase' as its domain, but this seems both inapplicable (consider the example of, for instance, *expectation*) and inelegant: it seems just as easy to invoke a more-or-less direct reference to surface syntax instead of a higher-level phonological constituent. Moreover, S claims that the existence of the 'phonological phrase' is highly suspect, since 'syntactic timing', reflected in grids that give positions to silent demibeats – see again (5.46), gives (she argues) a more appropriate representation to junctural phenomena (which might have been conceived in terms of supra-word constituents), and one conceptually simpler than importing yet another prosodic category into the model.

Finally, what of the 'intonational phrase'? We have deliberately avoided discussing the 'grammar of intonation' in any detail, but it does seem as if the intonational phrase, unlike the phonological phrase, is a well-motivated supra-word constituent of a phonological grammar. An intonational phrase is not, for example, necessarily correspondent with syntactic phrasing. Although sentences consist of one or more intonational phrases (compare the two representations of, for example, *My sister who lives in Edinburgh brought the wine*), these intonational phrases may be associated with syntactic strings that are not themselves syntactic constituents (compare the 'intonational' representations that may be given to *Batman and Robin meet the Yellow Peril*). In addition, it seems as if the grid itself defines no such unit in the characterisations it gives to higher-level phonological structure. Therefore, S claims, a high(est)-level intonational phrase constituent is a well-motivated part of a prosodic hierarchy. In S's model, then, the hierarchy consists just of the syllable and the intonational phrase: these are the only units that need to be given definition independent of other grid-based rules.

Before we turn to investigating how the revised model operates, let us summarise the main features of S's model as they are distinct from, say, P's.

(1) Grids in the revised model consist of rows and columns of beats and demibeats. Demibeats are aligned with syllables on L1 of the grid. These demibeats may be aligned with grid positions at higher metrical levels, in which case they are defined as (weak or strong) beats (or demibeats). A 'weak beat' is a beat not aligned with any higher grid position – recall the discussion at (5.45).

(2) The 'syllable level' (row of demibeats) forms in every case the lowest level of each grid. The syllable is independently defined as a prosodic constituent, and is crucial, S suggests, in any analysis of word/ phrase-stress:

The internal structure of syllables and the number occurring within a particular syntactic domain are reflected in the rhythmic patterns of English words. The syllable sequence provides the anchor, so to speak, of that rhythmic patterning: the representation of the stress pattern of an utterance on our theory is the alignment of the syllables of the utterance with a metrical grid. The syllable, then, has a solid place in the theory of the phonological representation of English words. (S: 140)

(3) Other grid positions at higher levels (strong demibeats, strong and weak beats) are determined by reference to the internal composition of syllables and/or their positions in syntactic domains. Therefore, it is claimed, notions such as 'stress foot' and 'word' play no part in the revised model: their special properties, if any, are determined simply by the alignment, the height and adjacency, of syllables at certain grid levels.

(4) Revised grid theory also provides a place for representations that include silent grid positions. These are relevant as indications of syntactic timing and juncture (pausing, final lengthening). Such silent grid positions also bear on point (3) above, by rendering the notion of 'word' doubly unnecessary.

(5) Intonational structure also finds a place in the revised theory: the intonational phrase – the second and only other constituent in the prosodic hierarchy – is not only relevant to the analysis of such phrases as 'sense units' but also serves as the domain with respect to which patterns of rhythmic prominence are defined (S: 28).

Features (1) to (5) are relevant to TGA rules; after these rules have applied, they will have constructed underlying (or perhaps 'partial') grids which are then completed by (6).

(6) Phonological rules of Movement, Addition, or even Deletion themselves apply in accordance with the PRA. Thus such prosodic rules may be regarded as rules of euphony (S: 55). However, note that the PRA is not itself a representation: it characterises a certain type of rhythmical organisation to which possible grid alignments, at each successive level above L1, aspire.

So much for a bare outline of some central tenets of S. Our job now is to look at how such rules work in practice. Again we must first look at word- and phrase-stress in the revised theory before we pass on to discuss higher-level rules of rhythmic phonology.

5.7   Word-stress

Q. Bearing in mind the features of S's model outlined above, and ignoring for the moment rules of syntactic timing (silent demibeats), suggest how the revised grid model might construct partial grids for the words *expect, chimpanzee, prognostication* by TGA rules.

A. Let us take the example *expect*. Since syllables (demibeats) form the lowest elements of the revised model, we must map the two syllables of *expect* onto the bottom level of the grid:

(5.47) a.   x   x
            ex pect

A syllable-mapping procedure of this kind is universal; S dubs it *Demibeat Alignment* (DA), and formalises it (S: 57) as follows: 'Align just one demibeat with every syllable.' Notice that if the DA rule were to provide for 'derived' representations including silent demibeats, then the rule might be recast as less restrictive, possibly 'Align at least one demibeat with every syllable' (provided that no demibeat is aligned with more than one syllable).

The next highest metrical level is the level of strong demibeats or 'basic beats'. Recall that we mentioned earlier that syllables were aligned on a second level of the grid because of their type of internal composition, because of their position within a given domain, or possibly because of both these factors. That is, rules which construct a second metrical level are rules which appeal to 'type and position' distinctions (S: 59). Now recall from chapter 2 how distinctions in syllable type were to be made: in terms of the notions 'light' and 'heavy' syllable. Heavy syllables were syllables with branching rhymes. In terms of grid theory, it is just these syllables – most clearly, CVV and CVC(C) syllables – that get mapped onto a second grid level (although see S: 59 where the issue of syllable 'geometry' as a precondition for 'stress' is discussed in rather more detail). In *expect*, then, and working from right to left, we can view the final syllable as heavy; it contains a branching rhyme. This leads us to construct the partial representation (5.47b):

(5.47) b.　　　　x　　　by Basic Beat rule(s) (BBR)
　　　　　　x　x　　　DA
　　　　　　ex　pect

But remember that rules which construct the second grid level (dubbed BBR by S) make reference to both type *and* position of syllables. What are we to make of the initial syllable in (5.47b)? We could view it, clearly, as heavy since it contains a branching rhyme. And because it is heavy, it might be aligned with a second-level grid position as in (5.47c):

(5.47) c.　x　　x　　　BBR
　　　　　x　　x　　　DA
　　　　　ex　pect

But there is another and more satisfactory way of arriving at (5.47c). If we are to derive all the word-stress patterns in English, we must include in the grammar a rule which will assign 'stress' (in grid terms, a basic beat) to initial syllables where they occur in the domain 'word' – or, preferably, 'root' (see especially S: 60, 84). This rule might be cast as a second part of BBR (a 'position', rather than a 'type' rule). Note at present that this second part of the BBR will indeed assign the incomplete pattern (5.47c) to *expect*. Note too that the BBR now falls into two distinct parts: the first part is the position rule we have just discussed, which S calls the *Initial Beat Rule* (IBR); the second part is the type rule which assigns syllables to basic beats when those syllables are heavy, and S calls this the *Heavy Syllable Basic Beat Rule* (HBR). We continue to use these terms in what follows.

So far, we have been able to construct two grid levels. We must now see how main word-stress is projected. S follows P in supposing that main word-stress is projected by a *Domain-End Prominence Rule* of very much the kind we examined earlier (P's End Rule). In English, for example, it is clear that such an End Rule (Main Stress Rule or MSR) operates on that basic beat that is last (rightmost) in each word. The MSR, then, enables us to construct the fully-formed (5.47d):

```
(5.47) d.      x     MSR
          x    x     BBR (IBR and HBR)
          x    x     DA
          ex   pect
```

The same principles are of course at work in analysis of the second example, *chimpanzee*. The derivation proceeds by DA, then by BBR which, in the case of *chimpanzee*, assign an initial beat by IBR, then two further basic beats by HBR (*-pan-* and *-zee* are both heavy syllables). These rules allow us to construct the partial grid (5.48a):

```
(5.48) a.   x     x     x     IBR, HBR
            x     x     x     DA
            chim  pan   zee
```

We must now look to the projection of main word-stress. Again this works quite straightforwardly: the MSR applies to promote the rightmost basic beat in the word(-sized) domain as in (5.48b):

```
(5.48) b.                x     MSR
            x     x      x     IBR, HBR
            x     x      x     DA
            chim  pan    zee
```

There are, however, two issues we must now consider. The first is a question which relates to the phonetic form of *chimpanzee* in American English (AmE), as opposed to British English (BrE). In BrE, but not, apparently, in AmE, the second vowel of *chimpanzee* reduces to schwa, [ə]; in AmE the same syllable appears to be phonetically [æ]. How is this variation to be accounted for? In BrE, and to some extent in AmE, there seems to be a 'medial destressing' rule at work in the (post-cyclic) phonology; examples such as *Mozambique, Kilimanjaro, confrontation*, *dispensation* etc. (see S: 124–5) tend to be structured with medial [ə]. That is, a medial destressing rule 'undoes' the stress assigned to each syllable immediately preceding main word-stress, and it is clearly the case that such a rule will be at work in BrE [tʃɪmpənzi]. In AmE, however, *chimpanzee* seems to be an exception to such a destressing rule (S: 124); as S writes (125): 'Whether or not a word is an exception to Monosyllabic Destressing is an important source of idiosyncrasy in the grammar of English.' (In this way S differs from Hayes 1982; as S notes (125) Hayes' word-stress rules cannot account for the medial stressed syllable in words such as *chimpanzee, Halicarnassus*; unlike the rules of the revised grid model, Hayes' rules must consider such examples as exceptional in bearing such 'medial stress'.) For a fuller discussion of Destressing, see again chapter 3 and the comments below. The second issue we must consider is again that of higher-level alternation. Surely, *chimpanzee* does indeed display alternation – that is, we must make provision for a word-stress analysis that allots a greater strength to *chim-* than to *-pan-* (where, of course *-zee* will remain stressed by the MSR). How are we to achieve this? In terms of the new model, alternation at higher levels (as well as at L2, as we shall shortly see) is achieved through Beat Addition, which, cast as a rule of grid euphony (GE), operates to ensure higher-level alternation.

In quite general terms, Beat Addition rules may be of two kinds which, following S, we might call 'left-dominant', as in (5.49a):

(5.49) a.   x

         x   x ⟶ x   x

Or 'right-dominant' as in (5.49b):

        b.   x

         x   x ⟶ x   x

Languages appear to select which of these two versions is applicable (S: 60–2). In English, Beat Addition is left-dominant, and applies right-to-left in the appropriate domain. This process can be seen in (5.50):

(5.50)   x   x   x

         x   x   x ⟶ x   x   x

or

                              x   x

         x   x   x   x   x ⟶ x   x   x   x   x

Starting from the rightmost edge of a domain, left-dominant, right-to-left Beat Addition will iterate on every grid position where this is possible, promoting as it goes every other grid position as in the SD/SC of the rule

(5.49a). Notice we have seen other rules of just this kind: at the word-level, for instance, Stress Retraction is a case in point (see again chapter 3). Although we shall discuss L2 Beat Addition shortly, at present let us simply confirm that Beat Addition (BA) applies at the third level of the representation of *chimpanzee*, on the initial syllable of the word, and that of course after BA has applied there, then main word-stress is adjusted onto a fourth metrical level: BA cannot apparently undo the effect of the MSR (and we might wish to incorporate a 'Textual Prominence Preservation' condition into the grammar to that effect). A full derivation of *chimpanzee*, runs, then, as follows (compare (5.51) with (5.48b) and our comments there):

(5.51)

		x	MSR
x		x	BA
x	x	x	IBR, HBR
x	x	x	DA
chim	pan	zee	

What of the final example, *prognostication*? Again DA will construct a partial grid:

(5.52) a.　x　x　x　x　x
　　　　prog no sti ca tion

And the IBR and HBR will operate to place basic beats on the initial syllable and on the penultimate syllable, which contains a bi-moric (VV) vowel. (Notice that we omit to mention the word-final syllable /ʃən/. Of course, this too is nominally a 'heavy syllable', but you will recall from the word-stress analysis of chapter 3 that extrametricality operates in such domain-end syllables so that they will indeed be scanned as 'light'. You should assume just for now that such an analysis is at work above.) The partial word-stress patterning is thus as in (5.52b):

(5.52) b.
x			x		IBR, HBR
x	x	x	x	x	DA
prog	no	sti	ca	tion	

Yet there is clearly a domain here where Beat Addition (BA) will apply: there is a grid 'lapse' between the initial and penultimate syllables. And it certainly seems to be the case that BA will not just apply at the word level (L3 and above), but will also assign basic beats. This is not in any way a controversial position: BA, operating on the level of basic beats, can be regarded as the grid equivalent of Hayes' rule of Stress Retraction. BA will operate to ensure that grid lapses are avoided, and that 'alternation' occurs at every grid level (above L1 of course!). Because BA works right-to-left, and is left-dominant in English, it will operate in (5.52b) by proceeding leftwards from the rightmost basic beat (the beat on *-ca-*) and assigning a basic beat to every second syllable it comes across; in (5.52b) operation of BA means that *-no-* will become basic beat-aligned, and the following grid is the result:

(5.52) c.   x   x   x   IBR, HBR, BA
            x   x   x   x   x   DA
           prog no sti ca tion

The MSR now operates on (5.52c) to project main word-stress onto the rightmost syllable that is aligned with a basic beat:

(5.52) d.   x   MSR
            x   x   x   IBR, HBR, BA
            x   x   x   x   x   DA
           prog no sti ca tion

And, at least in some English dialects, it is clear that after the lowest-to-highest, cyclic, rules have applied, (5.52d) might undergo an 'initial destressing' rule; alternatively, we could regard the word as patterning along with the rather curious *Ticonderoga* example(s) – see here S (102).

5.8   *Word-stress and extrametricality*

Q.   The grid-based rules that have been outlined – DA, the two Basic Beat rules (IBR, HBR), BA (applying at L2 and above), and the MSR – should allow you to construct the appropriate grid patterns for a fairly wide variety of English words. But now consider words such as *utensil, develop, America, mangrove*, and *asinine*. If you use the word-stress rules outlined above, you will find that in many cases you will derive incorrect scansions. Can you suggest how the correct representations of these words are arrived at in the revised grid model?

A.   The answer, of course, is through an analysis that makes use of extrametricality. There is very good evidence, as we have seen, that extrametricality operates on segments and syllables within the lexicon, and extrametricality plays an important role in grid-based word-stress rules. Consider firstly the word *Nantucket*. If IBR and HBR were to apply, the following partial grid would be constructed:

(5.53)   x   x   IBR, HBR
        x   x   x   DA
      *Nan tu cket
      CVC CV CVC

The final syllable, -cket, would be scanned as heavy. This is clearly incorrect. But if Consonant Extrametricality is allowed to apply and to precede all grid construction rules (see §3.6), then final VC syllables will be analysed as light. Operation of CE in (5.53) then gives us (5.54) by BA and application of the MSR:

(5.54)   x   MSR
           x   x   IBR, BA
           x   x   x   DA
          Nan tu   cket
          CVC CV CV(C)

The example *utensil* patterns similarly to (5.54):

(5.55)   x   MSR
           x   x   IBR, HBR
           x   x   x   DA
           u   ten   sil
          CVV CVC CV(C)

Notice one difference, however. In (5.54) penultimate stress was arrived at by scanning -*tu*- as basic beat-aligned by the operation of BA. In (5.55) -*ten*- is CVC and is thus basic beat-aligned by the HBR.

In *develop*, the patterning and derivation are similar to (5.54):

(5.56)   x   MSR
           x   x   IBR, BA
           x   x   x   DA
          de   ve   lop
          CV   CV CV(C)

Similar to (5.56) – although with operation of (initial) Destressing tending to alter the output patterns – are words such as *amalgam*, *astonish*, *electron*, *betrayal* etc. (S: 96).

Now let us turn to the third example, *America*. It is clear that neither the original word-stress rules nor CE can derive the correct pattern. An unrevised scansion, for example, might run as follows:

(5.57) a.   x   MSR
            x   x   IBR, BA
            x   x   x   x   DA
           *A   me   ri   ca
            V   CV   CV   CV

Obviously this is not what we want. Matters become clearer, however, if we follow Hayes (1982) in suggesting that the final rhyme of (many) nouns in English is extrametrical. In *America*, for instance, final-syllable extrametricality would allow us to derive (5.57b):

(5.57) b.   x
        x   x
        x   x   x   x
        A me ri ca
        V CV CV (CV)

(later /əmerikæ/ by Destressing; cf. *vanilla*, also S: 84–5).

Finally, let us look at the examples *mangrove* and *asinine*. Unlike *develop* and the *America/syllabus* examples, there is no way we can analyse the final syllable as 'extrametrically light' by CE (although the final consonant is indeed extrametrical), as the syllable in question here contains a bi-moric V. What S suggests is that in these examples we should regard the final syllable not as 'extrametrically light' but entirely extrametrical as in (5.58a, b):

(5.58) a.   x   MSR
         x x   IBR, HBR
         x x   DA
         man grove
         CVC(CCVV(C))

      b.   x   MSR
         x x   IBR, HBR
         x x x   DA
         a si nine
         V CV(CVV(C))

In both cases, since the final heavy syllable is entirely extrametrical (and this is relevant with respect to the MSR in particular), BA cannot operate (as it does in *America*, for example) to promote the penultimate syllable; in fact once a segment or syllable has been ascribed extrametrical status, it is clear that both BA and the MSR must ignore it in subsequent applications. Yet you may have noticed one or two difficulties with the analysis of final-syllable extrametricality. One particular problem runs as follows: if extrametricality precedes grid-construction rules (and S suggests that the extrametrical status of segments and syllables is marked in the lexical entries of words), how then can the HBR apply to align the final syllables of *mangrove* and *asinine* with basic beats? (And similarly, if syllables are defined as extrametrical in the lexicon, how are they then aligned with demibeats?) The answer to this particular question falls into two parts: we must consider both the idea of the *domain* on which word-stress rules are operative, and the 'type and position' distinction made by the stress rules themselves. We turn first to the 'domain' issue. Both segment and syllable extrametricality can be regarded, S suggests, as rules that in essence redefine the limits of a cyclic domain. For example, on a lower cyclic domain, a CVC syllable will be treated as CV; on a higher cyclic domain, the same syllable will be treated like any other CVC syllable:

$$\beta[. . . \alpha[. . . C \, V \, C_{em}] \; \alpha . . .]\beta$$ Cyclic domain α; CVC = CV

$$\beta[. . . \alpha[. . . C \, V]\alpha \, C_{em} . . .]\beta$$ Cyclic domain β; CVC = CVC on
that domain

A similar position applies with respect to syllable extrametricality. An extrametrical syllable will be treated as such in the 'lower' α-cycle; on the β-cycle, however, it will be treated like any other syllable:

$$\beta[. . . \alpha[. . . \sigma \; \sigma_{em}]\alpha . . .)]\beta$$

$$\beta[. . . \alpha[. . . \sigma]\alpha \; \sigma_{em} . . .]\beta$$

What does this mean in practice? Take the case of DA. DA is a grid-construction rule for which the location of the limits of a cyclic domain is irrelevant (S: 89); therefore it should not be affected by whatever extrametricality does to the limits of domains. And this is what happens: DA aligns syllables with the bottom level of the grid whether those syllables are extrametrical or not. Similarly, the HBR – a 'syllable type' rather than a 'syllable position' TGA rule – pays heed to the internal composition of a syllable but not to its position within a given domain. It is thus the case, S argues (90), that final syllables of the form CVV(C) and CVC(C) are stressed by the HBR, even though they are regarded as extrametrical by, for example, the MSR (a 'domain' rule) or indeed by BA (a 'position' rule):

Our theory is that syllable extrametricality is *relevant* only to grid construction rules for which the position of a syllable with respect to the limits of a cyclic domain is relevant, or to those grid construction rules whose structural descriptions refer to sequences of grid positions. . . . Into this category fall (i) position-sensitive basic beat rules, (ii) Beat Addition on the second metrical level . . . and (iii) domain-end prominence rules, such as the English Main Stress Rule. Thus it is entirely possible under this theory for a syllable to have been aligned with a beat by the HBR and at the same time for it to be extrametrical with respect to one of these other rules. (S: 90–1)

However, notice that S's conception of extrametricality is in this particular respect rather different from that of Hayes, who relies on a rule of Long Vowel Stressing and a separate 'extrametricality rule', to account for the fact that word-final CVV(C) syllables are stresséd but nonetheless potentially extrametrical; we ask you to comment again on this issue in the essay questions that conclude this chapter.

Q. Extrametricality, then, does a great deal of work in this analysis. Give grid scansions of the words *shampoo*, *vanilla*, *venison*, and *crocodile*, and in each analysis you give, indicate which rules, including rules of extrametricality, have applied, and how each output pattern corresponds, if at all, to examples (5.54–5.58).

A. *Shampoo* is not attested in patterns (5.54–5.58); but recall from chapter 3 that certain nouns in English (*shampoo*, *Berlin*, *canteen* etc.) do not carry extrametricality-marking in the lexicon. In *shampoo*, DA, IBR, HBR and MSR apply to give the end-stressed pattern characteristic of this section of the English lexicon:

```
(5.59)          x     MSR
          x     x     IBR, HBR
          x     x     DA
          sham  poo
          CVC   CVV
```

Vanilla patterns with those examples that undergo Consonant Extrametricality (compare *betrayal*, *amalgam*, *develop* etc.). DA, IBR, BA, MSR apply:

```
(5.60)          x           MSR
          x     x           IBR, BA
          x     x     x     DA
          va    ni    lla
          CV    CV    CV
```

Venison undergoes final-syllable extrametricality; compare *America* (5.57b). DA, IBR and MSR apply (BA is inapplicable because the final *syllable*, rather than the final *consonant*, is extrametrical – note *Pamela*; S: 85):

```
(5.61)  x                   MSR
        x                   IBR
        x     x     x       DA
        ve    ni    son
        CV    CV    (CV(C))
```

Crocodile should be compared with *asinine* (5.58b). DA, IBR, HBR and MSR operate to give the output pattern:

```
(5.62)  x                   MSR
        x           x       IBR, HBR
        x     x     x       DA
        cro   co    dile
        CCV   CV    (CVV(C))
```

In the word-stress examples we have looked at so far, we have seen how patterns of second-level basic beats are determined by reference to syllable type and position, how patterns of main word-stress are projected by a domain-end prominence rule, and how extrametricality plays a crucial part in how such TGA rules apply. To summarise: (1) Above the level of demibeats, two TGA rules are at work on the next level, the IBR (which, so S claims on page 86, is ordered before other rules operating at the basic beat level), and the HBR, which aligns CVV and CVC syllables alike with basic beats. (2) BA also operates at the level of basic beats; this can be most clearly viewed as a grid euphony (GE) rule, operating to prevent grid lapses. BA applies wherever its structural description is met, and (in English) operates right-to-left (ignoring extrametrical syllables) in a left-dominant fashion. Operating at this level of the grid, it is in a sense the grid equivalent of the Stress Retraction rule of Hayes' tree-based account of word-stress (see again section 3.6 if you need clarification on this point). (3) Main word-stress is projected by another TGA rule, the MSR, a domain-end prominence rule. Main word-stress is projected onto a minimal third grid level. (4) GE rules – in particular, BA – operate(s) at level 3 and above to ensure higher-level patterns of alternation within words (as in *chimpanzee* above). BA at this level and above does not undo the work of the MSR: main word-stress is always more prominent (by a minimal one level) than any other rhythmic stress projected on its domain by TGA and GE rules.

5.9 Nuclear Stress, Compound Stress and Beat Movement

In the foregoing, despite some oversimplification and omission, notably of her rules of Destressing (see S: 111–31, and compare the discussions of Destressing in chapter 3), we have seen how S's model is in some ways both more elaborate and more inclusive than the analysis presented in Hayes (1982) or in P. In particular, it seems that just as the outline we gave earlier of P's End Rule suggested that his grid-based rule could very adequately capture the properties of English word-stress, so S's analysis does a similar job. Indeed, S's analysis in some ways offers distinct improvements (although these are perhaps fairly general and conceptual, rather than technical improvements) over earlier metrical models. Yet problems remain for the grid-based analysis. In P's model, for instance, it seemed that the inadequacies inherent in a 'grid-level' formulation of Move x mirrored the difficulties encountered in equating grid levels with prosodic strata. Does S's model – despite the apparent adequacy of the word-stress rules – fare any better in this respect? There must remain the nagging suspicion that S's model encodes a prosodic hierarchy 'in disguise', and perhaps the best way to test this suspicion is to examine how S's model handles rhythmic restructuring.

Q. Because the rule that 'moves x' applies very largely at the supra-word level (although it does occur in 'words' like *expectation*) we must first discuss how TGA rules project Nuclear and Compound Stress (recall the discussion in the earlier part of this chapter). How would you formulate Nuclear and Compound Stress rules within the revised grid-only format?

A. It is a straightforward assumption that Nuclear Stress is normally projected onto the rightmost level 3 grid entry within a specified syntactic domain (phrase). Thus within the revised format the Nuclear Stress Rule most clearly applies as another domain-end prominence rule. In a sentence such as (5.63), for example, a grid-based NSR will apply three times, in each case cycling on the rightmost strong beat that was constructed by earlier TGA rules (in (5.63) we indicate what you must take to be L3 prominences on the bottom level of the grid for clarity):

(5.63)

```
                                          x
                    x                     x
    x         x         x         x       x
[[Batman and Robin]_NP [meet [the Yellow Peril]_NP]_VP]_S
```

Informally, S (147) states the NSR as follows:

Within a given phrase, the beat of the metrical grid aligned with the rightmost (immediate) daughter constituent of the phrase that is (a) the most prominent beat of (that part of) the grid and (b) on at least the third metrical level is made the most prominent beat of the metrical grid aligned with the entire phrase.

Given this formulation (and we leave it to you to confirm that such an informal statement will in fact apply correctly to (5.63)), it should be clear that the NSR applies cyclically, first on lower-level phrasal domains (*Batman and Robin, Yellow Peril*) and then on higher (the entire S in (5.63), whereby *Peril* becomes the 'strongest stress'). However, notice that the informal version of the NSR given above makes crucial reference to the notion of 'syntactic phrase': it was the explicit correlation between syntactic categories of this kind and particular grid levels that led to the various problems with P's Move x – where 'height' was defined by reference to constituency. It seems *a priori* desirable, then, to reformulate the NSR so that it applies solely in grid terms, making no (necessary) reference to the internal constituent structure of the phrase on which it is applying. S (149) reformulates the NSR in the following terms: 'Within a given syntactic phrase, the rightmost beat of the metrical grid (fragment) aligned with the (entire) phrase that is on at least the third metrical level is made the most prominent beat of that grid (fragment).' And such a formulation of the rule will indeed give the pattern seen in (5.63).

Q. There is, however, another problem with this revised formulation of the NSR. Making reference to (5.23) and the subsequent examples in this chapter if necessary, specify what this problem is.

A. The type of example that poses a problem for this version of the NSR is shown by *screenprint*, an N N compound. Just as we saw that P's. End Rule ran into difficulties with (5.23), so the NSR meets the same difficulty here: because, in compounds of the N N type, the rightmost word is given L3 grid-alignment by the rules of word-stress, the reformulated NSR will take that to be the 'rightmost beat' on which it is to apply within that grid (fragment):

(5.64)   x
         x   x   x   x   x
*(He confessed to liking) [Japanese screenprints]

Notice, however, that the 'informal' version of the NSR given above does not run into this problem: it makes reference to 'immediate (daughter) constituents'. In (5.64) *-prints* is not an immediate constituent of the phrase *Japanese screenprints*, and its own prominence will not therefore be discussion at (5.23) above): put in this way, the NSR and CSR would be but some ways preferable to the more concise, grid-based version. Yet, presumably the grid-based version could indeed apply if we assume with P that extrametricality operates at the 'word level' in compounds (recall the discussion at (5.23) above: put in this way, the NSR and CSR would be but higher-level reflexes of the MSR. As we noted earlier, if this assumption proves to be true it would be a striking result. This option is denied to S, however, who restricts extrametricality to segments and syllables, retaining the elaborate version of the NSR and a separate statement of the CSR. Both rules are formalised in terms of grid levels in (5.65) and (5.66) below (S: 151):

(5.65) *NSR* x_j
                                            :

$[\alpha \ldots [\beta \ldots x_i \ldots]\beta]\alpha \longrightarrow [\alpha \ldots [\beta \ldots x_i \ldots]\beta]\alpha$

The CSR is simply a mirror image of (5.65), and the conditions are the same as for that rule:

(5.66) *CSR* x_j
                                            :

$[\alpha [\beta \ldots x_i \ldots]\beta \ldots]\alpha \qquad [\alpha [\beta \ldots x_i \ldots]\beta \ldots]\alpha$

We assume that you will by now be familiar enough with these rules, and indeed with the rules that manipulate and interpret grids, for these formulations to be straightforward.

Having discussed the NSR and CSR, we must now move on to look at rhythmic restructuring at the phrasal level. By now it should be clear that, just as the other higher-level metrical rule, the Addition rule, we have looked at in the revised grid format is cast as a GE rule, so P's Move x will be recast as a GE, 'Beat Movement' rule, applying to alleviate grid clashes at higher metrical levels in the now familiar fashion:

(5.67) *Beat Movement*

$$
\begin{array}{ccccccc}
x_i & x & & x & & & x \\
x & x & x & \longrightarrow & x & x & x
\end{array}
$$

Condition: x_i is a weak beat (recall that a weak beat is simply a beat that is not aligned at a higher metrical level). Beat Movement works just as Move x works (and after all, they are almost identical rules) in phrases such as *next door neighbour, Modern English Dictionary* (some grid levels omitted for clarity):

(5.68)

$$
\begin{array}{cccccccc}
& & x & & & & & x \\
& x & x & & & x & & x \\
x & x & x\ldots & & x & x & & x\ldots
\end{array}
$$

next door neighbour $\longrightarrow$ next door neighbour

(5.69)

$$
\begin{array}{cccccccc}
& & x & & & & & x \\
& x & x & & & x & & x \\
x & x & x\ldots & & x & x & & x\ldots
\end{array}
$$

Modern English Dictionary $\longrightarrow$ Modern English Dictionary

What is significant at this stage is not how Beat Movement handles these straightforward examples, but how it operates on those examples that stymied P's Move x, the *Japanese bamboo* and . . . *hard-boiled egg* cases. It is clear that, on the face of it, these examples might form the same problems for Beat Movement as they did for Move x – unsurprisingly, since Beat Movement is 'the same rule':

(5.70)

$$
\begin{array}{cccc}
& & x & \\
& x & & x \\
x & x & x & x
\end{array}
$$

Japanese bamboo $\longrightarrow$??

(5.71)

$$
\begin{array}{cccccccc}
& & & x & & & & x \\
& x & & x & & & x & x \\
x & x & x & x & & x & x & x & x
\end{array}
$$

almost hard-boiled egg $\longrightarrow$ almost hard-boiled egg

In (5.70) the SD of Beat Movement is not met. In (5.71), Beat Movement will apply to promote *hard-*. How does S meet these problems? If we understand S correctly, cases like *Japanese bamboo* are to be taken as patterning with her examples *telegraphic communication*, *ideal editorial* etc., where 'the first beat in the second word is not a third-level beat, but only a second-level one. . . . Here there is no clash . . . yet Beat Movement is possible. . . . If a clash is a necessary condition for Beat Movement, how can it apply here?' (S: 189).

Look at the fully constructed grids for these problem cases:

(5.72)
```
                    x
           x        x
   x   x   x   x
   x x x   x   x
Japanese bamboo
```

(5.73)
```
                            x
           x                x
   x   x           x   x
   x x   x   x   x   x x x x
telegraphic communication
```

(5.74)
```
               x
       x       x
   x   x x   x
   x   x x x x x
ideal editorial
```

What S suggests is that representations such as (5.72–5.74) are 'not in fact the appropriate pre-Beat Movement configurations for the stress-shifted pronunciations of these phrases'. She claims that where Beat Movement does take place, the strongest beats of the first and second words bear 'pitch-accents', and are on these intonational grounds aligned with still higher fourth/fifth level grid positions. In such cases a grid clash will of course be defined and Beat Movement can apply. The central problem is – how? Although there is some evidence to suggest that the presence of pitch-accent produces greater rhythmic prominence (see S: 190), and although S goes on to defend a 'pitch-accent first' hypothesis wherein intonational structure is freely assigned to English phrases before phonological rules themselves come into play, it seems evident that the pitch-accent argument simply does not work to allow Beat Movement in (5.72–5.74). If we do assume that the relevant grid columns of these examples are strengthened by one level, then the pre-Beat Movement (?) structures are, respectively:

(5.72')
```
                    x
        x           x
        x           x
    x   x   x       x
    x x x   x       x
    Japanese bamboo
```

(5.73')
```
                            x
            x               x
            x               x
        x   x           x   x
        x x x   x   x   x x x x
        telegraphic communication
```

(5.74')
```
                x
        x       x
        x       x
    x   x x     x
    x   x x x x x
    ideal editorial
```

These structures are nominally clashing, but Beat Movement cannot, surely, apply: its SD (5.67) is not met, and there is nowhere for the clashing x to move. S's suggestion therefore seems, as we understand it, quite wrong – unless of course Beat Movement is licensed under these special conditions of 'pitch-accent' to move *two* grid rows leftwards. But it is clear that if Beat Movement is to be formulated elegantly, only one x must move at any one time, and stipulation of 'special conditions' makes the grid-based formulation ever more complicated, and has extremely undesirable repercussions elsewhere. (By way of contrast, notice how clearly a tree-based approach permits Reversal in these phrases.)

Q. What of the second range of problem cases, the *almost hard-boiled egg*, *slightly underripe pear* set? Take the example *rather lily-white hands*, and show what representation(s) Beat Movement will lead to.

A. After word-stress and phrase-stress rules have applied, the representation is that of (5.75a):

(5.75) a.
```
                    x
                x   x
        x   x   x   x
        x   x   x   x
        x x x x   x   x
        rather lily-white hands
```

Beat Movement will apply to shift the clashing topmost x on *white* leftwards (L1 and L2 structure omitted below):

(5.75) b.
```
                        x
          x             x
      x   x     x       x
      rather lily-white hands
```

Although we could regard a surface structure similar to (5.75b) as a possible output pattern for *almost hard-boiled egg* (and perhaps 'intonational phrasing' plays a role here too), it seems far more desirable to search for a more principled alternative, one that does reflect the 'eurhythmic' nature of the phrase(s) where the second greatest prominence is on the far left. In S, this alternative makes use again of BA, where it applies immediately after the 'word-stress' cycle(s) and first NSR cycle (S: 180):

(5.76) a.
```
      x       x   x   x
      x       x   x   x
      x   x   x   x   x
      almost hard-boiled egg ('word-stress')
```

b.
```
                      x
                  x   x
      x           x   x
      x   x   x   x
      x   x   x   x
      x   x   x   x
      [[almost hard-boiled] egg] (NSR, BA)
```

c.
```
                      x
      ←-----------x   x
      x           x   x
      x   x   x   x
      x   x   x   x
      x   x   x   x
      almost hard-boiled egg (Beat Movement)
```

d.
```
                      x
      x               x
      x   ←----x       x
      x   x   x   x
      x   x   x   x
      x   x   x   x
      almost hard-boiled egg (Beat Movement)
```

The output pattern to (5.76) is, presumably, the one we want; but it is derived at some cost. Notice that throughout the discussion of (5.72ff) various assumptions have been made about Beat Movement's application that are not entirely straightforward. First, the 'pitch-accent hypothesis': does it always apply? And if not, on what grounds are certain structures picked out for it? And is it not the case that the pitch-accent hypothesis, even in its 'optional' form, makes Beat Movement rather difficult to constrain? Doesn't it seem to be a case of 'going outside the grid' to find the information that grid structure itself lacks? Secondly, the role of BA in (5.76): by way of contrast, notice how clearly an LP-style derivation would proceed, by two applications of Reversal, [w s] $\longrightarrow$ [s w], triggered in each case by a clashing grid; even the pre-shift SD Kiparsky gives to Reversal (recall 4:20) seems preferable to the 'inter-cyclic' BA-triggered Beat Movement in (5.76). Both the earlier model (LP) and a tree-only model seem considerably simpler than S's derivation in (5.76), and this may lead us to suspect that the grid-only model is in fact insufficiently richly structured to handle cases like these. In fact, it seems to be true that the two crucial problems we have encountered with Move x/Beat Movement – the lack of sufficient (underlying) grid structure to permit movement in cases like (5.72–5.74), (5.76), and the lack of sufficient structure to allow formulation of the conditions under which movement is prohibited – are a direct reflection of the paucity of grid-marked phonological structure compared, for example, to the kind of structuring found in trees. In this sense, it is indeed arguable that the grid, hierarchised overtly or covertly, can only derive output patterns via Addition and Movement rules at considerable expense in terms of elegance.

Finally, recall that we mentioned earlier that S's model gave a place to intonational structure in the form of silent demibeats (see (5.46) and the brief comments there). We do not intend to discuss this issue in any detail here, but only S's claim that the presence or absence of silent demibeats 'will be responsible for a fair amount of the variability in Beat Movement' (S: 183), and that the silent (demi)beats introduced by Silent Demibeat Alignment (SDA) 'may in effect "undo" a clash that might have otherwise been present if the underlying metrical grid alignment of the sentence were simply the alignment of its syllables with the grid according to the principles outlined here' (S: 184). The minimal contrast is that between *Marcel Proust* where, it is claimed, Beat Movement is virtually obligatory, and *Marcel proved it*, where Beat Movement is apparently highly disfavoured (S: 184). Notably, the core theory of prominence relations, outlined in this chapter, will lead to an identical grid being constructed in both cases:

(5.77)
```
              x
         x    x
      x  x    x
      x  x    x
      Marcel Proust
      Marcel proved (it)
```

What, then, constitutes the difference in the likelihood of Beat Movement applying? S argues that it is precisely the presence or absence of silent demibeats. If silent demibeats are added optionally at the end of a word, at the end of a branching constituent, and at the end of a daughter of the sentence node (see S: 184 ff for a discussion and justification of these assumptions), then the phrases in (5.77) will bear different grid representations:

(5.78) a.
```
                  x        b.                      x
         x        x                    x           x
      x  x        x                 x  x           x
      x  x (x)    x                 x  x (x) x  x  x
      Marcel   Proust              Marcel       proved (it)
```

Grid structure (5.78a) is clashing, and will of course permit Beat Movement. But what about (5.78b)? In its present form, it too is clashing. Yet S argues (185) that BA applies here as well: 'Beat Addition knows nothing of the individual alignments of grid positions – it is an operation defined strictly on the grid, and hence will apply to silent and syllable-aligned positions alike.' In (5.78b), then, BA applies to 'undo' a potential clash:

(5.78) c.
```
                  x
         x        x
      x  x    x   x
      x  x (x) x  x  x
      Marcel      proved (it)
```

Again, we shall not discuss this issue any further here, but instead refer you to S (especially 197ff) for a much fuller discussion of the 'grammar of intonation'. You should note, however, that the grammar of intonation and the grammar of phonology are indeed linked (in phenomena such as intra-word pausing, final lengthening, and 'silent stress' – see also the following chapter), although to what extent the metrical models we are sketching here might represent this interrelationship is, we feel, another question that needs further research.

In sum, the formulation of a 'grid-only' phonology still contains many problems, largely because the metrical model is too powerful. When rules relating to the rhythm of English are formulated as Addition and

Movement rules on metrical grids, it appears that constraint is difficult – although S's hypothesis as to the constraining effect of silent demibeats is attractive. In addition, the fact that neither P's nor S's model can derive stress-shift in a collocation such as *Japanese bamboo* without appeal to the notions of eurhythmy or 'pitch-accent' seems to be a crucial shortcoming, for, in P's terms, eurhythmy is invoked when other grid-movement operations become impossible (thus making his model even more powerful, and even more difficult to constrain); in S's terms, the 'pitch-accent' theory simply leads to the inapplicability of Beat Movement. Further, particularly in the light of S's recent work on phonological structures, the equation P makes between certain grid levels and certain phonological constituents seems curious, since it leads – as we have seen – both to a problematic view of those constituents and to a rather arbitrary analysis of Iambic Reversal and its grid-equivalent, Move x, in English. However, S's model seems to make life little easier, largely because her TGA rules – and therefore the grid height and representation of lexical items – depend partly on morpho-syntax, and this may lead us to suspect that the grids of S's model encode a prosodic hierarchy 'in disguise'. In fact, the brief outline we have given of the grid-only model seems to suggest that a phonology expressed in terms of grids alone raises more problems – especially in the broad area of 'rhythmical well-formedness' – than these revised grid structures have so far been capable of solving. We might conclude this section by stating that the arguments put forward by P and S are promising, but not conclusive; if the consequences of abandoning tree structure are so problematic for a grid-only metrical model, then there seems to be a case for retaining the kind of prosodic organisation found in tree structures.

5.10   A 'tree-and-grid' phonology

This is essentially the position of Hayes (1984), who, as we noted earlier, argues for the retention of both the tree and the grid in a metrical phonology, relating linguistic stress to tree structure, and the 'level-and-pattern' aspects of rhythmic organisation (S 1984b: 162) to the grid. Initially, Hayes adopts almost unchanged LP's general scheme of trees and grids, with those grids built up by reference to tree structure. The way Hayes marks grids is similar, too, to that of LP: he marks every syllable on L1 of the grid, then, at a second level, assigns a grid mark 'to the strongest syllable of every phonological word' in conformity with the general requirement that 'content words' should be grid-marked. Hayes suggests, like LP, that the grid is completed by assigning sufficient additional marks so that the strongest syllable of every constituent labelled *s* has a higher grid column than the strongest syllable of its weak sister. Hayes then reviews the shortcomings and problems of LP's original theory, proposing rules of Beat Addition and eurhythmy to rectify LP's theoretical failures; he then gives an alternative account of stress clashes in terms of the grid and eurhythmic rules.

At this stage, what is significant for us is the later part of Hayes' 1984 paper, where he defends the role tree structure has to play in metrical description. He brings forward several important points relating to the *effect* of tree structure on those grid (re)configurations that have in the work of P and S been defined as operating on grid levels by making reference to the notion of euphony (the PRA) or to the syntactic structures that underpin each grid. In addition, if differences in tree structure can be seen to lead to differences in phonological behaviour, then we have even more of a case for retaining tree structure, as certain aspects of prominence relations will thus be uniquely defined.

Consider the examples which follow. (The particulars of these grids are rather different from those we have seen in the grid-only model; this is a consequence of Hayes' rules of grid construction. In particular, lexical monosyllables are marked, in Hayes' model, on only a second level in their citation forms.) In *Peter's three red shirts*, for instance, a grid-only model might derive the 'perfect' alternating rhythmical pattern by multiple applications of Beat Addition in accordance with eurhythmic rules (the PRA) as follows:

```
(5.79) a.                               b.                        x
                                              x                   x
                              x               x      x            x
        x         x   x   x           x       x   x   x
        x x       x   x   x           x x     x   x   x
        Peter's three red shirts      Peter's three red shirts
```

Similarly, a 'perfect' or eurhythmic grid identical to (5.79b) is arrived at in the output of our paradigm example *almost hard-boiled egg* as a consequence of two iterations through Iambic Reversal:

```
(5.79) c.               x
        x               x
        x       x       x
        x       x   x   x
        x   x   x   x   x
        almost hard-boiled egg
```

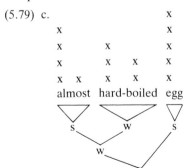

Next, consider the example *overboiled egg blues*. Notice that it, like *Peter's three red shirts* and *almost hard-boiled egg*, consists of five syllables – four 'modifier' syllables and a monosyllabic head, or designated terminal element (DTE). The reason we emphasise what seems to be merely a syllabic count is that, as we saw in chapter 4, four syllables constitutes a 'target distance' under Hayes' rules of eurhythmy; in quadrisyllabic concatenations such as *Mississippi (Mabel)* and *multilingual (text)*, these level-and-pattern aspects of rhythmic prominence seem almost certain to apply. Hayes formalises this principle in his Quadrisyllabic Rule, which posited, you will remember, that 'A grid is eurhythmic when it contains a row whose marks are spaced close to four syllables apart' (1984: 46).

But to return to our example *overboiled egg blues*. Reversal is apparently possible on two pairs of nodes (see Hayes 1984: 61):

(5.80) a.   b.

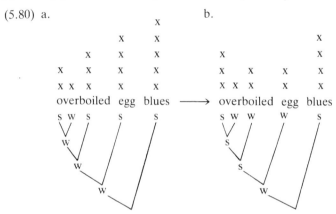

Look at the terminals of the tree of (5.80b). Like the terminals for an example such as *Peter's three red shirts*, they fall into an [s w w w s] terminal pattern and, again like (5.79a, b), it might appear as if (5.80b) would be susceptible to Beat Addition, since the output of (5.80b), augmented by Beat Addition, would be more eurhythmic under the terms of Hayes' second rule of eurhythmy, the 'Disyllabic Rule', where 'domains delimited on the level of scansion should be divided evenly by a mark on the next lower grid level' (Hayes 1984: 48).

A grid augmented in this fashion would appear as (5.80c), well-formed under the Disyllabic Rule but – surely – ill-formed in other respects:

(5.80) c.   x

    x------------------x   ('level of scansion')

    x-----x-----------x   (level of 'even division' – Disyllabic Rule)

    x   x   x   x

    x x x   x   x

    overboiled egg blues

Recall that we have seen a similar problem before: other modifiers appear not to undergo stress-shift operations, for example, when they are constrained by rules such as P's subjacency constraint on Move x. Similarly, here it is Beat Addition that must be prevented from applying in (5.80c). But why?

Q. Work out one reason why Beat Addition appears to apply straightforwardly in examples such as *Peter's three red shirts*, but not in *overboiled egg blues*.

A. The answer apparently lies in the *constraining effect* of tree structure on grid reconfiguration – in particular, of the type of branchingness dominating the modifier in question. In *Peter's three red shirts*, for example, the underlying tree structure was right-branching, but the constituent to which we might want to apply Beat Addition, *three*, is itself a left branch:

(5.81)

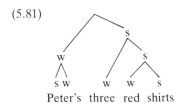

Peter's three red shirts

In *overboiled egg blues*, on the other hand, the tree structure is left-branching overall, but the (sub)constituent *boiled* is itself a right branch:

(5.82)

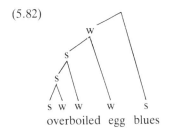

overboiled egg blues

Although we have seen that appeal to pseudosyntactic conditions similar to branchingness (for example P's subjacency condition on Move x) is problematic – and remember that the relationship of tree structure and syntactic structure is not, in any case, *necessarily* one-to-one; see chapter 3 – these examples suggest fairly strongly that the type of branchingness found in tree structures is *restrictive*, at least in terms of the applicability of Beat Addition. For Hayes, it is precisely the difference in tree shapes between:

(5.81')

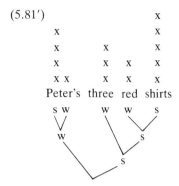

```
                    x
    x               x       ('level of scansion'; eurhythmic under QR)
    x       x       x       ('level of even division'; DR)
    x       x   x   x
    x x     x   x   x
  Peter's three red shirts
   s w     w   w   s
```

and:

(5.82')

```
                x
    x           x
    x   x   x   x
    x x x   x   x
  overboiled egg blues
   s w w    w   s
```

that permits Beat Addition in the former example, but debars it in the latter. The right branches of trees – more specifically, right branches of trees whose nodes are labelled [s . . w . . w] either in their citation forms or through node relabelling after Reversal has applied – apparently constrain Beat Addition, and this effect, writes Hayes, 'is robust and reproducible' (1984: 61). Further, he writes (1984: 62) that data of this kind:

. . . form a *prima facie* case that trees are necessarily involved in the formulation of the Rhythm Rule – the *constituent structure* of a phrase determines whether a specific grid target may be achieved. In particular, the following descriptive generalisation appears to hold:

Right Branch Constraint
Beat Addition may not add to a column if the maximal constituent of which it is the strongest element is a right branch.

From this, however, it is clearly but a small step to formulating Beat Addition not *solely* in terms of the grid, but rather, as an arboreal rule which adjoins certain nodes of the citation tree structure, grids being reconfigured simply in accordance with the demands of the recreated trees. Hayes casts this arboreal rule as a rule of *adjunction*, that is, as a rule which adjoins the nodes of the relevant tree. In *three red shirts*, for example, the metrical tree is structured initially as follows:

Q. How would you adjoin nodes on the above tree so that a grid of the following form would result from the adjunction?

```
            x
   x        x
   x    x   x
   x    x   x
   A    B   C
```

A. One possible answer might be to adjoin the two *w*-labelled nodes dominating *three red* . . . as follows:

(5.83)

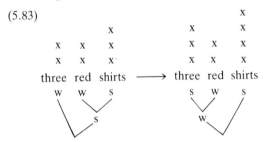

(As Hayes notes, adjunction of this kind presupposes that the adjoined node will always be (re)labelled *w* after adjunction has applied.)

Similarly, a derivation of the rhythmical patterning of *Farrah Fawcett-Majors* (see 4:33) would operate along the same lines, the grid reconfiguring after the adjunction of the two relevant *w*-nodes:

(5.84)

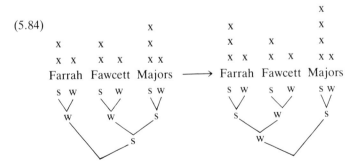

We think it is significant that Hayes uses tree structure to such effect in these and similar examples. Notice what it is that the grid now does: it simply duplicates the prominence relations expressed in the tree. In fact, it seems as if the grids above are not *linguistic* representations at all (if they are, they seem redundant because of the role of the tree from which they derive).

For Hayes, grids are *not* linguistic representations; rather, he argues, they 'represent rhythmic structure. They are projected from trees by convention . . . and they may influence the application of phonological rules through the rules of eurhythmy' (1984: 65). This definition of the role of the grid does not seem very satisfactory; we have already seen that the convention (which is essentially that of LP's initial theory) through which grids are projected from trees is problematic in nature. Moreover, Hayes' circumspect formulation above ('. . . they may influence . . .') seems to suggest that rules of eurhythmy are only appealed to when phonological operations such as Iambic Reversal are otherwise blocked (recall too our comments on this aspect of P's model). What Hayes *does* recognise is the importance of tree structure; grids merely reflect the 'level-and-pattern', the 'eurhythmic' aspects, of rhythmic structure in English; they are unavailable to the model in the statement of certain phonological operations, which Hayes argues should be defined uniquely on tree structure. The adjunction rule we saw in preliminary operation above, for example, is specified more formally as the phonological rule below, which can only operate on tree structure (although of course it will *affect* the grid). Notice that the formulation gives as its structural description a tree configuration relevant not only to the kind of [w w s] structures we have already discussed, but relevant also to the underlying [w s s] structure of the Reversal rule; notice, too, that the rule's output gives an alternating [s w s] pattern identical to the output of Iambic Reversal; perhaps this new rule could be regarded in the light of a general 'Rhythm Rule' of English, of which Reversal and 'W-pairing' (as, following Giegerich (1985), we will call the specific adjunction [w w s] ⟶ [s w s]) form subparts:

Rhythmic Adjustment
In the configuration . . . X Y . . . DTE, adjoin Y to X

As noted, such a rule will apply to all structures of the kind:

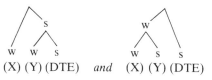

   (X) (Y) (DTE)   *and*   (X) (Y) (DTE)

Q. However, as Hayes (1984: 65) points out, the rule as it stands 'overgenerates wildly'. Using your own data as far as possible, specify in what ways such a rule will overgenerate and lead to ill-formed output structures.

A.   You may have noticed that the rule would (since it is formulated in terms of variables X and Y rather than in terms of specifically labelled tree nodes) allow adjunction of terminal *s*-nodes as well as applying to pairs of *w* terminals standing in the relevant configuration. For example, the rule would operate to adjoin *ss* in the following tree – remember that the dots in the original formulation of the rule (. . . X Y . . . DTE) in principle allow any material to intervene between the element Y and the DTE:

(5.85)

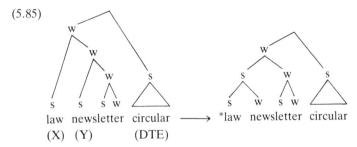

law newsletter circular ⟶ *law newsletter circular
(X)   (Y)   (DTE)

Similarly, Rhythmic Adjustment allows left-branches that terminate in *w*-labelled syllables to be reconfigured: in Hayes' theory the phrase *overboiled egg blues*, after two applications of Reversal, is seen as in (5.80b). However, Rhythmic Adjustment allows a still further reconfiguration:

(5.86)

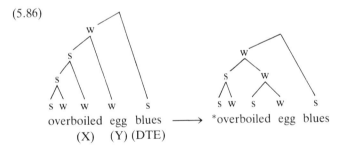

overboiled egg blues ⟶ *overboiled egg blues
(X)   (Y) (DTE)

We have noted before that tree structures of this kind constrain phonological processes such as Beat Addition (see also 5.80 and what follows it). Such data might form a fairly strong argument *against* casting Rhythmic Adjustment as an arboreal rule. For Hayes, however, this is not so. He introduces one further principle that constrains still further the prolific effects of Rhythmic Adjustment rule. This principle he calls the 'Maximality Principle' (Hayes 1984: 66), which we cite below for convenience:

Maximality Principle
Rules that manipulate tree structure must analyse maximal terms.

'Maximality' is formally defined by Hayes as follows:

Let R be a rule whose SD contains the terms $t_1, t_2 \ldots t_n$
Let T be a tree containing the constituents $c_1, c_2 \ldots c_m$ ($m \leq n$), matched up to the appropriate terms of R.
c_i of T is *maximal* iff there is no node c_j that
  a. satisfies R
  b. dominates c_i
  c. does not dominate any other member of the sequence $c_1, c_2 \ldots c_m$.

Such a formulation seems fairly complex; but as Hayes notes, the sense of such a principle is fairly simple: '. . . rules will not apply to small constituents if larger ones are available that do not overlap' (Hayes 1984: 66).

Q. Check for yourself that the Maximality Principle will in fact debar Rhythmic Adjustment of the kind we noted in (5.85) and (5.86).
A. Let us take the specimen examples, and work through the principle in an ordered way.

(5.85)

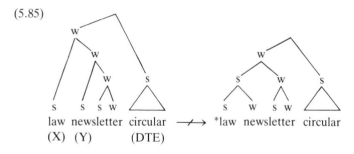

law newsletter circular $\longrightarrow\!\!\!/\!\!\!\longrightarrow$ *law newsletter circular
(X) (Y) (DTE)

In (5.85) Adjustment is blocked since the Adjustment Rule, supplemented by the Maximality Principle, cannot analyse Y as a maximal term; there *is* a node that dominates other members of the citation sequence, the node that dominates *newsletter* without dominating *law* or the DTE, *circular*.

The Maximality Principle will also block Adjustment in examples such as (5.86):

(5.86)

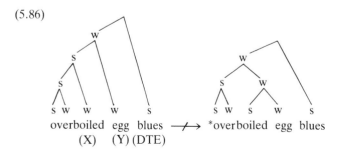

overboiled egg blues $\longrightarrow\!\!\!/\!\!\!\longrightarrow$ *overboiled egg blues
(X) (Y) (DTE)

The Adjustment Rule cannot analyse -*boiled* as X since, again, there is a constituent, *overboiled*, which dominates -*boiled* without dominating *egg* or *blues*. It appears, then, as if the Maximality Principle 'correctly trims back . . . cases of overgeneration' (Hayes 1984: 66). In addition, as Hayes notes, use of the Maximality Principle makes explicit formulation of the Right Branch Constraint unnecessary, since the Maximality Principle automatically excludes such potential violations. It also – and this is of relevance to the next chapter – obliges a metrical derivation to proceed from the 'largest' or uppermost set of nodes where the SD of metrical rules is found.

In sum, Hayes' arguments towards the retention of tree structure seems quite convincing. But notice that the metrical grids above simply duplicate the prominence relations expressed in tree structure(s). For Hayes, of course, grids are necessary as devices from which information concerning eurhythmy may be obtained (or upon which, perhaps, information concerning eurhythmy may be defined). In this sense, the grids of this model are *illustrative*. But the question now arises as to whether the kind of grid structures we have looked at here are 'merely' illustrative, and whether rhythmical well-formedness could be equally and with less cost defined upon tree structure alone. It is to this question that we turn in the following chapter.

Notes and further reading

5.2   Both this and the following three sections lean heavily on the first part of Prince (1983). For useful criticisms of Prince's theory see Giegerich (1984, 1985), especially §4.3 of the later work.

5.6   The elaboration and revision of grid-only theory in Selkirk (1984b) is absolutely essential reading. Both this reference and Prince (1983) are indispensable for understanding what a grid-based 'metrical phonology' can do – and what it can't. You should also read §4.1.2ff in Selkirk (1984b), which is a thorough examination of the 'grammar of intonation' as it may be expressed in a metrical model.

5.10 The most important paper on tree-and-grid phonology is again Hayes (1984). On a possible application of such a phonology to the scansion of verse, see Hayes (1983).

Essay and discussion topics

1. Selkirk (1984b: 70) claims that 'the patterns of rhythmic prominence in language can be insightfully characterised by a set of quite general grid-based rhythmic principles, the rules of grid euphony, in conjunction with a set of syntactic-structure-based principles, the text-to-grid alignment rules'. How far is this claim justified?

2. What representations may be given to simple compounds in the grid-based metrical model(s)? Which representation seems to be the most descriptively adequate? What conclusions do you draw from this?

3. Which analysis of final syllable extrametricality is preferable – that of Hayes (1982) or Selkirk (1984b)?

4. Compare the rules of word-stress given in chapter 3 here with the grid-based rules of word-stress presented in Prince (1983) and/or Selkirk (1984b). Which metrical analysis is to be preferred, and why?

5. What problems have you encountered in trying to formalise Move x/Beat Movement?

6. How far is the 'grammar of phonology' related to the 'grammar of intonation'?

7. Hayes (1984: 59) argues that trees and grids 'represent different things'. What are these things? Is Hayes' argument well-founded?

8. Giegerich (1984: 31) suggests that grid-only phonology 'won't come to grips with' phonological structure. On what grounds do you think this suggestion was made?

9. Choose any *one* of the metrical models discussed so far (LP; Prince 1983 and/or Selkirk 1984b; Hayes 1984). Show why the model you have chosen gives a more adequate representation (or solution) to any one phonological issue or problem that particularly interests you.

6   *The phonology of rhythm (3):*
'tree-only' metrical phonology

6.1   *Introduction*

In chapter 5 we saw that a wholly grid-based metrical model might prove to be descriptively inadequate. In our review of Prince's Move *x* (Selkirk's Beat Movement), for example, we saw that that rule failed to capture well-attested insights about the phonological structures involved in stress-shift operations: not only did Prince's assumption of a grid-aligned prosodic hierarchy seem arbitrary (and to some extent the same charge may be brought against Selkirk's model), but the failure of his model to derive Move *x* in *Japanese bamboo* seemed theoretically critical – particularly since that example, and others like it, can be shown to undergo Reversal in a tree-based format in a relatively unproblematic fashion. Moreover, the rules that manipulated grid structures were, as we saw, difficult to constrain or order. For example, various 'repair strategies', or 'housekeeping rules', are necessary in Prince's model; but as Dogil has written, 'In all cases . . . the choice of any of these repair strategies would be totally unmotivated.' In addition, Dogil continues, Prince's model '. . . provides no evaluation measure stating which of the additional devices like extrametricality, initial beat addition, forward clash override, etc., take priority in application. . . . [O]rdering relations and mode of application of rules are nowhere evaluated, although the results very much depend on specifications of them.' (1984: 289–90).

In the last chapter, then, as a consequence of the various apparent shortcomings of the grid-only approach advocated by Prince, and by Selkirk (1984b), we saw that it would be difficult to abandon tree structure altogether, especially if – and this was Hayes' point – trees express things about phonological structure that go uncaptured in a grid-only model. Indeed, it might well prove to be the case that a revised concept of tree structure would be able to do the job at least as well. Since, apparently, we cannot abandon tree structure, might it not be worthwhile to reconsider its nature and scope? Giegerich's work on phonological structure is to some extent based on those concepts of phonological structure expressed in LP's initial model, chief of which is the idea that phonological constituency and prominence relations are best expressed in binary-branching metrical trees. His interpretation of tree structure, of the rules that manipulate it, and, in particular, of rhythmical structure, is, however, different from that of LP, Prince (1983), Selkirk (1980, 1984b) or Hayes (1984). It is this difference that is our concern here, for Giegerich's is the fullest expression so far of a metrical phonology without grids.

In Giegerich's model, two phonological constituents receive special attention: the syllable and the foot. We have already seen in chapter 2 how important the syllable is in metrical description; it is seemingly crucial to retain this constituent in any metrical model (cf. Selkirk 1984b: 22–6). In chapter 3 we also saw that many generalisations concerning word-stress could arguably be captured by viewing the stressed-stressless distinction as a corollary of the contrast between unstressed syllables and stress feet, which invariably imply at least underlying prominence. This distinction is preserved in Giegerich's work – but the foot is given, as we shall see, a rather different emphasis. For the moment you should simply note that the syllable forms the 'lowest' constituent in word-level metrical structure; feet are the next 'highest' constituents at the word level, and their labelling, determined in LP's model by the LCPR, is of course relevant at the phrase level too. The point of drawing such a distinction is as follows: Giegerich suggests that word-level metrical structure, and operations consequent to its origination, is defined in the lexicon. Phrase-level metrical structure, on the other hand, is produced after the completion of the syntactic surface structure; this enables us, for example, to construct right-strong, phrase-level metrical trees by reference to the appropriate syntactic constituency.

After word-level and phrase-level features of the phonology have been derived, what we have are phonological underlying forms. But as we have seen, such base forms undergo various metrical transformations so that rhythmically well-formed phonological surface structures get produced. These transformations, Giegerich argues, form a separate *metrical component* of the grammar, a component which motivates the production of quasi-autonomous phonological structures that in turn undergo phonetic interpretation before the rules of segmental phonology (assimilation, aspiration and so on) come into play (G 1985: 17–18). You will of course notice that what Giegerich calls the 'metrical component' is directly comparable to what Selkirk calls 'phonological rules' proper, that operate after those rules which construct or define each representation; see again §5.6 for further discussion.

Two points arise from Giegerich's assumptions. The first relates to the phrase 'quasi-autonomous' used above; we use this specific term since we assume, with Giegerich, that structures derived via the metrical component of the grammar gradually become 'more and more remote from syntactic structure' (G 1985: 17; also Selkirk 1984b: 31–5). That is, while base forms of the phonology are (must be) congruent in important respects with syntactic surface structure, phonological surface structure is not necessarily congruent with, and conceivably does not make reference to, syntactic information of any kind. It is in this sense that metrical derivation is 'quasi-autonomous'.

The second point relates to the interrelationship between the phonetic interpretation of fully derived metrical structures, and the rules of segmental phonology. As yet there has been comparatively little study of the precise relationship between metrical structures and segmental rules (although see Kiparsky 1982; Leben 1982; Halle & Mohanan 1985, for some proposals). Since this is so, Giegerich's assumption (1985: 18) that the metrical structure which eventually undergoes phonetic interpretation is completed before the rules of the segmental phonology come into operation remains an undefended hypothesis. The precise relationship between 'metrical' and 'segmental' is an issue which we will not discuss further here, but see the discussion of the relation between syllabification and stress in chapter 2. Let us instead start a preliminary investigation of the two most important elements in Giegerich's prosodic hierarchy, the *syllable* and the *foot*.

6.2   Syllables and (stress) feet

It is the syllable that forms the lowest element in the prosodic hierarchy. Giegerich assumes the existence of a syllable template of the type discussed in chapter 2. Thus, for example, *drink* has the structure:

(6.1)

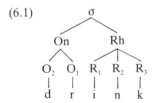

Such a description of syllable structure is, as we have seen in previous chapters, useful in various ways. Perhaps most importantly, syllable-internal structure can be shown to have relevance to the stress rules of English. For example, in LP's treatment of word-stress, we saw that the ESR assigned [+ stress] to certain vowels, working from right to left within each word; the resulting metrical trees were organised into feet. However, as we saw in chapter 3, subsequent work on word-stress has suggested that the phonological feature [stress], and the rule which assigns it, are in fact superfluous. Indeed, we can regard word-stress rules as rules that 'decide', principally on grounds of syllable structure, where arboreal *s* (or its grid-equivalent) should be placed within each word; these *s*s will form foot-initial terminals. For instance, as we have seen, Hayes (1982) suggests that the construction of feet in English makes reference to notions such as 'light syllable' and 'heavy syllable'. With our discussion of syllable structure in chapter 2 in mind, let us recall the interpretation of the terms 'light syllable' and 'heavy syllable'. Ignoring onsets, a light syllable will be represented as a simple non-branching rhyme (e.g. /a/ in *about*); heavy syllables, on the other hand, will contain a branching rhyme (long (VV) vowels, e.g. /dey/ in *Daytona*, or closed syllables, e.g. /bʌst/ in *robust*, /lim/ in *limpid*). There is strong evidence that such a description of the syllable is useful: in the first place, it allows us to specify just what the unit, syllable, is associated with – a sonority peak in a string of segments; secondly, we can claim that the sub-constituents we have specified as heavy syllables are (and again, roughly speaking) aligned with *stress feet*. That is, syllabic composition can be seen as forming one precondition for specification of the next higher category in the prosodic hierarchy.

Given, then, that the syllable is the lowest element in the hierarchy, we must now ask how Giegerich connects up the roots of such syllable trees so that feet are formed. Giegerich dubs this process *pedification*, and we continue to use this ugly but descriptive term in what follows. First, however, we must make a few pre-theoretical comments about the terms 'foot' and 'stress foot'.

We have come across the term 'stress foot' several times. In terms of the analyses outlined, stress feet will reflect the correct weight of syllables when they occur in isolation, as lexical monosyllables, or when they occur within words (note the *modest/gymnast* distinction we commented upon in chapter 3). We saw that it was also the case that, by using a prosodic hierarchy of 'syllable:stress foot', the phonological feature [stress] was rendered superfluous. This is essentially the position of Selkirk (1980), for example, who – like Giegerich – assumes that prosodic structure at the word level and below (including stress feet and syllables) forms part of the lexical representation of a word (Selkirk 1980: 596). This position, we have assumed, is relatively uncontroversial. Matters become problematic, however, when we reconsider the notion of (stress) foot. For Selkirk (1980) the stress foot is a phonological prime; like Hayes (1982) and Prince (1983), Selkirk assumes that the stress foot is a phonological entity independently needed in prosodic description. However, in these works, the stress foot is given no specific phonetic interpretation (although such interpretation is available by inference, as it were); Giegerich's work, in contrast, assumes a specific phonetic interpretation of the foot. Such a phonetic interpretation stems largely from work on 'stress-timed' languages by Pike (1946), Abercrombie (1965) and others.

Although the issues raised by the terms 'stress foot' and 'foot' are complex, let us try to clarify matters further. There seems to be a fairly general agreement that (stress) feet are needed in prosodic description (but see again the discussion of Selkirk 1984b in section 5.6), and that these feet are 'left-headed' – each of these units will begin with a terminal *s* syllable and include other *w* terminals rightwards. However, there seem to be limits to the domain of the foot. We could assume, with Hayes (1982), that feet are disyllabic, [s w], and that potential trisyllabic feet are somehow to be treated as special cases (Hayes 1982: 243ff). Or we can assume that trisyllabic feet are – in some sense yet to be defined – 'maximal' (you will recall that this was the largest foot built up by the rules of word-stress). Or we could look to the phonetic facts of 'stress-timing' and assume with phoneticians such as Classe (1939) that quadrisyllabic feet are maximal in English, with the proviso that such quadrisyllabic feet are often felt to pattern as two disyllabic feet.

To understand Giegerich's position with regard to interpretation of the foot we need to look towards the issue of 'stress-timing' noted above. While Giegerich gives a structural description of the foot which is similar to the descriptions of LP, Hayes (1982), Selkirk (1980) and others, the unit thus constructed is interpreted in a rather different way, in line with the phonetics of speech production and perception. This difference in turn circumscribes how we interpret feet as constituents in a prosodic hierarchy. Therefore, to make the provenance of the two terms 'stress foot' and 'foot' clear, the term *foot* in this chapter is restricted to our consideration of Giegerich's work, in line with his theoretical assumptions. In a sense, we can regard the two different terms as expressions of the concerns of two different linguistic traditions: 'stress foot' might be regarded as a reflection of the structural concerns of American linguistics; 'foot', on the other hand, while still a structural, phonological unit, is often interpreted by many British linguists in a specifically phonetic way (see, for example, Abercrombie 1965, 1976; Halliday 1970).

Having noted that the terms 'foot' and 'stress foot' are not mutually exclusive, but that various pre-theoretical problems arise from their precise interrelationship (or lack of it), let us return to the main concerns of this chapter by giving a theoretical analysis of the foot as a constituent of Giegerich's tree-only phonology. You may remember that at the beginning of chapter 1 we suggested that there was a perceived regularity about the rhythmical stressing of English. In fact, the last sentence is almost tautological: 'rhythm' could hardly be said to exist without such a perceived regularity. For instance, in our examples:

'Presidents 'Gorbachev and 'Reagan are to 'meet next 'month

and:

The 'goal of the de'scriptive 'study of a 'language is the con'struction of a 'grammar

we could see (and hear) that the stressed syllables tended to follow one another at roughly equal intervals. Despite the fact that the interval between one stressed syllable and the next varies from two syllables ('*meet next 'month*) to five syllables ('*language is the con'struction* . .) it is still possible to perceive a fairly regular succession of stresses, or rhythmic beats, in each example.

This characteristic of English has been called the *isochronous* movement of the language; the term 'isochronous' is usually glossed as 'having equal intervals, equal in duration'. However, as various scholars have pointed out, the term is not entirely accurate; it is better to invoke, less elegantly but more accurately, the *isochronously-tending* movement of English rhythm. In the first example above, for instance, it seems clear that the disyllabic interval '*meet next 'month* is in some way temporally equivalent to the quadrisyllabic interval '*Reagan are to 'meet* . . .: the unstressed syllables -*gan are to* are apparently 'crushed into' a particular stretch of time so that the tendency towards isochrony can be maintained.

Although there has been some debate concerning isochrony (see, for example, Lehiste 1977; Roach 1982; Dauer 1983), the notion seems to hold as a valid generalisation concerning the rhythmical structure of English, German, and other stress-timed (or 'stress-based': Dauer 1983) languages. Even if *phonetically*-equal intervals between stresses or rhythmic beats do not exist, as Giegerich writes:

Lehiste (1977) has shown that isochrony, while it cannot be interpreted as the objective measure in speech production, is nevertheless valid as a linguistic reality somewhat obliterated by the psychology of time perception. . . . We can thus, following Classe, Lehiste, and also Halliday (1967: 12) speak of 'phonological isochrony' without stronger claims towards acoustic exactness. (G 1985: 185)

Why should this concern us here? The answer relates directly to our comments on the terms 'foot' and 'stress foot', and to the difference in emphasis which British linguists have given to the foot. For the foot, in addition to being a constituent of the phonology through which 'stress' is expressed, can also be regarded as the unit through which the 'phonological isochrony' of English and other stress-timed languages is established. It is therefore, among other things, to be regarded as a unit of phonological timing: 'Speech is . . . divided up into "feet", where each foot begins at the onset of a stressed syllable and ends just before the onset of the next one. Foot boundaries are prosodic boundaries' (G 1985: 15).

In addition, Giegerich suggests that the foot is a constituent through which the relationship between 'metrical' and 'segmental' may in part be specified. Some evidence, although not apparently crucial (see Selkirk 1984b: 31), for the foot as a constituent in the phonology may be found '. . . in the structural descriptions of processes in the segmental phonology. The flapping of alveolar stops in some English dialects, for example, can be attributed (in part) to their foot-medial position' (G 1985: 15). And other segmental processes – among them the aspiration of voiceless stops in English, and the placement of pre-vocalic glottal stop in German – can be described very elegantly (it is claimed) by making reference to the foot (see also Selkirk 1980; Leben 1982; Giegerich 1983; and compare here chapters 2 and 5).

Since we have spent some time discussing the theoretical characteristics of the foot, we must now turn to examination of the precise structure of the foot, and how this is expressed in metrical tree structures. Let us make the fairly straightforward assumption that feet are represented as follows (G 1984: 8).

(6.2)   a.   b.   and (possibly) c.

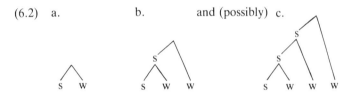

In these foot trees, the bottom nodes are interpreted, of course, as the roots of syllable trees.

Trees (6.2a, b) are relatively uncomplicated. A disyllabic structure is perhaps the most common type of foot span (recall Selkirk's (1984b) PRA, and the fact that almost all the metrical transformations we have discussed so far have led to the creation of neatly alternating [s w s . . .] structures); a trisyllabic foot, (6.2b), can be regarded as occurring with some frequency within the isochronously tending movement of English; it is the quadrisyllabic foot, (6.2c), that forms a problem. This is due to the fact that (as we have noted before) potential quadrisyllabic feet are often (if not always) interpreted as two disyllabic feet. However, if the foot is regarded as the carrier of isochrony in English, then we are obliged to assume, with Classe (1939), that quadrisyllabic feet are the 'largest' feet that occur with any frequency in English. For instance, both:

'many 'linguists 'go to 'Essex
(where each foot is disyllabic)

and:

'many 'linguists go to 'Essex
(where one 'quadrisyllabic' foot is bounded by two disyllabic)

are apparently plausible rhythmical structures (although one is more *likely* to turn up than the other; see here Selkirk 1984b: 36–43 for further discussion). To make this point clearer, consider the following phrases (see Pike 1946: 34). Try repeating them aloud, tapping to coincide with each foot-initial syllable:

(6.3) a. the 'man's 'here   (two monosyllabic feet)

   b. the 'manor's 'here   (one disyllabic foot; one monosyllabic foot)

   c. the 'manager's 'here   (one trisyllabic foot; one monosyllabic foot)

   d. the 'manager's not 'here   (one quadrisyllabic foot; one monosyllabic foot)

You will find (we hope) that you will have tapped twice in each case, possibly with the exception of (6.3d), where (although matters are complicated by possible 'emphatic stress') there is a conceivable 'tri-pedal' rhythmical structure. This is in line with our comments on quadrisyllabic feet; it is precisely because their span is relatively large that such putative 'feet' tend to restructure. English and other stress-timed languages appear to disfavour such long intervals between rhythmic beats; we are more likely to structure *Many linguists go to Essex* as 'quadri-pedal' than 'tri-pedal'. Nevertheless, we hope we have made our point: in terms of isochrony, what the constituent foot does is embody the claim that a disyllabic foot [s w], a trisyllabic foot [s w w], and – possibly, particularly at rapid tempi – a quadrisyllabic foot [s w w w], each occupy a phonologically equal time interval.

We must now turn to the representation of the foot in monosyllabic lexical items (see *The man's here*, above). This is one of the first important questions raised by postulating the foot as the next higher phonological constituent above the syllable. A second important and awkward question relates to the status and representation of weak word-initial syllables, *de-* in *detergent*, *pho-* in *phonology*, and so on.

Q. Taking these questions contrariwise, try to work out: (a) what representation is given to word-initial weak syllables in terms of foot structure; and (b) what representation might be given to lexical monosyllables.

A. (a) Despite the fact that there remain one or two doubts concerning the representation of word-initial weak syllables – doubts that we expressed in our consideration of Initial Destressing in chapter 3 –

throughout the greater part of this study we have made the assumption that words such as *appealing, excitement, phonology* and so on have had trees such as those seen in (6.4) assigned to them by convention:

(6.4)

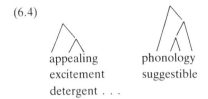

appealing   phonology
excitement   suggestible
detergent . . .

But what evidence is there that the weak, word-initial syllables of these and similar examples are in fact linked with the material on their immediate right in each tree? We could, for example, appeal to the notion of 'word', and suggest that the 'word' or mot formed a kind of constituent of the phonology above the foot level.

Now, such lexical items are indeed 'words'; we have used the term 'word' in the description of stress assignment rules, and we further need the term in consideration of certain segmental processes. Moreover, appeal to the idea of '(prosodic) Word' is made throughout *SPE*, LP, Selkirk (1980), Prince (1983) and Hayes (1982, 1984): in these models, the word is crucially assumed to be a constituent of the phonology. Giegerich's view, however, is that:

There is no evidence to support the claim . . . that the binary tree linking *de-* [in *detergent* and the similar examples above: RMH/CBM] with the material on its right governs a phonological constituent that has a place in the hierarchy of phonological constituents. . . . [The] lexical word does not have the same phonological integrity as, say, the foot. It therefore may not form a metrical tree. Indeed, in the case of *detergent* it doesn't. (G 1984: 9)

Giegerich's point is that the 'word' cannot be viewed as the next higher phonological constituent above the foot (in his view, there may not necessarily be *any* further higher-level phonological constituents above the level of the foot). What we are dealing with, in his tree-only model, are simply relationally defined concepts such as the syllable and the foot; see also Selkirk (1984b: 30–1).

Accordingly, there are two possible solutions to the issue raised by representation of word-initial weak syllables. Firstly, we could simply assume that such syllables are given no representation at all in terms of foot structure, as in (6.5):

(6.5)

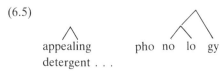

appealing   pho no lo gy
detergent . . .

The words in (6.5), and others such as *Monongahela, vanilla* are the product of post-cyclic Initial Destressing. In all these cases, word-initial syllables have already been (re)labelled as weak by the rules of word-stress; it would seem rather curious if we labelled such syllables by Destressing only to ignore such labelling in later stages of the metrical derivation.

Let us assume, then, that the word-initial syllables in (6.5) are indeed labelled as weak. But in each case we cannot directly adjoin such syllables to the foot-material on their (immediate) right. We must posit that such syllables are quite literally 'stray', and looking for a home, so to speak, within a preceding foot – since all word-initial weak syllables must be, in Giegerich's analysis, sisters of a preceding *s*-node. Therefore we might want to take the position that all such syllables are in fact weak, final elements of a preceding foot which, following Abercrombie and Giegerich, we can define as a 'silent stress'. We will discuss this issue again shortly, but let us now turn to the issue raised by (b) in our last question: this concerns the representation of feet in mònosyllabic lexical items.

You will have noticed that throughout our analysis of the role the grid had to play in metrical phonology we were uncomfortably aware of the way in which lexical monosyllables formed a problem for the model. In LP's analysis, for example, the only way such lexical items could be appropriately grid-marked was if the grid-construction rules made reference to information not contained in tree structure itself. And in the grid-only model, the various prosodic strata were a fairly direct reflection of information derived from the (morpho-)syntax; yet marking monosyllabic lexical items on a second or, more clearly, on a third level of the grid seemed essentially ad hoc: a direct reflection of the problem involved here was seen when we considered 'Addition' and 'Movement' rules within the grid-only framework. For Giegerich, though, the solution to the problem posed by lexical monosyllables follows quite naturally from the assumptions he makes about the phonological structure of the foot, and the kind of phonological relationships into which feet enter.

In every treatment of word-stress in English, some provision is made for the strength of monosyllabic lexical items. *SPE*-type phonology, for example, represented such items as invariably receiving [1stress] pre-cyclically, and in preceding chapters here we have seen various attempts – none of them entirely satisfactory – to ensure that such items are represented as (underlyingly) 'stressed'. Giegerich's approach is rather different.

6.3   'Zero syllables' and cliticisation

Q. Recall that word-stress rules can be regarded as rules that state which syllables in any given string have the capacity for being foot-initial. Such syllables will always be labelled *s*. How, then, do we represent lexical monosyllables in terms of a revised tree structure?

A. The first point to consider is that such items are indeed 'lexical'; they are 'mots'. This only suggests that since they are lexical category words, we cannot mark such items merely as *w*, for every such word (i.e. mot) must contain at least one *s* syllable – which is the same thing as saying that each such word must contain at least one foot. And further, within the assumptions of Giegerich's theory we must claim that such items are always associated with a pair of terminal nodes configured [s w], since the *s* we assign to such items obligatorily has a *w* sister to its immediate right. (This has to be the case whatever prominence relations hold at higher levels in each tree.) Therefore the tree structure relevant to monosyllabic lexical items is, provisionally, something like (6.6):

(6.6)

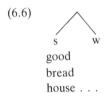

```
   s      w
  good
  bread
  house . . .
```

But how do we regard the *w*-labelled node? Is it merely vacuous, or is it associated with any particular feature of stress-timed phonology? The reason we cast the preceding question in this way, invoking again the issue of stress-timing, is that such *w*-nodes are indeed given a specific interpretation in Giegerich's work, one that stems directly from phonological properties of English syllables and words as they participate in stress-timed rhythmical organisation.

We have seen that there is a phonological regularity about feet; among other things, they are the carriers of isochrony and therefore units of phonological time. This being so, it seems plausible to suggest that a 'monosyllabic foot' and a disyllabic foot (for example) each respectively occupy the same 'phonological time': *the 'man's 'here* patterns with *the 'manor's 'here*; *'good 'work* patterns with *'better 'work*. We can claim, therefore, that a 'monosyllabic' foot is in this sense, at least, equivalent to a disyllabic foot. One of the strengths of Giegerich's model is that such equivalence is theoretically and practically demonstrable, since the 'monosyllabic' foot aligned with lexical monosyllables branches [s w]. Accordingly, since there is a phonological equivalence between 'monosyllabic' and disyllabic feet, we can specify that the *w*, 'empty' foot-final element of the tree structures dominating *good, bread* etc. is to be defined as a *zero syllable*, symbolised as Ø (hence our use of the term 'monosyllabic' foot above within inverted commas).

How are we to define these zero syllables? In the first place, we have already seen that such 'empty' nodes have some structural validity – and recall Selkirk (1984b) on silent grid positions. As Giegerich (1983: 6) notes, '. . . zero syllables have been shown . . . to have interesting empirical justification: they give a place in the grammar for those pauses (or lengthening phenomena) that, in stress-timed languages, occur between adjacent salient syllables (Abercrombie 1967; Pike 1946) . . .'

You can test this fairly easily for yourself. Try repeating the phrase *two black cats*. We think you will find that this is a 'bi-pedal' phrase (and of course this is in line with the spirit of Hayes' Rhythmic Adjustment, which – among other things – adjoined the second of a pair of *w*-nodes in the tree to the first, creating a [s w] constituent (a foot) at that arboreal level): in this instance, *two black* can be regarded as forming just one foot by such an adjustment. But now try repeating the phrase *two big black cats*. You should find that *two, big black*, and *cats* each form a foot (or foot-initial element, since *two* and *cats* are both followed by zero syllables). *Two* and *big* are 'adjacent' salient syllables, and therefore the tree-only model as we have outlined it predicts that here *two* will behave unlike the same word in *two black cats*: it will either be lengthened, or followed by an (optional) pause. We might represent the difference between the phrases as follows:

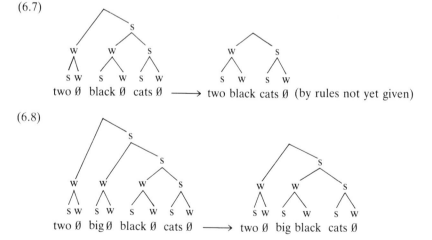

(6.7) two Ø black Ø cats Ø ⟶ two black cats Ø (by rules not yet given)

(6.8) two Ø big Ø black Ø cats Ø ⟶ two Ø big black cats Ø

Although we have not yet given the precise details of the metrical rule relevant to these examples within Giegerich's theory, what is important at this stage is that you notice the different representation given to *two* in each output tree. This rhythmical behaviour is correctly predicted by Gieger-ich's model, and seems to be in line with the ascertainable facts of stress-timing in English.

Q. Recall that in our discussion of word-initial weak syllables above, we posited that such syllables, already labelled weak, were in fact 'stray', and looking for a home within a preceding foot. Construct a metrical tree for the word *good*. Then construct trees for the phrases *good detergents* and *better detergents*. Do you notice anything significant about these representations?

A. Representation of *good* is as predicted; it is a lexical monosyllable, and will therefore (in isolation) be automatically followed by a zero syllable:

(6.9)

```
      /\
     s  w
   good  Ø
```

In *good detergents*, though, the picture is rather different. Rather than represent *good* here as being automatically followed by a zero syllable, it would make more sense, following on from our previous comments on word-initial weak syllables, if we suggested that any unattached material in a given string (*de-* here) formed a weak element of a preceding foot. As Giegerich writes (1984:9): 'The zero syllable following *good* [in the underlying structural representation of *good detergents*: RMH/CBM] . . . will be automatically filled by any unattached material in the next word . . .' This is achieved, Giegerich suggests, by 'right-to-left pedification'. Hence the representation given to *good detergents* will be as in (6.10), and *better detergents* will have the very similar structure (6.11):

(6.10)
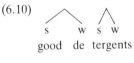

```
    /\   /\
   s  w s  w
 good de tergents
```

(6.11)

```
        /\
       s   \
      /\    \  /\
     s  w    w s  w
   better   de tergents
```

Q. But what happens when a *w*-labelled syllable is not part of a following word? What happens, for example, when nonlexical items appear in the terminal level of the tree? Bearing in mind the formal

properties of Giegerich's model that we have discussed above, suggest some possible tree representations for the phrase *fish and chips*.
A. You might have drawn up trees such as the following:

(6.12) a.   b.

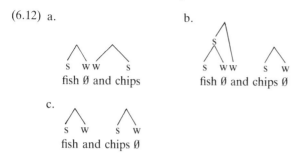

c.

Analyses (6.12a, b) seem rather odd, the first since *chips* is a lexical monosyllable and therefore should have a sister zero syllable to its immediate right, and the second since, by allowing a zero syllable to intervene between a monosyllabic lexical item (*fish*) and a following terminal *w*-node, we have called into question the phonological status of the zero syllable, which has been identified with pauses or lengthening phenomena. In (6.12a, b), not only does a zero syllable crop up between *s* and *w* terminal syllables, but it would seem merely perverse to interpret the same zeros as 'pauses', given the usual phonetic form of the phrase in question, which is usually something like (fɪʃntʃɪps], *fish'n'chips*.

In fact there is good evidence to suggest that analyses (6.12a,b) are indeed ill-formed, and that we should prefer analysis (6.12c). This evidence comes from a process called *cliticisation*. (En)*clitics* can, provisionally, be defined as 'elements that . . . combine phonologically with words with which they do not form morphological constructions' (*OED*, Supplement). In English, for example:

. . . unstressed syllables in some way hang on to preceding stressed ones and become enclitics. This is probably a generalisation that holds for all stress-timed languages. Thus, we are familiar with *bread'n'butter*, *Drinka pinta milka day*, and so forth. Note that this process of cliticisation works across syntactic boundaries, being – at least in these instances – altogether insensitive to syntactic structure. (G 1985: 12; cf. Selkirk 1984b: 383–406 for a rather different account of (en)cliticisation)

With these points in mind, we shall reanalyse our structural descriptions of *fish'n'chips*, and see that the preferable structure is that given in (6.12c). Precisely because of the phenomenon of cliticisation, it seems wrong for us to allow a zero syllable to intervene between *fish* and the following conjunction. It would be more descriptively adequate to suggest that clitics such as *and* (in *fish'n'chips*), *of* (in *pinta milk*) and others should form a weak, final element of the preceding foot.

Q. You should now think of a range of examples where a structural description such as (6.12c) would be appropriate. What do your examples and their structural descriptions tell you about the distribution of zero syllables? Can you formalise a constraint on their distribution?

A. In examples where cliticisation operates (such as *John O'Groats*, *bread'n'butter*) it seems to be necessary to restrict the environments in which zero syllables can occur. Apparently, we need a constraint on the distribution of such elements. You will have noticed that throughout our discussion of zero syllables and foot structure(s), zero syllables are never allowed to be present between adjacent *w*-terminals (recall (6.12c) in the analysis of *fish'n'chips*). Therefore we give a provisional statement of the 'constraining' rule as follows (Giegerich 1985: 14 dubs this rule the *Zero Syllable Constraint*):

(6.13) *Zero Syllable Constraint* (provisional)
Of two adjacent terminal *w*-nodes, neither occupies a zero syllable

Such a constraint will automatically rule out structures such as those seen in (6.12a, b). Moreover, a constraint of this kind allows an elegant account of cliticisation. Notice that the terminal structures that get produced as a result of (6.13) are always configured [s w] (*fish'n, pinta, bright'n* in *fish'n' chips, Pinta milk, bright'n'early*); allied with Giegerich's rules for building foot-level trees, which make reference to fixed prominence contours (feet always begin with a terminal *s*), both features of the phonology rule out the production of many [(w) w s] strings in the terminal level of trees altogether. (Of course, certain [(w) w s] structures *do* get produced in underlying strings – as we will see. But Giegerich's point is that the metrical component of the grammar operates to convert such underlying representations into rhythmically well-formed output strings describable in terms of Abercrombian 'feet'.)

In terms of cliticisation, then, as Giegerich (1985: 14) writes, the tree-only model '. . . quite naturally bears out the claim frequently found in the literature that there are no proclitics in English, only enclitics (Abercrombie 1965; Selkirk 1972) . . .' That is, cliticisation is always leftward in English; the item (syllable) that is cliticised always attaches itself to the preceding stressed (foot-initial) syllable.

6.4 W-Pairing and Defooting

Q. We shall shortly discuss a modified version of (6.13), but let us now reconsider the phrase *three blind mice*. (For this exercise, you might like to look at our preliminary comments on *big black cats* in (6.7).) Using zero syllables, draw up a tree for the phrase, and suggest a way in which rhythmic alternation might be produced among the (terminal and non-terminal) nodes of the output tree.

A. Recall that in Hayes' treatment of similarly structured phrases (*three red shirts*), a rule of Rhythmic Adjustment was proposed that would adjoin the second of a pair of (terminal or non-terminal) *w*-nodes to the first, creating an alternating [s w] structure at the appropriate level in the tree. According to Giegerich's rules of tree/foot construction, however, we are unable to describe *three* or *blind* as terminally *w* in the underlying tree structure. Because they are lexical monosyllables, and because cliticisation does not operate in this example (there are no nonlexical items on which it might apply), both *three* and *blind* must be foot-initial, and followed (therefore) by zero syllables, as shown in (6.14):

(6.14)

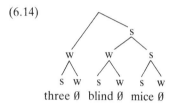

Given the underlying tree structure (6.14), it seems possible to proceed in the spirit of Hayes, and propose a transformation that will adjoin the higher-level *w*s so that an alternating [s w s] pattern is produced at this level in the tree. Giegerich calls this transformation *W-pairing*. It operates as in (6.15):

(6.15)

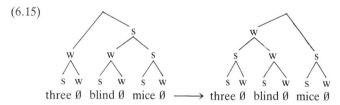

So far, so good. But what such a transformation won't do is get rid of those foot-internal zero syllables that are defined on the terminals of the output tree. Of course, there is nothing to prevent us saying ʹ*three* ʹ*blind* ʹ*mice* rather slowly, putting prominence on each syllable; but we must also make provision for an alternative surface structure, one that is alternating on the terminal level of the tree. We are supported in making such a provision by the fact that it seems *a priori* necessary to restrict the occurrence of zero syllables in any given string; this was essentially the motivation behind the Zero Syllable Constraint. In addition, it is arguably the case that zero syllables, identified as 'pauses' or equated with 'lengthening phenomena', only have this status in speech uttered at a particularly slow tempo. At a 'normal' tempo, and in connected speech, it seems undesirable for such zero syllables to remain non-phrase-finally in the output of (6.15). A fuller analysis seems preferable, one that optionally deletes the foot-final zero syllables of *three* and *blind*, and transforms that

structure into a single [s w] foot.

Such an operation would leave us with the desired, terminally alternating output for *three blind mice*:

(6.16)

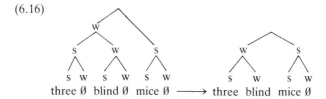

Q. Try to formalise such a rule.

A. Giegerich calls an operation of this kind *Defooting* (G 1983: 8–17 for a provisional account). We give the rule in its preliminary version below:

(6.17)

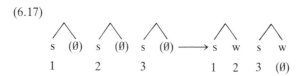

As we shall see directly, modifications to this rule will prove necessary (can you think why?). What seems important is the two-stage derivation for *three blind mice*, *two black cats*, etc.: a first transformation, which adjoins the pair of *w*-nodes in the (higher levels of the) tree; and a second transformation, which deletes all relevant foot-internal zero syllables.

We now need to give a final, fuller description of the Defooting rule. In the first place, we need to specify that the Defooting rule is given in a relationally defined form; secondly, we need to state that it is an optional rule; as we noted, it is still possible that phonetic surface structures such as *'three 'blind 'mice*, or *'Thieves 'stole 'Sue's 'new 'car* will turn up on occasion (particularly in slow speech). And further, there is a general consideration at issue here. Giegerich (1980: 189) writes, for instance, that it is arguable that the metrical phonologies of LP and others are, in a sense, over-determined: 'The major disadvantage of Liberman and Prince . . . is their failure to provide a sufficient amount of rhythmical options in their output strings.'

Bearing this in mind, Defooting may be reformulated as the rule given in (6.18):

(6.18)

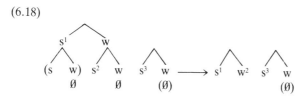

Rule is optional if s^1 branches as shown.

You will have noticed that the numbered structure relevant to the Defooting Rule above is configured [s s w . . .]. Such structures – with adjacent *s*-labelled nodes – are apparently objectionable in English, and they have a great deal to do with the next aspect of the tree-only model that we would like to consider: this is Iambic Reversal.

Q. Using the tree-only formalism as we have outlined it, construct a tree for the paradigm example *good-looking tutor* in its citation form.

A. You might construct the tree as in (6.19):

(6.19)

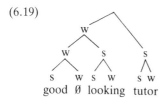

The word *good*, as a monosyllabic lexical item, will be described as the initial element of a foot, followed of course by a zero syllable; otherwise, the tree is unexceptional. On the face of it, the array of terminal labels on such a tree looks suspiciously similar to the SD of the Defooting rule; however, closer inspection shows that the SD of Defooting is not met here; we could not, for example, relabel *looking* as:

*looking

as we relabelled *blind* (in *three blind mice*) as *w* after Defooting had applied. Again, we need to look at higher levels in the tree structure, and there we find the familiar structure:

relevant in the SD of the usual Reversal rule. In (6.19), then, we assume that Reversal operates in the normal fashion:

(6.20)

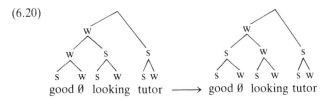

What is interesting here is the fact that we have no means of getting rid of the zero syllable in the phrase-initial foot. This is a point of some theoretical importance, and bears (as we will see shortly) on just how and where the Reversal rule applies. (For the present, try and work out whether this structuring of the phrase-initial foot is indeed formally relevant in the description or constraint of Reversal).

In the examples we have looked at so far in relation to Giegerich's work on metrical structure, we have noted the existence of four rules: one rule of constraint (the Zero Syllable Constraint), and three rules of transformation (respectively, W-pairing, Defooting, and Iambic Reversal). Before we proceed, we repeat the versions of these rules as we have given them so far:

Zero Syllable Constraint
Of two adjacent terminal *w*-nodes, neither occupies a zero syllable.

W-Pairing

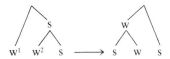

where nodes 1 and 2 branch [s w].

Defooting

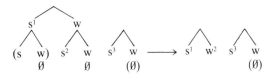

Rule is optional if s^1 branches as shown.

Iambic Reversal

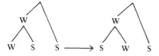

subject to constraint (to be further discussed).

Q. It seems plausible to assume that these rules are ordered intrinsically, in terms of their own mode of application, and 'extrinsically'. Using your own examples, describe how such rule-ordering might operate.
A. We approach this answer by considering at what level(s) of structure these rules apply.

Rule application and ordering: W-Pairing and Defooting

In chapter 4 we saw that in a tree/grid analysis of *almost hard-boiled egg*, Reversal was presumed to take place firstly on the largest (uppermost) tree domain where the crucial tree structure:

appeared. In this sense, the derived 'stressing' of a phrase appears to make reference to 'largest structure' before it makes reference to 'smallest structure'. A metrical derivation is thus quite unlike earlier generative work on stress phenomena which (as you will recall from chapters 1 and 3) made reference first to smallest constituents, then continued to erase syntactic brackets until the largest constituent was reached.

The picture with respect to metrical phonology – particularly the tree-only model – is, however, conceptually much simpler. In order to achieve a rhythmically well-structured phonological output, it seems desirable to restrict the ordering of transformations so that they may make reference to 'upper nodes first, lower nodes last' wherever this is possible. As Giegerich (1983: 17) writes, 'Rhythmic simplification . . . can . . . be viewed as a top-to-bottom flattening of metrical trees, formalized as a series of rules where those operating on terminal nodes presuppose application of "higher level" ones.'

Q. Show how such a 'top-to-bottom' process might work in the example *Thieves stole Sue's new car.*

A. This example is formed by a phrase (S) consisting solely of lexical monosyllables; the upper level nodes of the tree are all defined as right-branching [. . w w s]. Therefore it seems likely that one or more applications of W-Pairing will be required. The underlying tree structure is as follows:

(6.21)

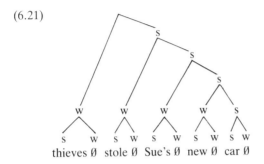

thieves Ø stole Ø Sue's Ø new Ø car Ø

We have a choice as to which nodes are relevant in any W-Pairing transformation. Notwithstanding Giegerich's comments on rhythmic simplification immediately above, and although we have seen the validity of such a view in consideration of, for example, Reversal, we shall take the position here that W-Pairing operates from right to left in each tree. In a sense this means working from the 'lowest' sub-tree to the 'highest', but such a process not only makes reference to the constituent structure where the rule's SD is met in the least controversial fashion, it also mimics the right-to-left iterations of the ESR itself. It remains to be seen, however, whether what we suggest is the right-to-left iteration of W-Pairing is any more than a stipulation. In (6.21), though, right-to-left iterations of W-Pairing do indeed give us the desired rhythmically alternating output:

(6.22)

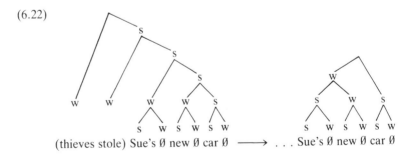

(thieves stole) Sue's Ø new Ø car Ø ⟶ . . . Sue's Ø new Ø car Ø

W-Pairing is also possible in another iteration leftwards, on the pair of *w*-nodes dominating *Thieves stole*. Once this operation has been carried out, we arrive at the mid-derivation structure (6.23):

(6.23)

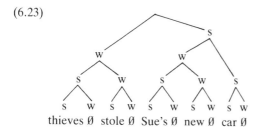

thieves Ø stole Ø Sue's Ø new Ø car Ø

Notice, however, that there is still another pair of 'highest level' nodes labelled *w*. We are, we think, unable to pair these nodes for two reasons: (1) once a derivation has started, we assume that the process is uniformly 'top-to-bottom'; (2) in line with the phonetics of stress-timing, potential quadrisyllabic 'supra-feet' (even assuming we could create them by disjunctive transformation) are felt to pattern as two disyllabic feet (cf. *almost hard-boiled egg*); but the tree of (6.23) is already alternating at the 'foot' level.

The mid-derivation structure above, however, still contains zero syllables. In (pre-head) feet of this kind, it is these we want to get rid of. Therefore we apply Defooting, again working right to left wherever the rule's SD is met:

(6.24)

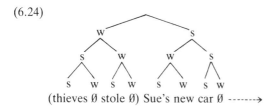

(thieves Ø stole Ø) Sue's new car Ø -------→

(6.25)

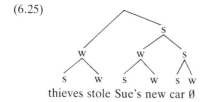

thieves stole Sue's new car Ø

That, we assume, is how the iteration of W-Pairing and Defooting takes place.

Rule application and ordering: Iambic Reversal and Defooting

So far in our review of Giegerich's work we have given no full account of the Reversal rule; in our preliminary analysis of *good-looking tutor* above, we simply assumed that the rule's SD is identical to that found in other treatments of Reversal, making reference to that critical underlying tree structure:

This is, indeed, more or less what happens, and the interaction of the Reversal and Defooting rules can be regarded again as a top-to-bottom flattening of metrical tree structure. The derivation of, for example, *home-made beer* is in these respects non-problematic: Reversal applies at a higher level in the tree, and Defooting operates – as it must – on the terminal level (Defooting operates to remove zero syllables, and these are of course only found at this level in each tree).

(6.26) a.

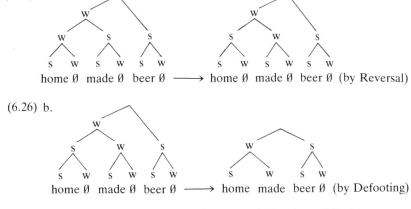

home Ø made Ø beer Ø ⟶ home Ø made Ø beer Ø (by Reversal)

(6.26) b.

home Ø made Ø beer Ø ⟶ home made beer Ø (by Defooting)

However, as we noted in our preliminary analysis of *good-looking tutor*, not all pre-DTE, foot-internal zero syllables can be deleted. The output of Reversal for this particular phrase was:

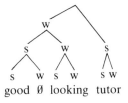

good Ø looking tutor

In fact, as Giegerich writes, it is actually highly desirable for this zero syllable to remain as the final element of the first foot in cases where the foot-initial element is either a lexical monosyllable (where Defooting cannot subsequently apply) or a Class II Prefix (G 1985: 215–16).

Q. Using the appropriate conventions of the tree-only model, give analyses of *well-funded bank* and *Montana bank*.

A. *Well-funded bank* appears to be straightforward:

(6.27)

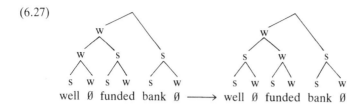

well Ø funded bank Ø ⟶ well Ø funded bank Ø

This example patterns along with *good-looking tutor*: the phrase meets the SD of the Reversal rule, the first element of the underlying structure branches, all is well. But we run into problems when we attempt to analyse *Montana bank*, where Reversal must (it is claimed – see LP: 321–3) be constrained.

The problem lies in the adequacy or inadequacy of three competing underlying representations that we might assign to the phrase. Firstly, we could assume that *Montana bank* simply fails to meet the SD of the Reversal rule, since its first syllable, *Mon-*, is labelled *w* and thus (in Giegerich's formalism) forms part of a preceding foot, as follows:

(6.28)

? s w s w s w
Mon tana bank Ø

The Reversal rule is, as we have seen throughout, always constrained from shifting stress onto weak, word-initial syllables (compare *Montana bank* with, for example, *appalling bank*). However, *Mon-* in *Montana* is rather unlike *a-* in *appalling*. In many dialects it is not a syllable containing the reduced vowel schwa, /ə/. Moreover, in terms of syllable structure, it is a closed syllable, with non-empty (onset and) coda; these features may lead us to suspect that *Mon-* is a 'heavy' syllable, like *prin-* in *princess* or *thir-* in *thirteen*. Accordingly, we cannot simply mark such syllables as terminally *w* in the tree. The alternative is to mark such heavy syllables rather as we did lexical monosyllables, as:

s w
Ø

If we make this assumption, it will lead to the following analyses:

(6.29)

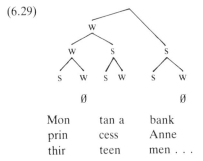

Mon	tan a	bank
prin	cess	Anne
thir	teen	men . . .

But several objections could be raised against such an analysis. The first relates to the status of the zero syllable. Recall that the zero syllable was equated with 'pauses . . . or lengthening phenomena' that, in English, tend to occur between adjacent stresses; it seems over-permissive to allow such 'pauses' to occur word-internally (and of course even if we wanted to get rid of such zero syllables by Defooting, this would be blocked in *Montana*, although Defooting *would* apply to the other items in the above list). A second objection relates specifically to *Montana bank*: it is assumed throughout the literature that Reversal does not take place in the phrase (*Montana bank, Montana cowboy*, etc.). Given the analysis above, however, *Montana* patterns with other items that almost obligatorily undergo Reversal.

Since it is *Montana* that seems to form the nub of the problem, let us search for yet another possible analysis. Notwithstanding our previous comments on the syllable structure of *Mon-*, we could, perhaps, regard it as forming a 'mot' constituent with the material on its immediate right, as follows:

(6.30)   Mot

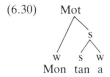

Although we have seen the objection that could be raised against such an analysis, it is in line with earlier work in this field – and in line with Giegerich's (1983) analysis of, for example, *thirteen* in *thirteen men*. Again, notwithstanding the syllabic structure of *Mon-*, we might object that we have created a [w s] constituent in the underlying representation, and that this runs counter to those foot-formation rules we have already discussed. However, certain [w s] constituents are unavoidably created elsewhere: strings of so-called 'function words' – auxiliaries, prepositions and so on – along with their heads in fact pattern out as [(w) w s] underlyingly before being converted by the metrical component into foot structures (rhyth- mically well-formed strings).

Let us assume, then, that the underlying representation of *Montana bank* might be shown as follows:

(6.31)

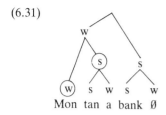

Mon tan a bank Ø

Reversal is now possible on the circled nodes. Or is it? Reversal would create the following structure:

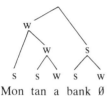

Mon tan a bank Ø

However, both Giegerich and Kiparsky have noted that Iambic Reversal 'usually does not apply when it would create a word-internal structure of the form

where the first *s* is non-branching' (Kiparsky 1979: 425). Giegerich elaborates on this, and generalises the statement so that it can be seen to apply to both English and German (you might like to check Giegerich's conclusions on this for yourself – see G 1985: 157ff for reference). There is something objectionable, apparently, about the creation of such word-internal

structures – unless (and it is an important proviso) such structures are subsequently going to be Defooted. If we analyse *thirteen men*, for example, in terms of our third possible analysis, we see that the derivation is as follows:

(6.32)

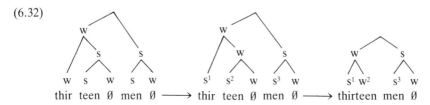

thir teen Ø men Ø ⟶ thir teen Ø men Ø ⟶ thirteen men Ø

thirteen men does undergo Reversal, and the mid-derivation structure above, that includes the 'problem configuration'

```
      /\
     /  w
    /  /\
   s  s  w
```

is subsequently Defooted (as it is in *Princess Anne, Skegness Rock*, etc.). No Defooting is possible in *Montana bank*, though, because the potential mid-derivation structure of this phrase does not meet the SD of Defooting. The conclusion, then, is that:

> . . . Reversal and Defooting interact in an interesting way: in all those cases where Reversal would produce a
>
> ```
>       /\
>      /  w
>     /  /\
>    s  s  w
> ```
>
> structure that doesn't meet the structural description of Defooting, it is blocked altogether. In phrases like *sensational claim* and *Montana bank*, for example, no Defooting would be possible after Iambic Reversal. Reversal doesn't apply . . . (G 1985: 214)

This state of affairs presupposes, however, that the syllables in question will be analysed as being assigned *w*, word-initial syllables. For the reasons we outlined earlier, an analysis such as this is problematic: here we are able to do no more than sketch the problem and suggest other possible analyses, for although the issue of a tree-only approach to these phenomena is highly interesting, no satisfactory solution has yet been found.

6.5   *Further constraints on metrical transformations*

In our work so far in this chapter, we have seen how Abercrombian 'feet' are constructed (and on what theoretical basis), how the zero syllables thereby produced are distributionally constrained (which constraint led to an elegant account of cliticisation), and we have described the application and interaction of three transformations: W-Pairing, Defooting, and Iambic Reversal. We would now like to discuss further constraints on Reversal and W-Pairing; we will, in addition, introduce two new transformations relevant to left-branching tree structures, and lastly, we will discuss how rhythmical alternation is produced in strings of nonlexical items by a transformation called, naturally enough, *Footing* (see G 1985: 246ff).

Further constraints on Reversal

Recall that in chapter 4 we saw that there were two constraints on Reversal: firstly, the syllable onto which stress is shifted by the transformation had to be specified as being in some way underlyingly 'stressed'. This constraint is naturally expressed in Giegerich's model, of course, by the stipulation that the initial element of a pre-shift phonological string must branch (*good-looking*, *well-funded*). The second constraint on Reversal presented in LP's initial theory is that, in the tree domain relevant to Reversal:

element 2 'must not be the strongest element of a syntactic phrase' (see (4.27), the subsequent example and discussions there). We saw that this constraint was potentially applicable in the iterative reversals through *almost hard-boiled egg*, but we escaped from the problem there by suggesting that, of the two applications of Reversal, the first made reference to that overall tree domain where *egg* was the strongest rightmost constituent (and therefore *-boiled* could not be analysed as the 'strongest element' of the phrase in that pass through the transformation). This seems, on the face of it, to be a partial solution. Giegerich notes a similar problem, one for which he suggests a different answer:

there appear to be some counterexamples to [the] claim that syntactic phrasing constrains Reversal. . . . Reversal is common in such phrases as *very good whisky*, *some more tea*, *Married Man's Allowance*, *Golden Gate Bridge*, etc. Cases like that are, of course, somewhat embarrassing for this model . . . [But] I believe that they can be accommodated in the account given here if we appeal to lexicalisation . . . (G 1985: 211)

That is, Giegerich argues towards interpreting such phrases metrically as either 'end-stressed compound adjectives' (*very good*, *some more*, *home-made*, *hard-boiled*, etc.), or as 'end-stressed compound nouns' (*Married Man's*, *Golden Gate*). In each case, Giegerich appeals either to the 'idiomatic character' of the 'phrase' in question, or to 'idiomatic character' coupled with 'sheer frequency of occurrence' (G 1985: 211). (Recall that we have cited before the comment that familiar lexical items tend to undergo Reversal more frequently than unfamiliar items.) Moreover, there seems to be some support for the idea of interpreting certain words as 'end-stressed compound adjectives'. Quirk *et al.* (1972: 1039), for example, observe that, while most compounds are 'generally stressed on the first element but with a strong secondary stress on the second element', there is a somewhat smaller number of compounds which have phrasal stress patterns (for instance *apple sauce*, *first rate*). 'Many of these', they continue, 'are often not nouns, but verbs (*back-fire*),

adverbs (*henceforth*), and especially adjectives (*knee-deep, flat-footed*).'
(See too Fudge 1984: 144ff, 196–7.) Notice that our much-used examples
hard-boiled and *home-made* fall directly into this class of 'end-stressed
compound adjectives'. The point of this discussion is as follows: in
determining constraint(s) on Reversal, we must appeal directly to the
lexical entry specified for the items in our string; 'compound' items are
rather ambiguous in terms of stress pattern, and in general it seems to be
the case that 'end-stressed compound' items undergo Reversal unprob-
lematically, while the (unambiguous) heads of syntactic phrases do debar
Reversal.

Since this appears to be the case, we can now, following Giegerich (1985:
211ff) give the structural description of Iambic Reversal in full:

(6.33)

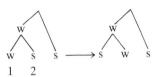

where (i) element 1 may branch [s w]
and   (ii) where element 2 is not the head of a syntactic phrase.

Further constraints on W-Pairing

The SD of W-Pairing is, you will recall, similar to the SD of Hayes'
Rhythmic Adjustment. Both are metrical transformations. Both make
reference to right-branching

structures, whose structural change is described roughly as follows:

(6.34)

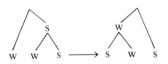

The question now arises whether such a rule is too powerful, and whether,
consequently, it needs to be constrained – either in the same sort of way as
the Reversal rule was constrained, or perhaps under the 'Maximality
Principle' (see again §5:10).

Q. Before we discuss this issue, can you specify in what way(s) W-Pairing might be seen as 'too powerful'? You might like to make reference to our comments on W-Pairing in the example (6.21) *Thieves stole Sue's new car* before answering this question.

A. One problem seems to be that W-Pairing produces a large number of possible outputs. Consider the phrase *seven pretty little girls*. This will have the underlying structure seen below:

(6.35)

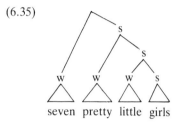

(where *pretty* is an adjective, rather than an adverbial). Multiple applications of W-Pairing are possible. As in the analysis of *Thieves stole Sue's new car*, we have assumed that the first pairing operation will take place on the nodes dominating *pretty little*. This would give us the output:

(6.36)

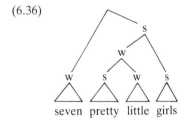

We might then assume that in order to derive further rhythmic alternation we should adjoin the *w*-nodes dominating *seven* and *pretty little*. Notice that such a derivation contravenes the putative 'uniformly top-to-bottom' mode of rule application – although not our 'right-to-left' mode; see again (6.21). Such a process gives us the maximally highly structured output:

(6.37)

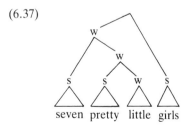

However, despite our assumption that the rule applies 'right-to-left', the structural description of the rule is also met elsewhere in the underlying tree structure (6.35). For example, according to the SD of the rule, we could adjoin the nodes dominating *seven pretty* in the first instance:

(6.38)

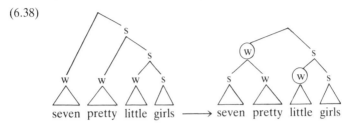

seven pretty little girls ⟶ seven pretty little girls

Yet the circled nodes of the output tree of (6.38) are also, nominally, candidates for W-Pairing. A second application of the rule would give us the following output:

(6.39)

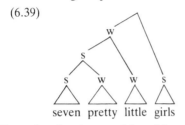

seven pretty little girls

But what has been achieved by this application of the rule? The answer, surely, is not much. The strength relations between the terminals of (6.39) are rather similar to those in (6.38); all that has altered is the 'higher-level' prominence pattern. What *is* significant is that two iterations through W-Pairing – those seen in the 'top-to-bottom, right-to-left' mode of application, and those seen in the unconstrained derivation above – lead to different results when applied in turn to any given string. (In case you are in any doubt about this, you should try the two modes of rule application on, for example, *John drinks cold lager* and *Sue wrote six good long papers*.)

On the face of it, then, W-Pairing appears to be a classic case for constraint. Giegerich's answer to this is in line with his earlier assumptions concerning the desirability of the model producing a range of possible phonetic surface structures. The metrical component of the grammar, it will be recalled, mediates between underlying phonological structures and their phonetic interpretations. And phonetically, *both* 'surface' descriptions of *seven pretty little girls* are possible representations. 'Of these', Giegerich writes (1985: 240), 'the one that alternates . . . is possibly the one that will be favoured, characterised by the alternation of *s* and *w* nodes on the word level and within words. But all the other structures are also permissible and will, I'm sure, be observed so long as *girls* remains the DTE . . .'

6.6 *S-Pairing and W-Pairing (left-branching)*

Bearing in mind this overall picture of constraint (or a necessary lack of it) on Reversal and W-Pairing, let us now introduce two new transformations which make reference to underlying, uniformly left-branching structures (W-Pairing has so far made reference just to right-branching trees).

Q. Consider the example *Sammy's father's dog*. As a preliminary, give the appropriate tree analysis of this phrase.

A. We assume your answer will be structured as follows:

(6.40)

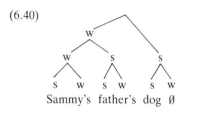

Notice that the 'higher' tree domain is w s s. This is of course the SD of the Reversal Rule. But Reversal cannot apply: *Sammy's father's* is a phrase, *father* is the strongest element of the phrase, and Reversal is thereby blocked. This is the correct phonological assumption. In embedded phrases of this kind, Giegerich notes, '. . . speakers will actually produce an increasing pattern . . .' (G 1985: 259).

Q. Now take the example *Sammy's father's brother's dog*, and construct the appropriate underlying tree.

A. Again, we will assume your answer is structured as follows:

(6.41)

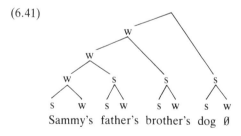

In this case, however, we might want to produce alternation; in such a multiply embedded phrase, an increasing prominence pattern like the one seen in *Sammy's father's dog* is, as Giegerich notes (1985: 258), 'shunned in English'. Similarly, LP assume that a grid analysis of such a phrase produces 'a rather unlovely "triangular" grid' (LP: 329). LP go on to produce alternation within the tree-grid format by 'a judicious application of Iambic Reversal', as follows:

(6.42)

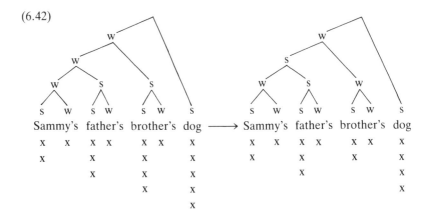

In the tree-only model, though, this option is denied to us. Even Reversal – however judicious – is ruled out. In the first place, we cannot relax the 'head of a syntactic phrase' constraint here; and there is no way we can analyse *Sammy's father's brother's* as, for example, an idiosyncratic 'end-stressed compound adjective' (even if we wanted to). In the second place, Giegerich, following Langendoen (1975) and Cooper (1980), assumes that intonation breaks occur in the phonetic interpretation of such tree structures. These intonation breaks mark certain constituent boundaries and, as Giegerich writes (1985: 259), 'It makes sense to assume that intonation breaks occur in a metrical tree at][-type metrical boundaries.' An LP-type (tree-and-grid) analysis defines no such bound- aries: in particular, the array of prominence on the grid seems ill-equipped to deal with this kind of constituency (although see Selkirk 1984b on juncture and silent demibeats). What we want, then, is a rule whose SD is different from Reversal, and whose output leaves back-to-back phrase boundaries that will be interpreted phonetically as the requisite intonation breaks. Such a rule will have to produce a surface output such as:

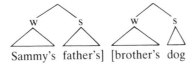

where the nodes dominating word trees alternate w s][w s. We can arrive at this output through a transformation Giegerich calls *S-Pairing*, which is as follows (G 1985: 259):

(6.43)

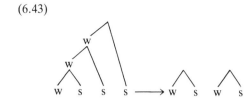

(You should check for yourself that such a transformation will in fact correctly apply to *Sammy's father's brother's dog*.)

Yet further questions remain. Reversal and S-Pairing are both transformations that produce alternating structures; they both apply on rather similar underlying tree configurations. They are conceptually different, however, insofar as S-Pairing applies to nested head-of-phrase elements, whereas Reversal cannot so apply. But what happens to the metrical derivation in nested 'word' constituents – in compounds? Does Reversal or S-Pairing apply? Or some combination of both?

Q.   Consider the example *Earl's Court Road Gardens*. Here, we must make reference to words in a compound structure. A morphosyntactically bracketed parsing runs as follows: [[[Earl's Court]$_N$ Road]$_N$ Gardens]$_N$. (Compare [[[Sammy's father's]$_{NP}$ brother's]$_{NP}$ dog]$_{NP}$).

Now construct a tree for *Earl's Court Road Gardens* (don't forget the zero syllables), and suggest how either S-Pairing or Reversal might apply.

A.   The underlying tree structure in this case is:

(6.44)

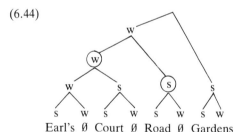

Earl's Ø Court Ø Road Ø Gardens

We now have a choice. Reversal can apply to the circled nodes (where *Earl's Court Road* is analysed as a compound) to give us the output:

(6.45)

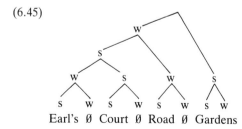

Earl's Ø Court Ø Road Ø Gardens

Or S-Pairing can apply, giving us the structure:

(6.46)

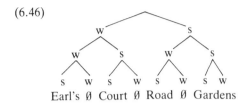

Earl's ∅ Court ∅ Road ∅ Gardens

Which process (if any) are we to prefer? Giegerich tentatively suggests that S-Pairing is debarred from applying to NSR-stressed embedded compounds; its domain is, he suggests, properly that of syntactic phrases. Moreover, the product of S-Pairing is, among other things, a pair of 'metrical brackets' (this constituency has been produced by the metrical component of the grammar) whose juncture is defined as an 'intonation break' (recall our discussion of Sammy's father's] [brother's dog). But no intonation breaks seem particularly evident in *Earl's Court Road Gardens*. Therefore, Giegerich suggests, Reversal applies. Notice that this presupposes that *Earl's Court Road* is a compound noun whose prominence is assigned by the NSR; if it is defined as a phrase (NP), then Reversal could not apply. But again, it is at least arguable that *Earl's Court Road* is indeed a phrase; for instance, we cannot entirely rule out a surface structure such as:

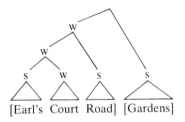

[Earl's Court Road] [Gardens]

with an (optional) intonation break after *Road*. (Our own informal observations lead us to suspect that this is in fact a strongly favoured perception of the string – possibly because Defooting applies to the structure above but not, apparently, to the outputs seen in (6.45) and (6.46) – and see G 1983: 26).

But if we cannot rule such a structure out, how are we to produce it? We could, perhaps, perform Reversal on the phrase *Earl's Court Road*. This is relatively unproblematic if *Earl's Court* is taken to be an end-stressed compound. But if we take the larger string into consideration, the picture is rather different:

(6.47)

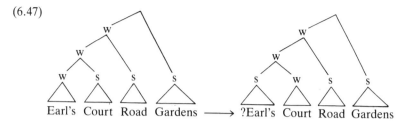

Earl's Court Road Gardens ⟶ ?Earl's Court Road Gardens

If we attempt to apply Reversal to the nodes dominating *Earl's Court*, then we are forced to ignore a higher-level set of nodes where the pre-Reversal domain

is defined. This is counter to what Giegerich suggests is the 'top-to-bottom' processing of tree structure, and of course in all the work we have done so far we have assumed an 'upper nodes first, lower nodes last' mode of rule application.

Like Giegerich, we can offer no direct solution to the theoretical problem raised by interaction of Reversal and the putative S-Pairing transformation. We can only suggest that the interrelationship of these two operations, or the lack of such a relationship, is of some importance within overall tree-only theory; you will find that the questions at the end of the chapter ask you to comment again on these aspects of the model.

In the same tentative spirit, let us discuss one further transformation relevant to left-branching structures. This is another 'pairing' operation, relevant to strings of compound nouns such as [[[law degree] requirement] changes], [[[[labour party] finance] committee] president], and so on. For the former example, you will recall from chapter 3 that LP give a tree analysis of the phrase as follows:

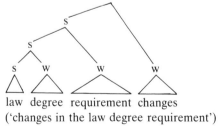

law degree requirement changes
('changes in the law degree requirement')

We might choose to analyse *labour party finance committee president* in much the same way, although the syntactic structure of the phrase is in fact ambiguous: is the committee a committee that rules on [labour party finance], or is the president a president of a [finance committee]?

If we choose to analyse the string as a compound throughout, however, the result is as follows:

(6.48)

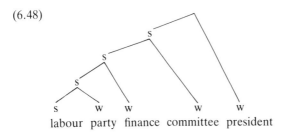

labour party finance committee president

This structure, like the one seen in *law degree requirement changes*, is uniformly left-branching at the higher arboreal level. But, just as we saw that alternation was produced in nodes dominating word trees in the controversial S-Pairing transformation, so we might wish to argue that the strings of *w*-labelled nodes in the examples above might be subject to some degree of alternation. And this in fact is Giegerich's position.

He proposes the transformation 'W-Pairing (left-branching)' to account for (re)structuring in cases such as these. This is the SD of the new rule (G 1985: 263):

(6.49)

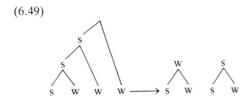

The rule would apply to *labour party finance committee* as follows:

(6.50)

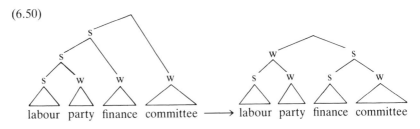

labour party finance committee ⟶ labour party finance committee

But as you may have noticed, there appear to be two problems with this rule. The first is its domain of application. Although the rule appears to work straightforwardly in the above example, what happens if we add *president*? Let us look again at that compound. If we work rightwards from the highest tree domain on which the rule's SD is met, we must make reference to the following circled nodes:

(6.51)

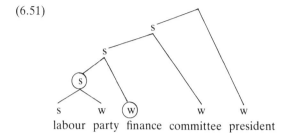

labour party finance committee president

Application of the rule would then give us the following output:

(6.52)

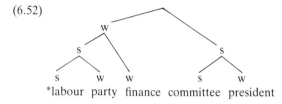

*labour party finance committee president

But this is surely ill-formed. And it seems apparent that, to get the result we want, a maximally alternating terminal set, then we must make reference to a lower-level set of nodes first, that is, the nodes dominating *labour party*. In this instance, application of left-branching W-Pairing would give us something like (see G 1985: 262):

(6.53)

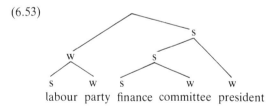

labour party finance committee president

We have seen before that such a mode of application is dubious. We can neither work where the rule's SD is met, nor on 'lower nodes first'. Of course, we could always say that a rule is relevant to 'lower nodes first' so long as its SC leaves no further higher domains on which the same rule can apply, but this would be something of a problem – as we shall shortly see – when we come to consider iterative applications of rules on other elements of phrase structure. And a second problem is this: W-Pairing (left-branching), as we have described it, has as one of its consequences the relocation of the strongest stress in a multiply embedded string of compounds. No other metrical transformation we have seen is allowed to do this. But not only does the new Pairing rule build a 'pseudo-syntactic' constituent (*finance committee president*), it is forced to define Nuclear Stress on *fi-* since the reconstructed 'constituent' branches.

In short, then, we have to regard the two new transformations we have introduced, S-Pairing, and W-Pairing (left-branching), as theoretical problems. This is not to say that they, or something like them, have no place in the metrical component of the grammar, but only to suggest that more work needs to be done on the mode of application of such rules. However, the questions raised by the precise status of these transformations are difficult to resolve, especially since crucial evidence is hard to come by.

6.7   Footing in nonlexical items

To conclude, let us examine a less problematic area, one rather better handled by the tree-only model: this is the rhythmic (re)structuring that takes place in strings of nonlexical items – or 'function words', as they are sometimes called. Two kinds of analysis are available to us. In the first place, we could assume that the nonlexical items in question – in particular, modals, auxiliaries, pronouns and prepositions – are underlyingly stressed. This is the position taken by Selkirk (1984b: 335–82), for example, who represents such items on at least level 2 of the grid, and who then proceeds to treat the rhythmical structuring in sequences of such items in terms of a cyclic rule of Destressing. Two factors govern her assumption that function words are underlyingly stressed. Firstly, she argues, many such words appear in both 'strong' and 'weak' forms in English: for example, the indefinite article may appear as both [ə] and [ej] in the phrase *a fence*; the personal pronoun *him* may appear as both the syllabic nasal [m̩] or as the 'strong' form [hɪm] in the phrase *need him*, and so forth. Secondly, function words seem to operate like 'real' words in that their syllabic structure(s) apparently constrain the Destressing Rule that subsequently works upon them. As Selkirk writes, 'a CV syllable . . . is the most likely to destress, a CVVC or CVCC syllable is the least likely to do so . . .' (1984b: 337); and in addition, a presumed *lack* of underlying stress in function words is, Selkirk argues, difficult to reconcile with a word-stress analysis that uses extrametricality as its *modus operandi* (although of course we might wish to argue that the ESR will in any case only apply to lexical items; there might be a sense in which function words are 'invisible' to the ESR – see Selkirk 1984b: 346). In Selkirk's basic analysis, then, function words are underlyingly stressed; they typically appear with second-level grid-marking (whereas lexical items are guaranteed at least a third-level prominence); monosyllabic function words are then destressed where appropriate, by cycles through a Destressing Rule that alters objectionable grid configurations.

However, we believe that this kind of grid analysis, which views function words as underlyingly stressed, is rather difficult to justify. The first difficulty is the assumption that function words exhibit 'strong' and 'weak' forms which are neatly related to one another. While it may be plausible to claim that, say, [him] and [m̩] are related, it is difficult to view [ðɛm] *them*, and [ɛm]/[əm] in the same way. Also, it seems apparent that certain so-called 'strong' forms of function words are historically derived from 'weak' forms, and not vice versa (for example, present-day English *I* < early Middle English *i* not *ich*); this may lead us to suspect that weak forms of such words are in fact the correct underlying representations. Synchronically we seem to be borne out in this suspicion: Gimson (1980: 261), for example, notes that of the 200 most common words in connected English speech, 42 are function words, 19 of which 'have over 90% unaccented occurrences with a weak form . . .' Gimson regards the weak form of such words as 'normal' and their strong forms as 'less usual'.

A second difficulty with Selkirk's favoured interpretation is this: a 'stress' analysis of function words is in essence more complicated than an analysis that reads such items as underlyingly weak; it seems unnecessary to posit that such forms are underlyingly stressed, then lose that stress by destressing, only to have metrical strength re-assigned to them by a cyclic rule of 'restressing' (in the grid-only model, by Beat Addition – see Selkirk 1984b: 362–5). Where such forms are considered as underlyingly weak, however, rhythmic restructuring may be produced by one iterative, externally motivated transformation; although we anticipate, it is not altogether true that 'making the assumption [that] function words are basically unstressed (and thus that their stressed forms are derived by rule in certain specified circumstances) . . . requires considerable ad hoc complication in the grammar' (Selkirk 1984b: 342).

A third and final difficulty lies in the path of Selkirk's model. The destressing of function words, as she sees it, is 'defined on phonological representation and is crucially governed by the junctural properties of the utterance' (1984b: 338). But it is open to question how far juncture may be represented in phonological structures of the type we have been discussing. In Selkirk's model, for example, the distinction between the 'minimal pair' *Take Grey to London* and *Take Greater London* is expressed, roughly speaking, in terms of the different alignment each phrase has with its corresponding metrical grid:

```
(6.54) a.             x          b.                x
              x       x                 x          x
              x       x                 x          x
              x x x x   x               x x x x   x   x
            Greater  London          Grey     to London
```

The claim is that 'a stressless syllable preceding a constituent break should be longer than a stressless syllable following one' (Selkirk 1984b: 324). In (6.54a) -ter is aligned with its following silent demibeat, whereas in (6.54b) to is aligned with just one grid mark and can therefore be viewed as juncturally close(r) to London (in these terms, to in fact acts as a kind of 'proclitic'; see Selkirk 1984b: 323–9 for a fuller discussion). But it is arguable that the distinction between these phrases can equally well be expressed in terms of intrasyllabic (CV) structure, and in terms of the representation each phrase bears in a tree-only model – specifically, in terms of the make-up of each foot and presence or absence of zero syllables at phrase-boundaries (see below for further discussion). It seems a little odd to make distinct claims about the length of an unstressed syllable (whose transcription is unambiguously [tə]) as a result of other, junctural properties of the phrase – particularly when this contrast can be expressed in terms of rather more general properties of a metrical model – and this may lead us to think that an analysis couched in different terms may be more explanatory. Accordingly, we shall examine the rhythmic restructuring of nonlexical items in terms of the tree-only model that has been our concern throughout this chapter.

Q. Consider first a phrase like *He must have been at home. Home* is the only lexical item in the string, and so will be aligned with the only terminal *s* in the tree (followed, of course, in a full representation, by a zero syllable). Construct the appropriate underlying tree for the phrase.

A. The answer seems to be a tree such as (6.55), although notice that even here there are difficulties in determining exactly what the correct constituency of the phrase might be:

(6.55)

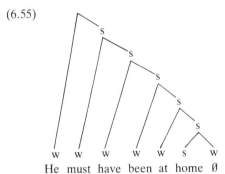

But metrical trees like this 'are not very satisfactory in that they are not sufficiently highly structured. They allow scansions, with the whole string of terminal W nodes unstressed, which one would not come across in speech – in other words, trees like that are (at least potentially) observationally inadequate . . .' (G 1985: 246).

Q. Consider how you might derive an alternative tree analysis, bearing in mind that it is 'rhythmic stressing' that appears to take place in strings of right-branching, *w*-labelled terminals.

A. Two principles seem to be at work. Firstly, you might have observed that, in the example above, *must* and *been* are far more likely to receive prominence in a restructured tree than *he*, *have* or *at*; and secondly, rhythmic prominence of this kind again seems to work so as to produce alternation in the tree. In any transformational process on the tree of (6.55) we must guarantee that prominence will never be defined on two immediately adjacent terminals (and as a corollary of this, we must ensure that the nonlexical item selected for prominence by such a hypothetical transformation will be followed by a *w*-labelled terminal).

Before we examine what such a rule might look like, let us go back to the claim that some nonlexical items are more likely to receive prominence than others. In *He must have been at home*, it seems clear that the modal, *must* and the last auxiliary, *been*, will receive a rhythmic beat. Modals, in fact, wherever they occur, seem very likely to receive prominence – consider phrases such as *You must be joking, He might have been drinking, He would have been thirty next birthday*. Certainly they receive prominence before a preceding pronoun might, or before an auxiliary verb. Next, consider phrases such as *He is a crook, You are no fun*. It seems fairly clear that in 'neutral' (non-emphatic) pronunciations, the personal pronoun, rather than the verb, is the best candidate for rhythmic prominence. Lastly, consider the phrase *They had been to the shops*. Again, the personal pronoun is a likely candidate for prominence; so is the second auxiliary verb.

What does this amount to? Although judgments are delicate, what seems apparent is that there is a hierarchy of nonlexical items, where highly-ranked items tend to receive prominence before items of a lower rank. Such a hierarchy might be roughly schematised as follows:

(6.56) Modal > Pronoun > Aux > Preposition

Where a modal occurs in a string, it is very likely to receive prominence before any of the other nonlexical items in the same string; where a pronoun occurs (and where it is not followed by a modal – although the hierarchy tells us this) it is likely to receive prominence before any other nonlexical item, and so on.

We shall go on to discuss the need for such an explicitly stated hierarchy a little later in this chapter, but, having spoken of certain nonlexical items 'receiving prominence' by magic as it were, we must now look at the mechanism by which such prominence is derived. We can be consistent in our claims about such a mechanism if we view it as another transformational rule that operates in the metrical component of the grammar.

Q.   Look again at the phrase *He must have been at home*. We have claimed that rhythmic prominence (more correctly, a sequence of rhythmic prominences) is achieved in the phrase through a transformational rule. Consider how you might formulate such a transformation, and in what manner such a rule might apply.

A.   The relevant transformation is one which Giegerich calls *Footing*. Essentially, what we need is a transformation that takes the first of a pair of terminal *w*-nodes (where these nodes are daughters of right-branches) and makes it strong, converting that underlying pair of *w*-nodes into a constituent, a (binary) foot. With this in mind, the Footing rule can be formulated as follows (G 1985: 247):

(6.57)

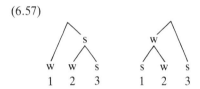

where 1, 2 are terminal nodes

You may notice that the SD of this new rule is very similar to the SD of the W-Pairing rule given earlier. We shall return to this point, but for the moment you might like to consider whether W-Pairing and Footing do in fact differ, or whether they are just separate statements of a single rule.

That, then, is a provisional statement of the rule. But how might it apply? A first hypothesis could be that Footing, rather like W-Pairing, applies iteratively wherever its SD is met. But this would lead to rather strange results. For example, in *He must have been at home*, the SD of the Footing rule would allow us to 'pedify' *He must* in the first instance, as follows:

(6.58)

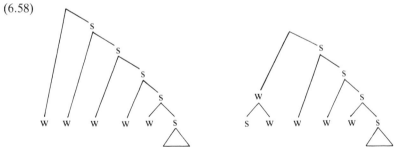

he must have been at home ⟶ *he must have been at home

If the Footing rule is so unconstrained, we could then go on to apply the rule again to, say, *have been*. This would give us the output tree:

(6.59)

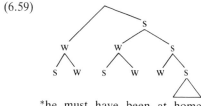

*he must have been at home

But such a tree is hardly a possibility. However, if the rule simply applies wherever its SD is met, we could come up with some equally perverse structures:

(6.60)

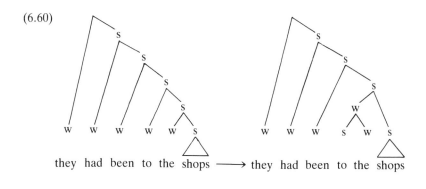

they had been to the shops ——→ they had been to the shops

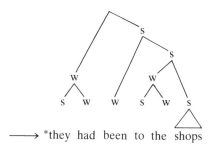

——→ *they had been to the shops

It seems, then, as if we must constrain the application of Footing. But how do we achieve this? Recall that we noted how certain nonlexical items were more likely to receive prominence than others; it would make sense, therefore, if we constrained Footing so that it applied iteratively along our putative hierarchy of function words – first on modals, next on pronouns, then on auxiliaries, and so forth, where the rule's SD is met.

This kind of constraint would give rise to the following analysis. In *He must have been at home*, the rule will first select the modal, *must*, as its 'target' item:

(6.61)

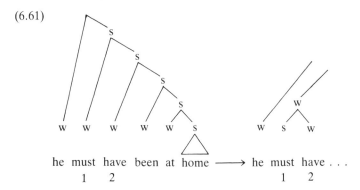

he must have been at home ———→ he must have . . .
  1   2   1   2

If we proceed according to the hierarchy proposed above, then pronouns will be the next candidates for receiving prominence. But as you will see, the nodes dominating *He must have* . . . in the output to (6.61) do not meet the SD of the Footing rule, which applies only to pairs of terminal *w*-nodes. Therefore an iteration of Footing on *He* is blocked. But there is still another pair of terminal nodes where Footing is possible. These are the nodes dominating *been at*, and Footing will apply here, too:

(6.62)

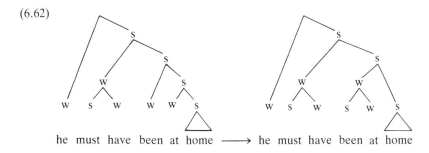

he must have been at home ———→ he must have been at home

This gives us a maximally alternating pattern on the terminal nodes of the tree (it might even be possible to argue that an iteration through W-Pairing on a higher level of this output tree could produce an even more richly structured tree, but we leave that possibility open for the present).

Q. You should now check that Footing, applying along the 'hierarchy of function words', produces uncontroversial results for the phrases (a) *They had been to the shops*, (b) *He might have been drinking*, and (c) *You are a doctor*.

A. Footing produces the following results:

(a)

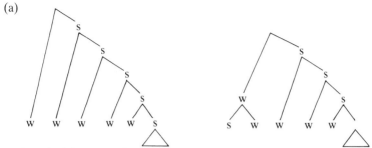

they had been to the shops ⟶ they had been to the shops
(Footing: Pronoun (>Aux) – 1st iteration)

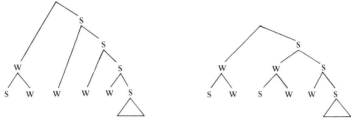

they had been to the shops ⟶ they had been to the shops
(Footing: Aux (>Prep) – 2nd iteration; no further Footing possible)

(b)

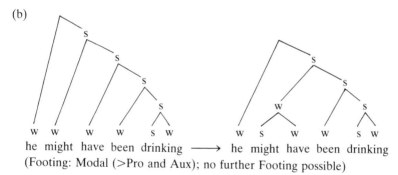

he might have been drinking ⟶ he might have been drinking
(Footing: Modal (>Pro and Aux); no further Footing possible)

(c)

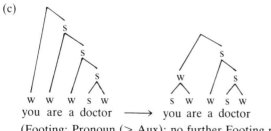

you are a doctor ⟶ you are a doctor
(Footing: Pronoun (> Aux); no further Footing possible)

It would appear as if Footing, by making reference to a hierarchy of function words, and by applying iteratively left-to-right, gives us the correct, maximally structured terminal output strings. That is, the hierarchy seen in (6.56) guarantees (with certain exceptions that we will discuss forthwith) that Footing will apply iteratively left-to-right.

There are still several problems that we have to contend with. The first problem is the ad hoc nature of the hierarchy we have been proposing; Footing has to 'know' which element stands where in the hierarchy, and this 'knowing' depends – it would appear, crucially – on morphosyntactic bracketing and labelling. However, all through this chapter we have kept noting (following Giegerich) how desirable it is for the metrical component of the grammar to be largely autonomous of syntax. Is Footing somehow a special case, needing special pleading? Or is Footing like the other transformations in the metrical component, needing no necessary reference to syntactic organisation? And if this is so, can we show that Footing applies in a principled way without the hierarchy? The second problem lies in the intractability of certain examples, such as *John must have been drinking, John must be joking, Mike has been asleep*. In these examples there are various rhythmical options that cannot be accounted for by the rules of tree construction and transformation as we have given them so far. How are we to account for them? A third problem relates to a point we made earlier: is Footing in fact a separate rule? Given that we already have one rule in the metrical component (W-Pairing) with a suspiciously similar SD, do we need Footing as well? If the rules are distinct, how do they interact? And if the rules are identical, can we reconcile their two apparently different modes of application? These questions are to a large extent related, so let us begin to answer them (or try to) by looking at what we called 'the intractability of certain examples'.

Q. Making reference to earlier work in this chapter if necessary, construct underlying trees for the phrases *Richard must be joking*, *John must be joking*, and *Mike has been asleep*. What do your representations tell you about the applicability of Footing?

A. *Richard must be joking* is relatively straightforward. The underlying tree is as follows:

(6.63) a.

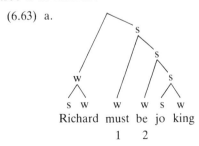

and Footing can take place where indicated, leaving us the well-structured output tree:

(6.63) b.

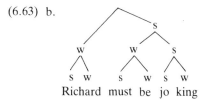

Richard must be jo king

But the underlying tree structure for *John must be joking* is different. *John* is a lexical monosyllable; it must be terminally *s* in the tree, with its sister to its right. According to the rules of tree construction we have given in this chapter, this *w* sister can only be *must* (it cannot be, for example, a zero syllable under the formulation of the Zero Syllable Constraint – see again (6.13)). These factors mean that our underlying tree structure for *John must be joking* is the following:

(6.64) a.

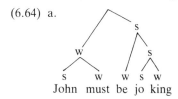

John must be jo king

This, of course, is a perfectly plausible – even preferable – tree. But the problem is that a scansion such as:

(6.64) b.

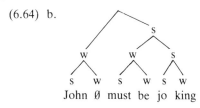

John Ø must be jo king

might equally well turn up in performance. Similarly, it seems possible that both structures:

(6.65) a.   b.

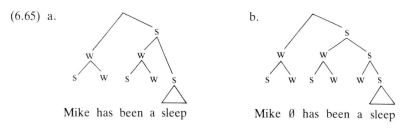

Mike has been a sleep   Mike Ø has been a sleep

will occur quite naturally. But if this is indeed the case, how are we to account for the presence of the zero syllable, and the consequent Footing that may then take place?

What seems apparent, in examples like:

John ∅] [must be joking

and:

Mike ∅] [has been asleep

is that a back-to-back boundary -]$_{NP}$ $_{VP}$[- occurs between the phrase-initial NP and the following items. Given this environment, and given the fact that cliticisation may fail to take place across this environment (compare the two analyses of *Mike's/has been asleep*, above), it seems necessary to modify the Zero Syllable Constraint so that zero syllables, under certain specified conditions, are permitted to occur to the left of other terminal *w*-nodes.

Recall that the Zero Syllable Constraint was originally formulated as follows:

(6.13) Of two adjacent terminal *w*-nodes, neither occupies a zero syllable.

All that seems necessary is to include some addendum concerning the] [boundaries we have been discussing. The new formulation of the Zero Syllable Constraint would run, therefore, as follows – see Giegerich (1985: 249):

(6.66) *Zero Syllable Constraint*
Of two adjacent terminal *w*-nodes not separated by a]$_P$ $_P$[boundary, neither occupies a zero syllable.

Q. Given this reformulation, provide full derivations of the phrases *John must be joking* and *Mike has been asleep*.

A. The first and in some ways the most straightforward analysis of *John must be joking* uses the unmodified conventions of tree-only theory. That is, we are able to assume that *must* 'cliticises' to *John* in the underlying tree structure, and if this is the case, *must* is no candidate for Footing at all:

(6.67) a.

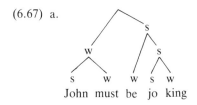

However, since *John* and *must* are separated by a]$_P$ $_P$[boundary, we are also able to construct the following underlying tree, licensed by the new version of the Zero Syllable Constraint:

(6.67) b.

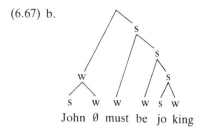

John Ø must be jo king

Given this tree, *must* is now a candidate for Footing:

(6.67) c.

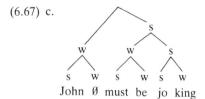

John Ø must be jo king

The position with respect to *Mike has been asleep* is a little more complicated. Again, the new version of the Zero Syllable Constraint allows us to construct two well-formed underlying tree structures, (6.68a) where *has* cliticises to *Mike*, and (6.68b) where *Mike* is followed by a zero syllable:

(6.68) a.   b.

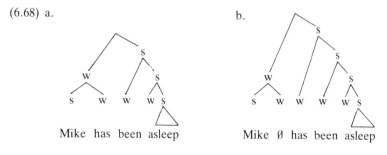

Mike has been asleep   Mike Ø has been asleep

Footing is again possible in these underlying trees. In (6.68a) it applies to promote the auxiliary, *been*:

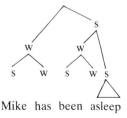

Mike has been asleep

In (6.68b), however, two applications of Footing are possible, according to whether the Footing rule selects *has* or *been* as its leftmost element. We illustrate both derivations below as (6.68c) and (6.68d):

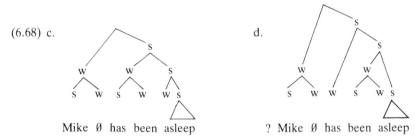

Mike Ø has been asleep   ? Mike Ø has been asleep

(At this stage you might also like to use the reformulated Zero Syllable Constraint to construct the appropriate trees for *Take Grey to London* and *Take Greater London*. See also the questions at the end of this chapter.)

Q. Given the reformulated Zero Syllable Constraint, and given that Footing seems to work iteratively left-to-right (with the exception of the queried derivation above), where does this leave our hierarchy? Do we still need an explicit statement of the hierarchy to guarantee correct application of Footing? Give two analyses of the phrase *Ruth must have been drinking*. What do your derivations suggest to you about the necessity of retaining an explicit 'hierarchy of function words'?

A. Two underlying structures are possible. The first derives straightforwardly, via Footing left-to-right:

(6.69)

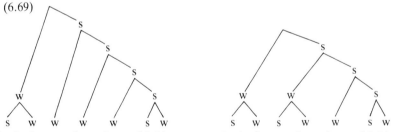

Ruth Ø must have been drinking ⟶ Ruth Ø must have been drinking

But consider the following underlying structure:

(6.70) a.

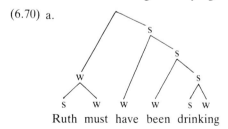

Ruth must have been drinking

If Footing applies iteratively, left-to-right, regardless of the kind of nonlexical item it comes across, then from the last underlying structure we could generate:

(6.70) b.

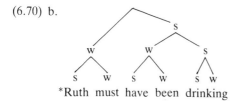

*Ruth must have been drinking

Such a derivation should be ruled out. *Have* rarely seems to acquire 'stress' by transformation when it is surrounded by other nonlexical items (modals, auxiliaries); yet if we abandon the notion of hierarchy, then there is no way of ruling out the deviant scansion above. Giegerich (1985: 252) suggests, in fact, that we retain the hierarchy, simply adjusting its specifications, so that 'the last auxiliary in a string [is] a more likely candidate for Footing (if that isn't a modal) . . .' This 'adjustment' does indeed seem to work, but as we have noted before, and as Giegerich himself admits, 'the apparent ad hoc character of the hierarchy is at the same time its main weakness'.

We mentioned 'intractable examples' above, and we must look at one or two more of them before we end this chapter, if only to illustrate yet again the range of open questions metrical phonology generates.

Q. Consider the phrase *He will be asleep*. What derivation(s) might take place?

A. The underlying tree contains the expected string of terminal *w*-nodes:

(6.71) a.

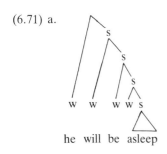

he will be asleep

Footing is possible on the pair *will be*, according to the hierarchy, and this will generate the output:

(6.71) b.

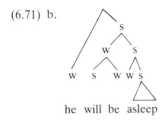

he will be asleep

As we saw above, modals and auxiliaries will cliticise to a preceding lexical item (*John must, Mike has* . . .); yet additionally, it seems as if modals and auxiliaries will also cliticise to preceding pronouns: *He'll be asleep* seems just as likely a 'surface structure' as *He will be asleep*. But in this example, how are we to account for cliticisation? For *will* to cliticise, *he* must be marked as strong, but no provision has been made so far for marking pronouns as strong when they are phrase-initial (see *He must have been asleep*, for example).

Giegerich's solution to this problem involves the lexicon. He writes:

Certain pairs of nonlexical items, presumably ones that frequently recur, get shifted into the lexicon as some kind of idioms. Among those would be *he will, must not, must have, are not, want to, have to* . . . Whenever these pairs occur . . . they are idioms or at least somehow lexicalised. As lexical items they are subject to the rules of word stress and receive initial stress (G 1985: 254)

This is a radical solution to the problem posed by the rhythmic structuring of (some) function words (it is also a solution discussed by Selkirk (1984b: 386–9) with respect to *Not-* contraction and *To-* contraction). In effect, what such a proposal would mean is that very many underlying strings would display a great deal of rhythmic alternation, since word-stress rules, operating in the lexicon, would dictate that this was so:

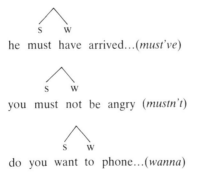

he must have arrived...(*must've*)

you must not be angry (*mustn't*)

do you want to phone...(*wanna*)

But if non-lexical items are thus marked in the lexicon, does that mean that Footing is redundant? Apparently not. Even given the 'lexical solution', there remain certain strings where further rhythmic alternation is only possible through the working of a transformational rule. Consider again the phrase we asked you to look at in the last question, *He will be asleep*. If we assume that *He will* is marked in the lexicon as bearing a [s w] pattern (> *He'll* by cliticisation), we are still left with the following underlying tree:

(6.72)

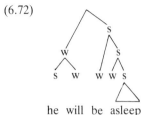

he will be asleep

Footing can still take place on *be a-* (there is no way this sequence could be 'lexicalised'!), and so we must conclude that Footing, albeit rather restricted in scope given the lexicalisation of certain function-word sequences, is a genuine metrical transformational rule in English.

We should conclude by returning to the last question we asked before embarking on these speculative forays: are W-Pairing and Footing the same rule? There are various differences. W-Pairing applies ('top-to-bottom') on nonterminal nodes, Footing on terminals. Yet the SD of the two rules is (near) identical, and it would not be too much to suggest that 'Footing' may conceivably be seen as the last iteration(s) of W-Pairing after it has worked its way across the tree (try this suggestion on, for example, *Farrah Fawcett-Majors wasn't in the picture*). We might relate this to another apparent difference between the two rules: W-Pairing applies wherever its SD is met, yet Footing – apparently – applies left-to-right according to the dictates of the function word hierarchy. But if we adopt the view that certain function words are listed with their 'sisters' in the lexicon, and are there appropriately stressed, where does this leave our need for a hierarchy? Will it not be the case that in many strings of function words there will only be one terminal domain left where Footing – W-Pairing – could apply? Since it is easy to collapse Footing and W-Pairing into one rule, applying top-to-bottom in tree structure, on what grounds should we keep the two rules apart?

You will have been aware that throughout this chapter we have been particularly closely concerned with the way in which the rules of the metrical component apply: do they apply iteratively top-to-bottom (Reversal), or 'top-to-bottom, right-to-left' (W-Pairing)? Can such transformations apply across prosodic levels in the tree, or is each transformation constrained so as to apply on one and only one level? Is the large number of possible output scansions an indication that the rules of tree-only phonology are too powerful, and need additional constraint – such as the Maximality Principle? And if constraint is needed, on what grounds are we to base it – morphosyntactic, phonological, or even lexical? As Dogil (1984: 286) puts it, 'the mode of application of rules, their order, and the constraints on them seem to be the weak point of this exclusively tree-based model. Some evaluation procedure must be found . . .' But where?

Notes and further reading

6.1 The key work for tree-only phonology is Giegerich (1985); you should look particularly closely at chapters 1, 4 and 5 of this work. You will in addition find useful short summaries of Giegerich's approach to metrical structure, and of many of the transformations discussed above, in Giegerich (1983, 1984).

6.2 The term 'foot' is troublesome. You will also be aware that the same term is also used to describe notional constituents of lines of verse. However, as far as we are aware, the evidence for such constituents – iambs, trochees, and so on – is scanty, at least as far as English is concerned. See Attridge (1982) on the 'Classical approach' to verse scansion for an excellent review and summary.

For a phonetic approach to the foot, see especially Classe (1939) and Abercrombie (1965); the essay 'Syllable quantity and enclitics in English' in this last work is particularly interesting.

6.7 Giegerich (1980) gives a provisional account of the rhythmic stressing of function words; although this account has been largely superseded by Giegerich's later work, it remains clear and interesting nevertheless. For an alternative account of stressing and cliticisation in function words, see Selkirk (1984b), especially chapter 7. Dogil (1984) questions the theoretical basis of tree-only phonology, and suggests a possible answer to the question with which we concluded the chapter. His paper is rather difficult, but his comments on the tree-only model are pertinent.

Essay and discussion topics

1. Look again at the final versions of the Defooting, Reversal, and 'S-Pairing' rules. Then give three possible metrical derivations of the phrase *Earl's Court Road Gardens*. To which derivations does Defooting apply? What conclusions do you draw from this?

2. Consider how word-initial weak syllables are represented in the tree-only model. (You should find that there are three conceivable representations.) Which representation are we to prefer, and why?

3. It has been claimed that 'Rhythmic simplification . . . can be viewed as top-to-bottom flattening of metrical trees' (G 1983: 17). Using your own range of examples, examine this claim and decide how far you think it is true.

4. Does W-Pairing need to be constrained? If so, why?

5. If you have read and completed this chapter carefully, following the hints contained in parentheses, you should find that the grid-only model and the tree-only model give rather different solutions to the problem posed by representation of the minimal pair *Take Grey to London* and *Take Greater*

London. In your opinion, which of the two models gives the better representation of the metrical structure(s) of this pair of phrases?

6. The notion of 'word-internal zero syllable' (see (6.29)) forms something of an embarrassment for Giegerich's model. How far do you think the word-stress rules of Giegerich (1985) are compatible with the account of word-stress given, for example, in chapter 3 here?

7. What advantages, if any, does the tree-only model have over grid-only, or grid-plus-tree, models?

Bibliography

Abercrombie, D. 1965. *Studies in phonetics and linguistics*. London: Oxford University Press.
— 1967. *Elements of general phonetics*. Edinburgh: Edinburgh University Press.
— 1976. 'Stress' and some other terms. *Work in Progress* 9: 57–9. University of Edinburgh, Department of Linguistics.
Anderson, J. M. & Jones, C. 1974. Three theses concerning phonological representations. *JL* 10: 1–26.
Aronoff, M. & Oehrle, R. T. 1984. *Language sound structure: studies in phonology presented to Morris Halle by his teacher and students*. Cambridge, Mass.: MIT Press.
Attridge, D. 1982. *The rhythms of English poetry*. London: Longman.
Bell, A. & Hooper, J. B. 1978. *Syllables and segments*. Amsterdam: North-Holland.
Butterworth, B. (ed.) 1980. *Language production. Vol. 1: Speech and talk*. London: Academic Press.
Chomsky, N. & Halle, M. 1968. *The sound pattern of English*. New York: Harper & Row.
Classe, A. 1939. *The rhythm of English prose*. Oxford: Basil Blackwell.
Clements, G. N. & Keyser, S. J. 1983. *C–V phonology*. Cambridge, Mass.: MIT Press.
Cohen, D. & Wirth, J. 1975. *Testing linguistic hypotheses*. Washington, DC: Hemisphere.
Cooper, W. E. 1980. Syntactic-to-phonetic coding. In Butterworth (1980).
Crystal, D. (ed.) 1982. *Linguistic controversies: essays in linguistic theory and practice in honour of F. R. Palmer*. London: Edward Arnold.
Dauer, R. 1983. Stress-timing and syllable-timing reanalyzed. *Journal of Phonetics* 11: 51–62.
Dogil, G. 1984. On the evaluation measure for prosodic phonology. *Linguistics* 22: 281–311.
Durand, J. 1986. *Dependency and non-linear phonology*. London: Croom Helm.
Fallows, D. 1981. Experimental evidence for English syllabification and syllable structure. *JL* 17: 309–18.
Fudge, E. C. 1969. Syllables. *JL* 5: 253–86.
— 1984. *English word-stress*. London: George Allen & Unwin.
Giegerich, H. J. 1980. On stress-timing in English phonology. *Lingua* 51: 187–221.
— 1983. On English sentence stress and the nature of metrical structure. *JL* 19: 1–28.
— 1984. *Relating to metrical structure*. Bloomington: Indiana University Linguistics Club.
— 1985. *Metrical phonology and phonological structure: German and English*. Cambridge: Cambridge University Press.

Gimson, A. C. 1980. *An introduction to the pronunciation of English.* London: Edward Arnold.

Halle, M. 1973. Stress rules in English: a new version. *L.In.* 4: 451–64.

— 1985. Metrical constituent structure. Paper presented to the Spring 1985 meeting of the Linguistics Association of Great Britain.

Halle, M. & Keyser, S. J. 1971. *English stress: its form, its growth, and its role in verse.* New York: Harper & Row.

Halle, M. & Mohanan, K. P. 1985. Segmental phonology of modern English *L.In.* 16: 57–116.

Halliday, M. A. K. 1967. *Intonation and grammar in British English.* The Hague: Mouton.

— 1970. *A course in spoken English: intonation.* London: Oxford University Press.

Hayes, B. 1981. *A metrical theory of stress rules.* Bloomington: Indiana University Linguistics Club.

— 1982. Extrametricality and English stress. *L.In.* 13: 227–76.

— 1983. A grid-based theory of English meter. *L.In.* 14: 357–94.

— 1984. The phonology of rhythm in English, *L.In.* 15: 33–74.

Hooper, J. B. 1976. *An introduction to natural generative phonology.* New York: Academic Press.

Hulst, H. van der & Smith, N. (eds.) 1982. *The structure of phonological representations* (Parts I and II). Dordrecht: Foris Publications.

Ingria, R. 1980. Compensatory lengthening as a metrical phenomenon. *L.In.* 11: 465–95.

Jespersen, O. 1905/1952. *Growth and structure of the English language.* 9th edn. Oxford: Basil Blackwell.

Jones, C. 1976. Some constraints on medial consonant clusters. *Language* 52: 121–30.

Kahn, D. 1976. *Syllable-based generalisations in English phonology.* Ph.D. dissertation, MIT, Cambridge, Mass. published (1980) New York: Garland.

Kenstowicz, M. & Kisseberth, C. 1979. *Generative phonology.* New York: Academic Press.

Kingdon, R. 1958. *Groundwork of English stress.* London: Longman.

Kiparsky, P. 1979. Metrical structure assignment is cyclic. *L.In.* 10: 421–41.

— 1982. From cyclic phonology to lexical phonology. In van der Hulst & Smith (1982) Part I.

Ladefoged, P. 1982. *A course in phonetics.* New York: Harcourt Brace Jovanovich, Inc.

Langendoen, T. 1975. Finite-state parsing of phrase-structure languages and the status of readjustment rules in grammar. *L.In.* 6: 533–54.

Lass, R. 1984. *Phonology.* Cambridge: Cambridge University Press.

Leben, W. R. 1980. A metrical analysis of length. *L.In.* 11: 497–509.

— 1982. Metrical or autosegmental. In van der Hulst & Smith (1982) Part I.

Lehiste, I. 1977. Isochrony reconsidered. *Journal of Phonetics* 5: 253–63.

Liberman, M. 1975. *The intonational system of English.* Ph.D. dissertation, MIT, Cambridge, Mass.; published (1979) New York: Garland.

Liberman, M. & Prince, A. 1977. On stress and linguistic rhythm. *L.In.* 8: 249–336.

Nespor, M. & Vogel, I. 1982. Prosodic domains of external sandhi rules. In van der Hulst & Smith (1982) Part I.

O'Connor, J. D. & Trim, J. L. M. 1953. Vowel, consonant and syllable: a phonological definition. *Word* 9: 103–22.

Pike, K. L. 1943. *Phonetics*. Ann Arbor: University of Michigan Press.

— 1946. *The intonation of American English*. Ann Arbor: University of Michigan Press.

Prince, A. 1980. A metrical theory for Estonian quantity. *L.In.* 11: 511–62.

— 1983. Relating to the grid. *L.In.* 14: 19–100.

Quirk, R., Greenbaum, S., Leech, G. & Svartvik, J. 1972. *A grammar of contemporary English*. London: Longman.

Roach, P. 1982. On the distinction between 'stress-timed' and 'syllable-timed' languages. In Crystal (ed.) (1982).

Saussure, F. de 1966. *Course in general linguistics* (trans. W. Baskin). New York: McGraw-Hill.

Schane, S. A. 1972. Noncyclic English word stress. Mimeographed paper, La Jolla, California.

Selkirk, E. O. 1972. *The phrase phonology of English and French*. Ph.D. dissertation, MIT, Cambridge, Mass.; published (1980) New York: Garland.

— 1980. The role of prosodic categories in English word stress. *L.In.* 11: 563–605.

— 1982. The syllable. In van der Hulst & Smith (1982) Part II.

— 1984a. On the major class features and syllable theory. In Aronoff & Oehrle (eds.) (1984).

— 1984b. *Phonology and syntax: the relation between sound and structure*. Cambridge, Mass.: MIT Press.

Siegel, D. 1974. *Topics in English morphology*. Ph.D. dissertation, MIT, Cambridge, Mass.; published (1979) New York: Garland.

Trager, G. L. & Smith, H. L. 1951. *An outline of English structure*. Studies in Linguistics, Occasional Papers 3, Washington DC.

Vennemann, T. 1972. On the theory of syllabic phonology. *Linguistische Berichte* 18: 1–18.

Wells, J. C. 1982. *Accents of English* (3 vols). Cambridge: Cambridge University Press.

Zonneveld, W. 1976. Destressing in Halle's English stress rules. *L.In.* 7: 520–5.

Zwicky, A. 1975. Settling on an underlying form: the English inflectional endings. In Cohen & Wirth (1975).

Index

277